Where
the
Wild
Things
Grow

David Hamilton is a forager, horticulturist and explorer. He started experimenting with wild food as a teenager, making soup from nettles found in his family garden and has been foraging seriously for more than 25 years. He has hitched, walked, cycled and driven all over the world in search of wild food and has taught Mary Berry, Ben Fogle and thousands of others how to forage. He holds a degree in food science and nutrition and a diploma in horticulture and leads the Guardian Masterclass on foraging. He is the author of several books, including *Wild Ruins* and *The Self-Sufficientish Bible*, and lives in the south west of England with his partner and two young sons. They are keen foragers and refer to wild food as 'Daddy food'.

Where the Wild Things Grow

A Forager's Guide to the Landscape

DAVID
HAMILTON

Illustrations by
May van Millingen

HODDER

First published in Great Britain in 2021 by Hodder & Stoughton
An Hachette UK company

This paperback edition published in 2023

1

A CIP catalogue record for this title is available from the British Library

Paperback ISBN 978 1 529 35107 1
eBook ISBN 978 1 529 35106 4

Designed by Nicky Barneby, Barneby Ltd

Printed and bound in Great Britain by Clays Ltd, Elcograf S.p.A.

Hodder & Stoughton policy is to use papers that are natural, renewable
and recyclable products and made from wood grown in sustainable forests.
The logging and manufacturing processes are expected to conform to
the environmental regulations of the country of origin.

Hodder & Stoughton Ltd
Carmelite House
50 Victoria Embankment
London EC4Y 0DZ

www.hodder.co.uk

For the Mountain Men

Contents

Introduction

WHEREVER YOU ARE reading this, you are almost certainly just a short walk from a source of wild food. Find your nearest patch of greenery, whether it's a garden, wild woodland or the patch around a car park, and look down. At first it may seem like an indistinguishable mass of weeds, shrubs, flowers or trees. But once you know what to look for, a whole new world of exciting tastes will open up to you. You might find edible weeds like dandelions, shepherd's purse or nettles. If you look closer, you might see bittercress, a plant with cross-shaped flowers and a mustard-like flavour that goes beautifully with feta and walnuts. Perhaps there's a blackthorn bush, with sloes that can be used to make gin or cured like olives for a melt-in-the-mouth flavour. Or a patch of wood sorrel, which can give a tzatziki-style dip a sour, lemony bite.

Foraging has become fashionable in recent years – it can sometimes seem as though every hipster from Hoxton to Houston has picked up a foraging basket – but it is not a new trend. For most of human history, we have eaten wild food. The first anatomically modern humans evolved more than 200,000 years ago but agriculture is a much more recent invention, dating back around 12,000 years. Early humans survived by tracking herds of mammoth, buffalo and deer for meat. But a large proportion of their diet would also have been leaves, roots, shoots, flowers, stems, bark, sap, nuts, berries and seeds. They had intimate knowledge of the landscape and their nomadic lifestyles allowed them to move with the seasons and forage when food was abundant.

The variety of plants we consume today has diminished dramatically. While our early ancestors would have made use of thousands of types of plant, as people settled and began to farm this fell to the hundreds. Today humans only consume 3 per cent of the world's farmable plant varieties, with twelve species providing three-quarters of our food. In fact, at least half of all calories we consume come from just three crops: rice, maize and wheat.

Most of us will walk past wild foods every day without noticing them. I recently tested this on a short walk from my home to the local park. In around one thousand steps, I counted sixty different plants and trees with edible parts. Every few paces a different weed, flower, tree or shrub suggested a new dish. I found dandelions, sow thistles, wild lettuce and countless other green leaves waiting to be thrown together in a salad. Rowans and hawthorn berries were in fruit, ready to be made into vividly coloured jellies and jams or a delicious, thick ketchup. Wild foods can bring us flavours and tastes as exotic as any you could find on an adventurous foreign holiday. In your back garden there might be potato-like tubers beneath day lilies and dahlias that can be roasted until they are soft and creamy and served with melted butter. The bright-green tips of conifer branches in spring have a unique citrus tang, between rosemary and lemon, and make a mouth-watering ice cream. Along a rocky coastline there are seaweeds that taste just like fried bacon, and others with the pungent kick of black pepper.

It feels a lifetime ago that I took my first steps toward foraging. In my early twenties I took a trip to South Wales where my host lent me an antiquated wild food guide and took me for walks along the nearby hedgerows and lanes. We ate gorse flowers from prickly bushes, picked wild garlic from the woods and made pasta with nettle sauce. It was a world away from the oven chips, spaghetti rings and crispy pancakes of my childhood. I was hooked. I ended up walking, hitching and cycling all over the UK, foraging from roadsides, lay-bys, hedgerows and headlands. In the years that followed I travelled further afield, and picked prickly cactus pears in the Yucatán Peninsula, wild herbs in India, chickweed and walnuts in the Pyrenees, carob in Spain and pine needles for tea in Germany. I learnt all I could from books, other foragers and experiments in the poky kitchens of shared houses. I studied nutrition and food science at university, took a diploma in sustainable gardening and eventually began to write and teach others.

Over the years I've taught everyone from celebrity chefs and soldiers to hen parties and office workers. My way of teaching has always been to tell stories about the plants – where they are from, how they are used in different cultures, what they taste like and how to prepare them. My hope is always that my students start to see distinct characteristics and exciting opportunities, instead of just 'plants'.

Regardless of where you live or can travel to, I hope these pages will show you the bounty of wild food that surrounds us. This book is rooted in the habitats of these foods – the *where* of the wild things. It is a suggestion for how to read a landscape and an exploration of why things grow in the way they do. It comprises four principal sections, each dealing with a different landscape: man-made, rural, woodland and water, with smaller chapters within. In each chapter are the plants most commonly found in that location, organised roughly in order of seasonal relevance. There are instructions for how to identify them, when and how to pick, and what to do with them, including recipes.

A quarter of a century of foraging has taught me plenty of tips and tricks, which I've included throughout. For example, a traditional foraging guide might suggest you gather beech nuts from a beech forest, but I've discovered it's far easier to sweep them up from a tarmac path or quiet roadside. And some of the best places to look for cherry trees or *Rosa rugosa* bushes are housing estates, because they are commonly used by landscape architects.

The book is also full of nuggets that fascinate me about these plants – their surprising histories, recent scientific discoveries about them, and snippets of folklore, myth and legend. It reflects on the human cultures that have thrived on the wild plants, trees, mushrooms and seaweeds of the northern hemisphere, alongside recipes from medieval Europe, modern-day Japan, Soviet Russia and precolonial North America.

You can read the book from cover to cover, flick through it at random or look up wild foods in the index. You might like to read through a chapter prior to or during a visit to a particular habitat. The hedgerow or meadow chapters could be read on a train journey out to the countryside; the fresh water chapter would make ideal reading on a narrow boat holiday; and the coast or rocky shore chapters might nourish a weekend by the sea. Do bear in mind that the wild foods are listed where they are most commonly found, but this is by no means the only place to find them. Pignuts, for example, are as likely to pop up in a meadow as they are in open woodland, and nettles are found just about everywhere, not just edgeland.

When harvesting wild food you should always keep the conservation of the crop in mind. In recent years headlines have appeared in the media telling of 'gangs' of foragers stripping the forest bare. Foraging bans have been put in place in areas such as the New Forest and Epping Forest, and while the 'gangs' are often nothing more than small groups of Eastern European families reported by xenophobic visitors, as the popularity of foraging increases it is very important to be mindful of sustainable foraging practices. And for professional foragers it makes little sense commercially to destroy their future source of income by over-picking.

To be sure of a supply of mushrooms the following year, for example, you should always leave some of the biggest to continue to spore and some of the smallest to grow. Although it's worth remembering that considering the number of spores mushrooms produce and the amount of life that occurs underground, you are unlikely to harm them by picking alone. Sadly, loss of habitat, climate change and pollution are all much more likely culprits for the fall in numbers of fungi.

With other wild foods, take what you need and leave the rest for the animals, birds and insects that rely on them to survive. Some people follow rules with numbers and ratios, such as only picking one plant in seven, but you can also just use common sense and err on the side of caution. For trees such as elder, for example, pick the berries at ground level but leave the rest for the birds. If you find signs of rare animals, such as otter scat by a riverside or nut shells nibbled by a dormouse, then it is best to gather from elsewhere. In areas where a plant, fungus or seaweed is scarce, move to where it is more abundant.

You should check the local laws in your country or region before you set out foraging. In most of the world, it is illegal to dig up any plant without the landowner's permission, including common wild foods such as burdock and horseradish. And there are often separate laws for seaweed. In Britain, it is legal to pick (but not dig up) any mushroom, fruit, foliage or flower as long as it is for personal consumption, with the exception of protected land such as that of special scientific interest. I always ask a passing farmer or a warden before digging – and they often respond with a laugh and grant permission. If they refuse I either move on, or pick something I don't have to dig up, like blackberries or sorrel.

The other golden foraging rule is: be sure that what you are picking is what you think it is. You need to be 100 per cent certain, so if in doubt leave it out! While there are detailed descriptions, tables and illustrations to aid with identification in this book, no single guide can give you all the information you need. You should cross-reference with the internet and guides from your region. Video guides can also be helpful to see plants and especially mushrooms from all angles – check the Further Reading section at the back of the book for suggestions. Foraging apps can be a useful starting point but should never be relied on. I have tested apps on poisonous webcap mushrooms and deadly hemlock, both of which were incorrectly identified as edible. Be sure you're aware of regional differences too. Although there are no poisonous seaweeds in Britain, for example, there are in France and elsewhere. Common names of plants can also vary, so check them against the Latin or scientific name.

Some people are allergic to certain wild foods, so eat just a ittle of something to begin with and try not to mix too many different foods in one sitting. Always wash what you have picked, especially if is growing at ground level in areas where dogs are exercised. And watch out for warnings in this and other guides you use – certain wild foods are not recommended for pregnant and breastfeeding women, for example.

With all those things in mind, my hope is that foraging will transform your experience of your garden, your journey to work, your favourite woodland or a beloved stretch of coast. Over time you will remember where the sweetest raspberries and blackberries grow, in which part of the woods the mushrooms are most abundant, or where to pick the most aromatic herbs.

Wild food has had me in its thrall for most of my adult life. Every year I discover a new plant or recipe. It can be a lifelong gastronomic journey that will change the way you look at both the world and the way you eat. And like any journey, it begins with a single step.

Equipment

FORAGING NEED NOT be an expensive hobby – in most instances it is totally free. However, there are a few things that make life a little easier. It is not essential to rush out and buy all these things at once; a plastic bag, rather than a basket, will suffice for early foraging trips and a blender and sieve can take the place of a juicer.

Essential equipment

The most important thing to bring with you on a foraging trip is something to carry your wild food home in. Wicker baskets or wooden trugs are both traditional and useful, especially for mushrooms and seaweed. These are suitable for short trips, close to a car park or bus/train station, but on long hikes they can be cumbersome to carry. I tend to fill my pockets with plastic bags and have a backpack with a few Tupperware tubs. I also carry a canvas or sturdy paper bag for mushrooms, as they can sweat in plastic.

A knife is useful for cutting mushrooms and sharp scissors or secateurs are good for seaweed and herbaceous plants. A pair of protective gloves will also help when picking nettles or prizing open chestnuts – I use gardening gloves.

Waterproof wellington boots are great for shallow rivers or rockpools.

Kitchen equipment

The more you forage, the more you might want to invest in certain labour-saving devices. Buy cheap, buy twice as the old saying goes, so look around for good-quality second-hand items rather than buying something new and cheap. New initiatives where you can borrow expensive equipment are popping up all over the place. In my town we have a shop called Share, where you can borrow dehydrators, apple presses, brewing barrels, jam pans and blenders for a small fee, and there are lots of online equivalents which lend or give away unwanted equipment.

DEHYDRATORS

A good dehydrator is perfect for drying mushrooms, seaweeds and herbs for tea, or making fruit leather. Price is not necessarily the best guide, so read reviews and make an informed decision.

GRINDERS

It can be useful to grind or powder wild foods in order to make things like burgers, coffees or condiments.

A pestle and mortar works well to powder most mushrooms, seeds, seaweeds and nuts. You can also use them to make pesto – it takes longer than a food processor but the grinding motion crushes the cells of the leaves, releasing more flavour and creating a superior, creamy consistency.

Another handy tool is a coffee or seed grinder. Either electric or hand cranked, these can be bought separately or as an attachment to a food processor. The more powerful the better, though to protect the motor you will need to chop larger, hard nuts such as acorns first. If buying new, look for grinders with removable blades as these can be sharpened, increasing the lifespan of the motor.

The oils within nuts can damage the insides of a grinder, so make sure it is cleaned and dried between uses or it will rust.

BLENDERS AND FOOD PROCESSORS

For soups, smoothies and nut milks, a blender or food processor can be invaluable. Look for those with a high wattage. A handheld blender is best for soups but make sure it is made from a durable material; those at the lowest end of the market are often made from cheap plastic, which can melt in hot soups. A kitchen-top processor is best for jobs like smoothies or preparing ingredients for ice cream. You can use these in combination with a sieve to remove fruit pulp, skins and seeds. The pulse option is handy for tough stems and plant matter and will help the motor last that little bit longer.

JUICERS AND PRESSES

To juice hard fruits, such as apples or pears, you can use a centrifugal juicer or a good old-fashioned apple press. Look for them in second-hand shops and online, as used juicers go for far less than they would new. Again, go for something powerful: an 800 W juicer will burn out in no time, so I would go for 1000 W and up (preferably over 1200 W).

An apple press is a useful bit of kit that should last for ever. It will press soft fruit as well as apples and can double up as a cheese press. I have a solid metal one which is very easy to clean and after more than thirteen years of use it looks as good as the day I bought it. The wooden ones are considerably cheaper and nicer to look at, but are harder to maintain and can stain. Think about capacity before buying; a five-litre press is great for the odd few glasses of juice but if you are bringing home apples by the sack load it will begin to seem very small, very quickly.

HOME-BREWING EQUIPMENT

Brewing can be a good way to preserve wild ingredients. To do it, you'll need storage containers to ferment your creations. I would recommend you invest in a brewing bucket (if you don't have anything else you can improvise with) and a couple of glass brewing vessels, or demijohns, fitted with airlocks. When you're ready to bottle up, you can buy bottles or reuse those that come with a fitted bung.

Be honest with yourself about how much you'll drink. If you're a 'glass of wine once a year after Christmas dinner' sort of person then home-brewing might not be for you. Home-brewing can also end up being a passing fad, leaving buckets and demijohns cluttering up spare rooms and garages. Only invest in the equipment if you think you will use it.

MUSLIN CLOTH

A piece of muslin cloth or a woven jelly bag is essential for sieving out fine pieces of plant matter, such as the hairs around the seeds of a rose hip or hard raspberry seeds. You'll find muslin cloth in haberdashery shops, and jelly bags are sold as filter bags in kitchenware shops and some bigger supermarkets around jam-making season. The cloth can be cut down to make bags for bouquets garnis or used for cheese making.

SIEVES

Your sieve will come in for some punishment. Often you will be pushing down or rubbing on the mesh to force through your pulp. New cheap sieves, especially those made of plastic and nylon, are not worth the money; one season of pushing hawthorn pulp through the mesh and it will break away from the upper ring. Look for a good-quality, heavy-duty sieve. Aim for at least 20 cm (8 inches) diameter – smaller ones mean pushing through in multiple batches.

Sterilising equipment

From jams and jellies to chutneys, pickles and ketchups, all jars and bottles need to be sterilised before use to minimise the risk of spoilage. This also goes for the lids. Sterilising needn't be an onerous task – here are four easy methods:

- Submerge the jars in water and bring it to the boil.
- Wash the jars in the dishwasher on a hot setting.
- Soak the jars in a sterilising solution, such as Milton, and rinse.
- Microwave the jars for 30–45 seconds on high power (you will need to boil or sterilise the lids separately, as you cannot put metal into a microwave).

Other equipment you may need

- **Jam pan** – A large saucepan or a specialist jam pan for processing large amounts of foraged food.
- **Cooking thermometer** – For making jams and jellies.
- **Jars, jars and more jars** – Jams, jellies, pickles, dried mushrooms and dried seaweed are all best stored in jars. Save all your old jars and thoroughly wash in the sink or dishwasher. Think also about investing in some Kilner/Mason jars.
- **Berry picker** – A comb berry picker is useful for small berries such as bilberries and cranberries (see pages 205 and 215).
- **Foldable trowel** – These come in handy for wild roots such as dandelions, chicory and Jack-by-the-hedge. You'll find them in most camping shops.

Base Recipes

ALTHOUGH THIS BOOK deals with a wide variety of foods, many are prepared and preserved in the same way. For example, watercress and nettles can both be made into a hearty soup using a thick base of potatoes and onions, and elderberries, raspberries, blackberries and blackcurrants can all be made into a delicious jam in exactly the same way. This chapter is here to give you the tools to prepare or preserve the majority of wild foods you may come across, within the pages of this book and beyond.

Using green leaves

During the spring, several different species of leaves start to rise up from their dormant roots or burst their buds to make the most of the returning sun. During this time of year, it's useful to have a few catch-all recipes to make good use of the abundance of succulent, young leaves.

SALAD

Foraged salads are a little different from those you might buy ready prepared in packets from the supermarket. Leaves can range from bland to bitter to nose-scrunchingly spicy. The secret is to use milder leaves such as lime (*Tilia* spp.) or mallow for the main bulk of the salad and then mix in stronger flavours like wild mustards, chicory leaves or rocket to add depth. Edible flowers don't add much in the way of flavour, but they are wonderful for colour. Dress the whole mixture with olive oil and lemon, or use a flavoured vinegar (such as spruce tip).

PESTO

Pesto can be made with nearly any green leaf, with flavoursome herbaceous leaves among the best. The leaves are macerated, mixed with an oil and toasted seeds or nuts, and then seasoned with salt, pepper and grated parmesan. For picky eaters (i.e. children) you can 'cheat' by adding a teaspoon of shop-bought pesto to homemade recipes – trust me, they don't always notice the difference!

Traditional basil-leaf recipes use uncooked leaves, which works fine for thin, herbaceous leaves such as rocket or wild garlic. However, thicker leaves like mallow, lamb's quarters/goosefoot (which make a particularly good pesto) or stinging nettles need to be treated a little differently. Any thick stalks should be removed and the leaves steamed or boiled in just enough water to cover them. You can also try mixing different wild leaves, such as wild garlic and nettle or ground elder and chickweed. The recipe below serves 4–5, over pasta.

FOR A BASIC PESTO RECIPE, YOU WILL NEED:

- 2 handfuls of wild leaves (gloved hands for nettles!)
- 50 g (2 oz) toasted nuts or seeds
- ½–1 tsp lemon juice (or generous pinch of sumac powder)
- A good pinch of salt
- 1–2 tbsp olive oil

METHOD:

1. Cook the leaves if necessary (see above).
2. Grind the toasted nuts/seeds.
3. Roughly chop the leaves and remove any tough stalks.
4. Place all the ingredients in a high-powered food processor or pestle and mortar and work into a smooth paste. Note: stringy

leaves can burn out the motor of a food processor, so use the pulse function and prepare your leaves beforehand.

5. Serve on pasta, with crusty bread, as a pizza topping in place of tomato paste, as a sandwich filling or drizzled over couscous.

COOKED GREEN LEAVES

In medieval England, most households would prepare 'buttered wortes', a mixture of wild and domestic seasonal leaves boiled and flavoured with butter. In Greece they cook a near identical dish called 'horta', with olive oil and lemon in place of dairy. Greens prepared this way are great as a side, or on toast with a poached egg or fried tempeh. Use just a little water to cook your greens as this preserves the nutritional content.

Any of the following leaves can be mixed together: beet spinach, dandelion, mallow, hollyhock, thistles (spines removed), nettle (blanch in boiling water first to remove the sting), wild garlic (in moderation), wild mustard, Jack-by-the-hedge, docks (leached). Or experiment with what you have to hand.

YOU WILL NEED:
- 1–2 handfuls of mixed leaves
- 1–2 medium onions (optional)
- Oil or butter for frying
- Optional extras (see below)

METHOD:
1. Brown the onions on a low heat in a little butter or oil, stirring often (you can omit this step if you'd rather not use onions).
2. Remove any tough stems and shred the mixed leaves.
3. Stir the leaves into the pan and let them wilt.
4. Add a couple of tablespoons of water (or a bit more for thicker leaves). Season with salt and pepper. Flavour with optional extras from list 1 (see below).
5. Cover the pan and simmer for a minute or two.
6. Test for flavour and check leaves are sufficiently cooked.

7. Add optional extras from list 2 (see below).
8. Serve and top with optional extras from list 3 (see below).

OPTIONAL EXTRAS 1:

· **Start with 1 tsp per 250 g (9 oz) of leaves and add more to taste.**
· **Soy sauce**
· **Pine needle vinegar (see page 275)**

· **Liquid aminos**
· **Ume plum vinegar**
· **Balsamic vinegar**
· **Tabasco sauce**

OPTIONAL EXTRAS 2:

· **Butter and lemon juice**
· **Olive oil and lemon juice**

· **Olive oil and a light vinegar**
· **Sesame oil (use with soy sauce)**

OPTIONAL EXTRAS 3:

· **I recommend any of the following toasted in a dry pan:**
· **Flaked almonds**
· **Walnut pieces**

· **Crushed hazelnuts**
· **Sesame seeds**
· **Himalayan balsam seeds**
· **Hogweed seeds**

WILD GREENS SOUP

Soups can be an improvised affair, using what you have to hand. Start with a base of fried onion and potatoes or rice (I bring cooked rice on camping trips for this purpose) in a good stock for a full-flavoured, filling soup. Play around with your ingredients; use a little more of this, or a little less of that the next time if it's not quite right. If your soup tastes too bitter add something salty, such as stock powder, salt, soy sauce or liquid aminos (a delicious soy sauce alternative). Alternatively, add something sweet such as honey or a good balsamic vinegar. If the soup is too thick add a little more water, and if it's too stringy return it to the blender.

YOU WILL NEED:

- Butter or frying oil
- 100 g (3½ oz) onions
- 150 g (5½ oz) potatoes peeled and diced
- 150–225 g (5½–8 oz) wild greens (such as wild garlic, nettle, watercress or a mix)
- 1 l (4 cups) stock (vegetable, chicken or mushroom) – or alternatively, for a creamier soup, 500 ml (2 cups) stock and 500 ml (2 cups) milk
- Salt and pepper

OPTIONAL EXTRAS:

- Vegetables: courgettes, squash, carrots, wild stems or shoots
- Mixed greens: dandelion, Jack-by-the-hedge, wild lettuce, hairy bittercress, chickweed, three-cornered leek
- In moderation: alexanders (stems or leaves), ground elder
- For flavour: powdered mushrooms and/or seaweed, liquid aminos
- Toppings: dairy or nut cream, or cheese (blue cheese works well with most greens); bacon; toasted and flaked almonds.

METHOD:

1. Prepare the base first by frying the onions in butter or oil until browned.
2. Add the potatoes and stock and simmer.
3. Add any vegetables you wish to use in order of cooking time (usually hardest vegetables first).
4. Once the potatoes are soft, chop your greens and add to the pan.
5. Check for seasoning add salt, pepper or flavourings (see above) if necessary.

MUSHROOM SOUP

To tweak the above recipe and make a mushroom soup, simply omit the potatoes (or equivalent) and wild greens. Make a roux by toasting 40 g (1½ oz) of flour in an equal amount of melted butter or margarine. Add the liquid stock, then simmer 400–450 g (14 oz–1 lb) of chopped mushrooms.

....

Preserving

During the late summer and autumn months, there is such an abundance of wild food available it is almost impossible to imagine the scarcity of the winter months ahead. The generations preceding us knew of these lean months all too well – being unprepared for them could be the difference between life and death. To ensure a year-round supply of sustenance, Iron Age people stored their food in chalk pits, the Romans salted fish and meats and the Saxons brewed mead and fruit wines.

Today food scientists have studied the reasons for food spoilage, and we know both how to effectively preserve our food and why it works. The backbone of any food preservation is to prevent the growth of micro-organisms such as moulds, yeasts and bacteria. The more methods we use to prevent this growth the longer the shelf life. Scientists call this hurdle technology. Sometimes one method of preservation or one hurdle is enough – for example, because micro-organisms need water to divide and grow, simply drying fruit or mushrooms will do the trick. At other times more than one hurdle is needed.

Hurdle (method of preservation)	Example
High acid environment	Vinegar – pickles and ketchups
High sugar content	Jams, jellies and cordials
Low water content	Fruit leathers, dried herbs and dehydrated fruits
Low temperature	Freezing
Bio-preservation	Fermentation – kimchi, sauerkraut, beers and wines
Oxidation prevention	Citric acid or lemon juice for cordials

The method of preservation you choose can be down to personal preference or just storage space. Here are my suggested methods for some of the more common wild foods.

Type of wild food	Suggested preserving method
Wild leaves	Lacto-ferment/kimchi, dehydrate (e.g. for wild garlic leaves)
Soft fruits	Jam, jelly, ketchup, freeze
Hard fruits	Pre-cook and freeze, ketchup, chutney, jam, jelly
Mushrooms	Dehydrate, pre-cook and freeze, ketchup, pickle (see below)
Wild vegetables (stems, bulbs, roots etc.)	Blanch and freeze, cold or warm pickle (see below)
Flower buds	Cold pickle (e.g. capers)
Seaweeds	Dehydrate, dehydrate and powder, warm pickle (tips or wracks, see page 373)

FREEZING

Soft fruit can be frozen without any prior preparation, but hard fruit, wild vegetables and mushrooms benefit from being steamed, blanched or pre-cooked prior to freezing. How long you blanch them for depends on how thick they are. As a rule of thumb, if you can easily push a fork into the food, it is ready to freeze.

To prevent foods, such as blackberries, from sticking to each other, freeze them on a flat baking tray. Once frozen remove them, store in tubs or bags and return to the freezer. Freezer food doesn't last for ever, so aim to eat your summer berries by Christmas and frozen dishes within 3 months of freezing.

JAMS AND JELLIES

Jams and jellies are fruit preserved in sugar. They're not only great as a spread on your morning toast but for all sorts of other things too, from sweetening yoghurt to baking into a pie. Jellies with a sharp flavour, such as cranberry, work well as an accompaniment to cheese or meat.

With jams, the whole fruit is preserved in sugar, including the seeds. Jellies have the same starting step but are strained through a muslin bag before being left to set. Unlike jams, which can contain whole bits of fruit, jellies have a smooth texture and if allowed to strain naturally rather than squeezed through the bag, they will be clear and not cloudy.

TO MAKE A JAM OR JELLY, YOU WILL NEED:

For soft fruit (raspberries, bilberries, etc.):

- Equal weights of cane sugar and fruit (e.g. 500 g (1 lb 2 oz) blackberries, 500 g (1 lb 2 oz) cane sugar)
- Pectin, which should be added according to packet instructions, or add a chopped full-sized apple (these will help the jam or jelly to set)

For hard fruit (pear, quince, apple etc.):

- Water and fruit. The volume of water should be around 1/3 the weight of the fruit (e.g. 166 ml (5½ fl oz) water for 500 g (1 lb 2 oz) fruit)

- Lemon juice or citric acid, if the fruit is prone to oxidising (e.g. apples). Use roughly 1 tbsp for every 500 g (1 lb 2 oz) of jam.

- Sugar (3 parts sugar for every 4 parts fruit pulp)

METHOD:

1. Simmer the fruit until it forms a pulp, adding water for the hard fruit.
2. Strain if you need to remove seeds (omit this step for jams with whole fruit).
3. Add the sugar.
4. Bring to the boil and cook to setting point: 104°C (220°F) (this normally takes around 10 minutes). Use the wrinkle test (below) if you do not have a thermometer.
5. Pour into sterilised jars, cover the top with a disc of waxed paper and screw the lid on tight.

This recipe will make about 4 small jars. In the absence of a thermometer, use the wrinkle test to see if jam is ready. Put a saucer in the fridge before you start cooking your jam (or put it in the freezer if you have just read this). Once it's cool, put a blob of jam on the saucer and run your finger over it; if it wrinkles, the jam is set.

KETCHUP

Ketchup is essentially preserved fruit in a semi-liquid form, a pourable chutney if you will. Elderberries, Japanese knotweed shoots, hawthorn berries, plums, apples and damsons can all be used – or experiment with mixtures of what you have to hand.

YOU WILL NEED:

- Fruit
- Sugar, around 1/3 of the weight of the fruit (e.g. 600 g (1 lb 5 oz) fruit, 200 g (7 oz) sugar)
- Water
- Vinegar
- An apple, cored and peeled (for low-pectin fruits)
- Spices of your choice, like coriander, chilli or cumin

METHOD:

1. Wash the fruit. Chop any harder fruits or vegetables, such as knotweed shoots or apples.
2. Put the fruit in a large pan on a low heat and cover with a half-half mix of water and vinegar.
3. For low-pectin fruits (e.g. elder or plum), add the cored and peeled apple.
4. Simmer to a pulp, continuously stirring.
5. Allow to cool and push the mixture through a sieve to remove any seeds and stalks.
6. Add sugar, to taste, to the sieved pulp.
7. Add your chosen spices (1–2 tsp per 200 ml (7 fl oz) of ketchup).
8. Simmer again until a thick puree is formed, adding more water if too thick or continuing to simmer if too thin (you can also add more apple to increase pectic content).
9. Pour into sterilised bottles and use within 6 months.

CHUTNEY

Sweet, sour and a little spicy; a good chutney goes well with cheese in a sandwich, meat or a curry, and can add interest to a winter dinner table when foraged goodies are thin on the ground. This is the basic recipe for chutney.

YOU WILL NEED:

- 4 parts fruit or vegetable
- 2 parts onion
- 2 parts vinegar – or a mix of vinegar and lemon juice
- 1 part sugar
- ½ part sultanas (optional)
- Spices (such as ginger, chilli, coriander, cumin, fennel seeds, hogweed seeds, carrot seeds)
- Salt and pepper, to taste

METHOD:

1. For harder fruit and vegetables, such as roots, boil until tender prior to making the chutney.
2. Simmer all the ingredients together in a pan on a low heat until they have formed a puree. Add a dash of water if too thick, or if too watery continue to simmer until it has thickened.
3. Check the seasoning and store in sterilised jars. Use within 6–12 months and refrigerate once opened.

PICKLES

Pickles are foods preserved in vinegar and/or salt solution, sometimes with the addition of honey or sugar to sweeten and spices to flavour. You can 'hot pickle' foods, which means to seal in a jar covered with warm vinegar solution (just off the boil). This makes for a tender pickle with a full flavour. Alternatively, you can 'cold pickle' foods by sealing them in a cold vinegar solution, which keeps them crisp. Or you can ferment them in brine (see kimchi below). Whichever method you choose, never use an aluminium pan when pickling food, as it can react with and discolour the ingredients.

When it comes to flavouring, spices (both wild and shop bought) can give pickles an added piquancy, while sugar and honey may be necessary to sweeten or balance bitter compounds. Aim to use a total of around 1–2 tsp of spice mix for every 200 ml (7 fl oz) of liquid. For a sweet pickle, add 1 tbsp of sugar or honey for every 200 ml (7 fl oz) of liquid. Making your own spice mix can be useful if preparing a lot of food at once. Use any of the following in your mix:

· Fresh or powdered ginger
· Whole allspice (not powdered)
· Coriander seeds
· Nigella seeds
· Hogweed seeds
· Mustard seeds

In addition, you can add:

· Spruce tips (2 per 100 ml (3½ fl oz))
· Wood avens roots (1 tsp) or 2–3 cloves

To make a basic warm pickling solution, mix equal amounts water with equal amounts brine, then sweeten or flavour.

FOR EXAMPLE:
· 100 ml (3½ fl oz) vinegar (i.e. apple cider, white wine)
· 100 ml (3½ fl oz) water
· A pinch of salt
· 2 tsp spice mix
· 1 tbsp sugar

METHOD:
1. First remove any dirt or debris from your wild food.
2. Sterilise your jars (see page 11).
3. Prepare as below. For foods soaked in brine use a 5 per cent solution – 1 teaspoon for every 100 ml (3½ fl oz).
4. If pouring boiling liquid into jars, ensure they are first warmed or they will break.

Wild food	Preparation	Method of pickling
Leaves	Soak in brine for 2 hours, rinse	Fermentation
Stems	Peel any tough skin (i.e. thistles, burdock). Boil or steam until tender (unless stems are already tender, e.g. wild garlic)	Fermentation or warm pickling For tender stems, cold pickling
Mushrooms	Boil for approximately 10 minutes then discard the water. Pat dry	Warm pickling
Seaweed	Soak in brine	Warm pickling
Buds	Rinse in fresh water	Cold pickling
Marsh samphire	Rinse in fresh water	Cold pickling
Roots	Boil or steam until tender	Warm or cold pickling

KIMCHI

Kimchi is traditionally made with crisp Chinese cabbages, but it can be made with any wild leaf. Wild garlic kimchi is a particular favourite in our household.

Kimchi is a popular dish in Korea, where it is served prior to a meal to help with digestion. Fermentation breaks down the leaves to create a creamy texture with a little sourness, and spices can be added to enhance the flavour.

The sour environment not only flavours the food but also promotes the growth of good bacteria. These in turn prevent the growth of bad bacteria, preserving the leaves for an extended period of time (three to six months in the fridge). This recipe makes one jar.

METHOD:

1. Pick and wash two handfuls of wild edible leaves.
2. Cut into 2-inch pieces and place in a bowl with a handful of salt between each layer. I include the stalks if you wish, as this will give the kimchi a good crunch.
3. Add water just to cover and place a plate on top, ensuring all the leaves are submerged. Weigh the plate down with a tin or heavy object and leave until the leaves begin to break down and become floppy; this can be anywhere between 2 hours to overnight, depending on the leaf.
4. Drain, setting aside a cup of the liquid.
5. Rinse in a colander, squeezing the leaves.
6. Add red pepper powder and a little sugar (chilli flakes and miso work well too).
7. Cram it all in a jar. The leaves should release liquid as you do – the leaves should be submerged in this liquid, so if they aren't, add some the solution you set aside earlier.
8. Put the lid on loosely. Leave the jar out for a day to a day and a half.
9. Open the jar and press the leaves down with a clean object. If bubbles are released, the kimchi is ready.
10. Put the jar in the fridge. The kimchi will be ready to eat after a week, but will improve with age.

CORDIAL

Cordials are sweetened, flavoured liquids. My rule of thumb is one part sugar for every two parts liquid. This will make a reasonably thick syrup. Increased sugar will aid preservation but will also rot your teeth! Citric acid and/or lemon juice can be added to both preserve and bring a sour note to subtle flavours such as elderflower.

Store your bottled cordial somewhere cool and out of direct sunlight. Although some cordials keep for months, many begin to ferment after two weeks to a month and become decidedly boozy.

Fermented elderberry cordial is delicious but I wouldn't recommend it for children's parties! The recipe below makes one bottle.

YOU WILL NEED:

- 400 ml (13½ fl oz) water infused overnight with the herb/flower of your choice, or alternatively 400 g (14 oz) pulped and strained fruit

- 200 g (7 oz) sugar or honey or 240 ml (1 cup) maple syrup (or half of each)
- Juice of one lemon (optional)
- Citric acid (if preserving)

METHOD:

1. Infuse the herb of your choice in the water or simmer your fruit until it forms a pulp.
2. Dissolve the sugar in the liquid.
3. Test for flavour and add the lemon if needed.
4. Strain through a sieve and/or muslin cloth if needed.
5. Pour into sterilised bottles.

FRUIT LEATHER

Fruit leather is a sheet of chewy dried fruit. It is a useful way of preserving fruit, especially berries, long after picking. It makes a good snack when out hiking, a handy addition to a lunchbox or a healthy treat for children. Sometimes it is flavoured, sometimes it is sweetened with sugar or honey. Aside from the water-soluble vitamins diminished through heating, dehydrated fruits contain much the same nutrients as fresh fruits. A food dehydrator makes the process a lot easier but an oven on its lowest setting also works.

METHOD:

1. Either mash in a bowl or simmer the fruit on a low heat, until it breaks down into a pulp.
2. For fruits with low water content, such as hawthorn berries, add a little liquid (no more than 1 part liquid for every 8 parts

fruit) to help them break up. You can use apple juice to add sweetness, or just water.

3. Push the resulting puree through a sieve to remove stones/pips and the skin. For fruits with hairy seeds, such as rose hips, squeeze through a muslin cloth.
4. Test for sweetness and add sugar, maple syrup or similar if necessary.
5. Spread the puree in a very thin layer (about 3–6 mm) on a baking tray if using an oven, or on parchment paper/silica trays if using a dehydrator.
6. Dry in an oven on a very low temperature (an Aga is ideal) or in a dehydrator. You can also dehydrate on top of a night storage heater.
7. Once the surface is smooth rather than sticky the leathers are done (this should take around 6–8 hours in a dehydrator) and can be wrapped up and stored.

Fruit leathers keep for up to a year (unless you have children who know where you hide them . . .).

HOME-BREWING – WINE

Brewing to create wine is one of the most ancient ways to preserve a harvest. The process is straightforward and can produce full-bodied reds and sweet white wines with flavours you won't find anywhere else.

METHOD:
1. Clean and prepare your wild food to remove dirt and bugs.
2. Create the liquid for brewing. For herbs or delicate flavours like elderflower or rose petals, this means steeping overnight. If using soft fruits such as berries or plums, juice or press them. Harder fruits, such as apples, should be boiled in water. Roots or stems should also be boiled to extract their flavour.

3. Once the flavours are in liquid form, strain the liquid, add sugar (around 1 kg per litre or 2 lbs per 4 cups) and heat until the sugar is dissolved.
4. Fruits such as apples and hawthorn berries, which contain pectin, should be prepared with pectic enzyme. This is best added to the liquid once it has cooled.
5. Also add a Campden tablet at this stage if possible, as this kills off any natural yeasts which can lead to unpredictable flavours.
6. Pour the mix into a fermenting bucket and add yeast. Use 1–2 packets (7–14 g or 1½–3 tsp) per 4–5 litres (gallon). You can also add extra flavours at this stage. For flowers and herbs, you can add a green or black tea bag for tannins; for fruit wines, raisins or grape juice can be added.
7. Cover the bucket and leave to brew somewhere warm for 2–5 days, until the bubbling stops or significantly slows.
8. Strain the liquid into a demijohn fitted with an airlock.
9. Once the bubbles have stopped rising in the demijohn you will need to rack the wine. Let the wine settle on a high table and siphon the liquid with a piece of tube into another sterilised demijohn placed on a lower chair, ensuring you leave any sediment behind in the upper demijohn.
10. Let the wine mature for 6–8 weeks and then repeat step 8, this time siphoning the wine into sterilised wine bottles. Cork the bottles and store for at least 8 months to a year (or more) before drinking.

Dehydrating

Mushrooms, seaweeds and wild leaves (for tea or culinary herbs) can all be dehydrated and stored in sealed jars or Ziploc bags.

Seaweeds are best dried outdoors on a washing line or rack. If you lack outside space you can hang them above a bath, but the humidity should be kept low – so remove the seaweed before having a bath or shower and ensure the steam has dissipated before rehanging.

You can dry herbs and leaves for tea by tying them in bundles and hanging in a ventilated space or spreading them out on newspaper on a windowsill. They will take two to three days or more to dry completely, at which point they will be brittle to the touch.

Mushrooms can be dried on a convection radiator or in a dehydrator. The larger the surface area the longer a foodstuff will take to dehydrate, so cut foods into thin slices.

Alternatively, arrange your wild foods on a baking tray and put them in the oven on the lowest possible setting. Regularly check the tray to prevent burning and keep the oven door ajar.

When the time comes to use your dried foods, soak mushrooms and seaweed in warm water prior to use in soups, stews, pâté and risotto (mushrooms), setting aside the liquid for use as a stock for soups. Alternatively, powder the seaweed and mushrooms and use as a flavour enhancer in soups and stews.

MAN-MADE

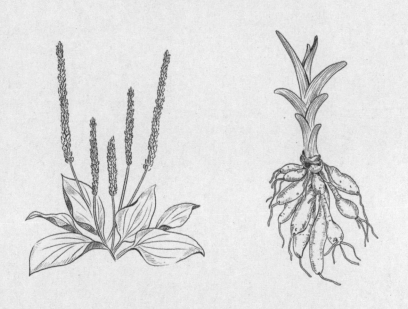

CHAPTER ONE

Gardens

L EFT UNATTENDED FOR just a few weeks, a garden will rebel against its constraints. The grass is usually the first to kick off. Defying the absent mower, it rises up to long and straggly heights, dotted with daisies, clovers, dandelions, buttercups and speedwells. Weeds such as bittercress, ragwort, willowherbs and enchanter's nightshade begin to multiply and spread through an unattended border. Ivy, goosegrass and bindweed climb any shrub within reach, eventually depriving them of light and locking them in a chokehold. If neglected for months on end, even intentionally grown plants, such as wisteria or Virginia creepers, will pull down guttering, roof tiles and downpipes, eventually erasing all signs of human occupation.

And yet, gardens give us the illusion of control over nature. We shape and encourage, producing patches of land in an effort to reflect who we are. We sow, plant, pot and propagate; we deadhead, clip, prune, mow and mulch; we tie up, train, feed and water.

The earliest examples of gardens, where plants were intentionally selected and grown within an enclosed space, seem to have emerged between 6,000 and 10,000 years ago, in two separate regions. These early gardens marked a move away from hunter-gatherer lifestyles, to a more settled society where people lived in small village-like groups. At this time, in Mesopotamia (which roughly corresponds to modern-day Iraq), cereals and pulses were selected from the wild and domesticated in garden-like plots, transforming them into many of the crops we know today, such as chickpeas, lentils, wheat and barley. Around the same time, in southern Mexico, similar small plots developed and wild forms of maize became domesticated. Crude fences enclosed these gardens, keeping marauding tribes and wild animals at bay.

When societies outgrew these small villages, people formed towns and cities and set up gardens as we know them today, where plants were grown not as food but for purely aesthetic reasons. In the eighth century BC, in a similar boast of wealth and power, King Sennacherib established his great royal garden in Nineveh, near Mosul in modern-day Iraq. The king's royal garden was so renowned that many now believe it to be the true site of the much-fabled Hanging Gardens of Babylon.

Ancient Egyptian, Greek and Roman gardens followed on from these traditions, selecting plants from different regions and placing them in new environments. The Romans were renowned for moving plants all over their vast empire. We can see the legacy of this in Britain today; celandine, a popular flower in the villa gardens of the Roman Empire, is now a common woodland plant, and ground elder, once a Roman pot-herb, is now a frequent hedgerow plant and garden weed.

In our modern gardens we usually separate what is edible from what is beautiful. We plant up a bed for the dahlias, peonies and fuchsias and another for the potatoes, peas and carrots. But this distinction is a blurry one. One of the oldest known food crops, the onion, has a very striking, pom-pom-like bloom when left to flower, and I like to imagine that even the earliest smallholdings would have been attractive in their own way.

And though we might not think of a beautiful garden as a source of food, the flowers of spring bedding plants such as violas, pansies and primroses make a colourful garnish to salads, cakes and pastries. Larger flowers such as the day lily and dahlia have edible potato-like tubers; fuchsias have edible berries; and the seeds of nigella flowers can be used to give a distinctive flavour to sweet and savoury dishes.

Children love eating from a garden, especially a flower bed, and your own garden can be a safe environment in which to teach them to distinguish the edible from the poisonous. From a young age, my own children would pull up random leaves and ask, 'Daddy eat?' waiting for the approving nod or the alarmed 'No!' The downside was that they were then quite happy pulling up primrose flowers in public gardens or edible leaves from friend's immaculate borders. I've since taught them to always ask before they eat.

BELLFLOWERS
Campanula spp.

Season for picking: all year
Where to find them: walls and pavement cracks
Main identifying feature: bell-shaped flowers and heart-shaped leaves
Best use: salads
Not to be mistaken for: monkshood, bluebells

Most garden campanulas have bell-shaped flowers and toothed heart-shaped leaves. The flowers and leaves of all campanulas are non-toxic and many have a mild, fresh flavour. Species such as adria bellflower (*Campanula portenschlagiana*), and the trailing bellflower *Campanula poscharskyana* grow as little clumps of blue flowers on walls and through cracks in paths and pavements. I nibble on them when passing or throw them into a salad to give a bit of colour. Most campanulas are clump forming or trailing; poisonous lookalikes such as monkshood or bluebells, in contrast, have flowers on stems.

HOSTAS
Hosta spp.

Season for picking: spring
Where to find them: garden borders
Main identifying feature: large, ovate leaves
Best use: shoots in stir-fry
Not to be mistaken for: arum lily

Hostas are prized for their foliage; they have large showy leaves, which are often variegated, sometimes vivid green or a light dusty blue. They grow well in damp and shaded areas so they suit gardens overshadowed by hedges or trees. During the spring the leaves push through the soil to sprout up in a neat clump before they begin to unfurl. This is when they are at their best for the kitchen table.

The flavour varies among different species, but generally they have a satisfying crunch to them, even after cooking. Asparagus, leek or lettuce are easy comparisons as they have a distinct springtime freshness.

If the thought of eating your prize hostas is a little horrifying, consider separating them to produce more plants. Large hostas can have substantial rootstocks which, like rhubarb, can handle being dug up with a spade and divided into two or more sections. One of these can be replanted in the border and the other in the vegetable garden for food.

In Japan, the hosta shoots intended as food are covered with a rice husk paper to blanch and soften them as they grow, as is often done with celery. Known as *urui*, *ginbo* or *giboshi*, hosta shoots (hostons) can be found for sale in Japanese food markets and are eaten in stir-fries or ramen noodle soups flavoured with soy or miso. *Hosta montana* is the most favoured but all varieties are edible.

Hostas can be confused with the similar-looking arum lily, *Arum maculatum*. The arum lily, however, has a glossy texture with arrow-shaped leaves, while hostas are more heart shaped, often with matt leaves.

PREPARATION AND USE
Hostas vary greatly in size and shape. For the chunkier shoots, boil or steam as you would asparagus until they are somewhat softened. For the smaller, thinner shoots, quickly fry in hot oil or even try crunching on them raw.

They are delicious dressed with lemon and butter, soy sauce and chilli or a sanbaizu sauce (made up commonly of one part soy sauce and two of vinegar and mirin).

Alternatively, for a fresher taste, lightly cook them in a pan, then quickly place in ice water before removing and dressing with a dashi sauce.

FLOWERING BLACKCURRANT
Ribes sanguineum

Season for picking: spring
Where to find them: shrubby borders
Main identifying feature: dusky-pink blossoms
Best use: cordial from flowers

Flowering blackcurrants bloom early in the season, as the days start to get longer and warmer around mid-spring. Swathes of dusky-pink blossoms hang pendulously, giving off a rich, musky aroma. They are usually pruned to waist or chest height, but they're tough old plants which can grow much larger if left to their own devices.

You will find them in gardens across the northern hemisphere, especially those which have elderly owners. Yet the flowering blackcurrant has a long history outside of chintzy gardens. It is native to the west coast of North America, growing wild along the coast from British Columbia down to central California.

PREPARATION AND USE

Although the berries are edible, they are insubstantial and not particularly flavoursome raw. I usually harvest the flowers to make a cordial or syrup with a complex, musky and herb-like flavour. Adding something sweet to bring out this flavour is essential and although sugar is the obvious choice, you can substitute the sugar for stevia granules or honey. A few sweet cicely leaves (see page 162) can also help to reduce the amount of sugar needed.

The cordial can be diluted to taste then frozen as a refreshing ice lolly, served as a cooling drink or used as a mixer for gin- or vodka-based cocktails.

FORAGER'S TIP

When I first experimented with flowering blackcurrants, I found dropping a little lemon juice into the syrup caused a magical, almost alchemical reaction, turning the mixture from a murky pink to a vivid one. This happens because the flowers contain a group of colour pigments known as anthocyanins. Heat breaks down these pigments, turning them from an acid into an alkali, and the colour fades. Adding lemon juice turns them back into acids, intensifying the bright pink colour.

İCE PLANT
Hylotelephium spectabile, syn. *Sedum spectabile*

Season for picking: spring
Where to find them: garden borders
Main identifying feature: succulent leaves and purple-red, flat flowers which remain over winter
Best use: salads
Not to be mistaken for: inedible sedums and succulents

The *Hylotelephium spectabile* (also known as the *Sedum spectabile*, or ice plant) is a popular garden plant that grows up to 45 cm (18 inches) high, with succulent green-grey leaves and a cluster of pink flowers which remain on the plant right through the winter. It is native to Korea and China where it is used in salads and stir-fries.

The leaves are best in the early spring, around the same time the primroses are in flower, and they remain good to eat right up until the flower buds form in the early summer. The flavour is mild and succulent, like a cucumber but with more of a crunch. Children seem to love them too; since I introduced him to it, my youngest son sets up camp next to the plant happily munching on the leaves as if they were sweets.

PREPARATION AND USE
In Korea they use a slightly different but similar tasting sedum with a yellow flower, called stringy stonecrop *(Sedum sarmentosum)*, to make a spicy salad called *dolnamul-muchim*. As it is far more common in gardens, *Sedum spectabile* can be substituted for the stringy stonecrop. Simply mix with fresh leaves, such as lettuce, and top with sauce made from vinegar, garlic, soy sauce, ginger, chilli, honey and sesame seeds. You can add shiitake powder (or boletus, see page 253), or powdered lotus root if you can find it in your local Asian food store.

MAGNOLIA
Magnolia spp.

Season for picking: spring
Where to find them: parks and gardens
Main identifying feature: large tree with pink-white blossoms
Best use: blossom pickle

All magnolia blossoms are edible, but in my view not all are worthy of your time. The best are the big, showy blossoms such as *Magnolia grandiflora* and *M. × soulangeana*. The flavour of the blossoms is not what you might expect. It's best described as spicy or gingery, but really needs to be experienced to be believed. Some find the taste overpowering and for a small minority magnolia can be an allergen. With this in mind, it's best to try a little before you harvest a lot.

PREPARATION AND USE
Pick the individual petals of the blossoms rather than the whole flower. Once harvested, magnolia blossom can be pickled in a solution of sugar, salt and a light vinegar, such as white wine or rice vinegar. Try in place of Chinese cabbage in a kind of floral kimchi (see page 24) or submerged in honey.[1]

Garden plants for tea

Gardens can be a source of refreshing caffeine-free alternatives to tea and coffee. Below is a selection of garden plants, including weeds, that can be made into herbal tea.

Brewing times vary depending on your taste. Bitter compounds tend to build the longer the herbs are allowed to steep, but pour the tea too soon and it can lack flavour. As a rule of thumb, I tend to brew most of my teas for around five minutes. For anything with a tough skin, such as rose hips, it's best to simmer in the water rather than infuse. For delicate herbs, especially flowers, use water which is just off the boil.

All can be brewed in a pot or in a cup and strained.

Name	Scientific name	Other information
Chrysanthemum	*Chrysanthemum morifolium* or *C. indicum*	Popular drink in China, where it is said to help lower blood pressure and reduce inflammation. Delicate but refreshing flavour. Use fresh or dried flower heads
Cleavers/ goosegrass/ stickyweed	*Galium aparine*	Leaves at any stage as a tea (good with mint or nettle). Seeds roasted and ground as a caffeine-free but refreshing coffee substitute
Dandelion	*Taraxacum* spp.	Leaves and/or flowers for tea, root for coffee (see page 124). Leaves are diuretic and the root is a probiotic
Evening primrose	*Oenothera* spp.	Leaves in tea used to settle stomach. Flavour best with other herbs/weeds such as nettle, mint or lemon balm
Fennel	*Foeniculum vulgare*	Seeds and/or leaves good to aid digestion as a tea after a meal. Seeds need to be steeped for a couple of minutes longer than the leaves. Seeds can be chewed following a meal as they often are in India
Ground ivy	*Glechoma hederacea*	Not actually ivy but a member of the mint family. Steeping the leaves makes a very refreshing and complex tea (see page 148)
Hibiscus	*Hibiscus syriacus*	Flowers and leaves – best dried first

Name	Scientific name	Other information
Common white jasmine	*Jasminum officinale*	Mix with green tea for a light, refreshing brew
Lady's mantle	*Alchemilla mollis* and *A. vulgaris*	May help with heavy menstruation and ease associated cramps. A very tasty tea
Lemon balm	*Melissa officinalis*	Light lemon flavour. Said to have calming and slightly sedative properties
Lemon verbena	*Aloysia citriodora*	Flowers used in tea (the leaves can be eaten). Oils contained in the leaves have been found to be calming.
Mint	*Mentha* spp.	Fresh or dried. Can be mixed with black tea and sugar to make Moroccan mint tea. Lab trials have found peppermint to boost memory.[2]
Nettle	*Urtica dioica* and *U. urens*	Flavoursome tea full of trace minerals, good with mint. Anti-inflammatory and said to enhance cognitive function.
Passionflower	*Passiflora*	Leaves and flowers. May relieve anxiety and improve sleep.
Peony	*Paeonia*	Petals – best dried first. A good flavour which goes well with rosebay willowherb tea (see page 97).

Name	Scientific name	Other information
Rose hip	*Rosa* spp.	For best results first boil the hips for a few minutes rather than infusing directly. High in vitamin C. Seeds are an irritant and should be avoided.
Rosebay willowherb	*Chamaenerion angustifolium*	Delicious caffeine-free substitute for black tea. Needs to be fermented (see page 99).
Rosemary	*Rosmarinus officinalis*	May help improve memory. Can be bitter so may need to sweeten or use in a mix with other herbs.
Thyme	*Thymus vulgaris*	Mix with honey and lemon for sore throats.

TORBAY, CABBAGE PALM
Cordyline australis

Season for picking: spring
Where to find them: gardens
Main identifying feature: palm-like tree with shaggy tops
Best use: roast the starchy hearts
Not to be mistaken for: dracaena

Used as an ornamental tree in faded seaside towns and villages, the cordyline or cabbage palm has developed a rather unfashionable image in some circles – unfairly in my view. It is unlike a typical palm tree as it does best in cooler maritime climates, growing well in coastal Britain, Canada and northern parts of the USA.

In its native New Zealand, it is far less fussy and can be found on forest edges, near swamps, on riverbanks and on open land.

Cordylines have long sword-shaped leaves which are usually green but sometimes variegated or purple. The tops have a shaggy appearance, like a singer in a 1980s hair band. Superficially cordylines resemble yucca plants, only far larger, with a trunk growing up to 20 metres (66 feet) high. The crown of older trees can divide in many heads on the single trunk and they can take up to twenty years to produce sprays of small white flowers. It is important you do not confuse cordyline with the poisonous dracaena, which has yellow to orange rather than white roots and is more commonly grown as a house plant.

For the Southern Māori of New Zealand, the cabbage palm was grown as a food crop. The roots of the plant, either in a mature or juvenile state, were removed prior to flowering and cooked in an oven or open fire and sweetened with honey. To ensure a continued supply, a portion of the root was left underground to re-sprout into a new tree. The tip of the plant was also eaten.

PREPARATION AND USE

Some years ago, I harvested the white heart of a cordyline the local council were weeding out. I used only the tip, the pale top section under the leaves. It was fleshy and white, similar to palm hearts sold commercially in cans. I found cooking greatly improved the flavour, which was starchy yet comparable to a rather sweet cabbage. I parboiled it before roasting it with chilli, coriander and cumin.

BAMBOO SHOOTS
Bambuseae

Season for picking: spring
Where to find them: parks and gardens – used in borders and as screens
Main identifying feature: hard tree-like grass
Best use: shoots in stir-fries
Not to be mistaken for: grasses

Bamboo plants have a bad reputation for escaping cultivation, popping up in neighbouring gardens or halfway down your own. They spread by sending up spear-like shoots – fortunately, these shoots are edible and so eating bamboo can be a simple way to keep them under control.

The shoots of all bamboos can be eaten and the larger the diameter, the more edible material there is. Different varieties shoot at different times of the year: some in spring and others as late as autumn. They send up shoots for two to three months and can be blanched then pickled or frozen for later use. As they do not grow in my garden, I harvest them from parks and public gardens with a good sharp pocketknife. Although you are preventing this potentially invasive plant from spreading, you should of course ask first before harvesting.

PREPARATION AND USE
The whole of the inner shoot, right back to the main root system, is edible, so either cut at ground level or follow the shoot right back to the rhizome. The shoots begin to harden, so only the top 30 cm (12 inches) or so is usable and the outer leaves need to be removed to expose the inner, pale-green-and-white centre. If the shoots taste bitter, blanch them for around five to ten minutes until soft.

A common recipe in India is Upkari, a fried spiced vegetable side dish using bamboo shoots. If necessary, the shoots are first blanched before frying in vegetable oil with mustard seeds and onion. Chilli flakes are often added for an extra kick.

Bamboo shoots have a pleasant flavour, rather like a slightly starchy pea. They go well with Quorn and tofu, with chicken or pork in a curry or added to a Thai or Chinese stir-fry. For a real wild food treat, use a good-sized tasty mushroom such as chicken of the woods, mix with bamboo shoots and wild leaves, and flavour with chilli, coriander and wild mustard seed. Serve with noodles or rice.

PANSIES, VIOLAS AND VIOLETS
Viola spp.

Season for picking: spring
Where to find them: borders, arable weeds, woodlands
Main identifying feature: petals in layers with yellow centre
Best use: as decoration

Pansies, violas and violets all have similar-shaped flowers with a yellow centre and layered petals. Pansies are the largest and often have a dark patch on the bottom-most petal.

Pansies do not exist naturally in the wild; they are hybrids, cultivated for their large showy flowers. Popular as bedding plants, they can be found growing on roundabouts, in pub gardens and in the ubiquitous hanging baskets that can be found throughout the UK. The diminutive violas and violets do exist in the wild and can be found across Europe, mostly as woodland flowers (see page 245).

PREPARATION AND USE
The flowers are mostly used decoratively, yet they have a delicately floral taste. They look beautiful crystallised, candied, frosted or frozen, spread out across the surface of a biscuit, bunched on the top of a truffle or crowning a cupcake. No wonder that food

photographers, Instagram users and restaurateurs adore them. They give depth to an otherwise uniformly green salad, break up the surface of a summer drink when frozen in an ice-cube and contrast beautifully with the rich brown of a chocolate cake.

The leaves are edible and have a similar fragrant flavour to the flowers. Use in salads.

HOLLYHOCK
Althea rosea

Season for picking: spring and summer
Where to find them: borders, kitchen gardens
Main identifying feature: large, top-heavy flowers
Best use: leaves in salad or as alternative to spinach

Hollyhocks are shamelessly ostentatious flowers. Towards the end of summer, the top-heavy blooms can fall victim to their own exuberance and come crashing down to earth. Like all members of the mallow family, which includes okra, most of the plant is edible.

PREPARATION AND USE

The big blooms can be thrown into a jug of Pimm's or used to brighten up cordials, jellies or salads. To make a cordial, infuse the flowers in a sugar solution or add pectin and a higher concentration of sugar to help this set into a jelly.

The leaves can be used in salads or as an alternative to spinach. They are best eaten during the spring before the plant comes into flower, at which point they get a little stringy. Although they do not have a strong flavour, they have a good texture and soak up other flavours well. Try them in mixed salads or as part of a cooked mix of leaves.

The immature seed pods (or 'cheeses') are small and circular, like a miniature cheese. They can be plucked from the plant before they set seed and have a nice crunch to them, reminiscent of water chestnuts in both taste and texture. Although they can be eaten raw, they benefit from a little steaming or a light boil to soften them. The season is short and you'll need to catch them before they start to separate out into seeds, as they can become very chewy.

LADY'S MANTLE
Alchemilla mollis

Season for picking: spring and autumn
Where to find them: gardens and woodland
Main identifying feature: nine-lobed leaves, yellow florescence
Best use: as tea
Not to be mistaken for: euphorbia

Lady's mantle species exist as wild plants in Britain, Europe and parts of northern USA and Canada. Yet most of us are familiar with the garden species, *Alchemilla mollis*, introduced from the Carpathian Mountains in Eastern Europe. Bearing clusters of yellow florescence, they have nine-lobed leaves which are toothed and slightly furry. At night these close to collect pearl-like droplets of morning dew. Superficially they can resemble euphorbia plants, which have toxic white sap. However, the leaves of a euphorbia are more lance shaped, whereas the lobes of lady's mantle leaves form a rough circle.

Throughout the Middle Ages and well beyond, a belief persisted that the dew on plants such as lady's mantle must have magical properties. Herbalists prescribed it for everything from wound healing and eye problems to impotence. The plant gets its scientific name, *Alchemilla*, from the Arabic word for 'alchemists', who, it has been said, would collect dew from the plant for use in their experiments. Medicinally, lady's mantle has a long history as a woman's herb, prescribed as a tea for heavy menstruation.

PREPARATION AND USE

The young leaves can be thrown sparingly into a salad and the older ones should be cooked.

Infuse the leaves in hot water to make a tea. This is a delicious drink, with a good full flavour. Women have drunk it for centuries as it is said to reduce menstrual cramps and help with conditions such as endometriosis. Similar to green tea, it has a pea-pod-like freshness.

LEMON BALM
Melissa officinalis

Season for picking: spring to autumn
Where to find them: herbaceous borders, herb gardens, parks, woodland, edgeland
Main identifying feature: nettle- or mint-like leaves, lemon scent
Best use: as tea
Not to be mistaken for: nettles

Lemon balm has a habit of self-seeding in and out of the garden, making it a potential weed, albeit often a welcome one. Outside of gardens I've found it wild in woodlands and edgeland. The sixteenth-century herbalist John Gerard recommended the plant, which according to him 'driveth away all melancholy and sadness'. Modern studies have found that extracts of lemon balm can be effective in treating mild anxiety, mild sleep disorders and even type 2 herpes simplex.[3] The plant has a pleasant flavour, like the zest of a lemon, with mild herbal notes and a tinge of bitterness. Although best in the spring before it goes to flower, it can be harvested any time of year the leaves are present.

PREPARATION AND USE

I mostly use lemon balm in the traditional way, steeping the leaves in hot water to make a herbal tea. During a stressful day, it can be just enough to take the edge off, still leaving me with enough energy to work.

Lemon balm can also replace basil in pesto, lemon in sorbet, or be added to traditional lemonade to increase the depth of flavour.

DAY LILIES
Hemerocallis spp.

Season for picking: flowers late spring/early summer, tubers autumn
Where to find them: borders
Main identifying feature: large (mostly) yellow or orange flowers. Long green leaves
Best use: flowers in salad, tubers roasted
Not to be mistaken for: other lilies, crocosmia

A few years ago, I was poised to remove the day lilies that had spread throughout my front garden when I discovered they are safe to eat and rather tasty. Now, rather than being annoyed by their mass of green for eleven and a half months of the year, I look forward to the blooms so I can add something new to the dinner table. The flowers are a good source of vitamin A and the edible tubers an excellent source of carbohydrate.

The tubers look like a bunch of tiny potatoes, growing horizontally from stalks attached to the plant. They normally come out as one big mass and can be harvested by getting a fork underneath the plant, pulling them up and shaking off the soil.

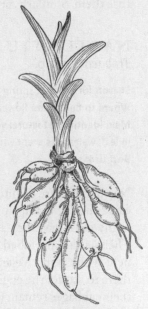

The tubers of day lilies are delicious and starchy.

PREPARATION AND USE

The flowers can be eaten straight from the plant or added to salads. The flowering buds are robust enough to be used in a stir-fry, added towards the end. The petals have a floral, bean-like taste and a satisfying crunch to them. They can be removed from the flower one by one for a bite-sized snack. They are very good deep-fried in batter and dipped in a satay sauce (though granted, most things are!).

The tubers are starchy and delicious boiled, roasted or baked. They taste very similar to potatoes but with a nutty rather than floury quality.

For an unfortunate few, the tubers produce excessive and sometimes painful flatulence, so should be eaten in moderation at first. Lilies that grow from a single bulb, rather than a cluster of tubers like the day lily, are poisonous, so be careful not to confuse them. Similarly, crocosmia grow from a flat, rounded corm.

NASTURTIUM
Tropaeolum spp.

Season for picking: spring to autumn
Where to find them: flower borders, vegetable patches
Main identifying feature: yellow, red or orange flowers, prominent veins in leaf, watercress scent when crushed
Best use: salads

Nasturtiums are beautiful red, yellow and orange flowers, which can either be clump-forming or trailing. They can self-seed but in the most part they are annuals planted from seed every year. Their leaves are lobed and roughly circular, often with prominent white veins. Vegetable growers sow them as a decoy crop, there to attract the eggs of the cabbage white butterfly, ensuring their cabbages remain uneaten.

Nasturtiums are native to South and Central America and were introduced to Europe as early as the sixteenth century.

Andean cultures grow a tuberous species of nasturtium called mashua (*Tropaeolum tuberosum*), which is eaten like a potato.

PREPARATION AND USE

Nasturtium leaves contain higher amounts of vitamin C than an average orange fruit. And as well as providing a vitamin boost, the plant's bright flowers make a spicy addition to any salad, tasting remarkably like watercress. The buds can be pickled like a caper: simply blanch in boiling water and add to a light vinegar (rice or white wine vinegar both work well).

When I was teaching at a college in Devon, the kitchen staff would macerate the whole plant, stalks and all, with a powerful blender to make a watercress-like soup (see page 15).

EVENING PRIMROSE
Oenothera spp.

Season for picking: summer
Where to find them: flower borders or as garden weeds
Main identifying feature: yellow flowers which unfurl in the evening
Best use: flowers in salads

The term 'evening primrose' actually covers a number of flowers within the *Oenothera* species. They are beautiful to look at and are delicious in salads. There is an apocryphal tale that the flower was once rare in the UK until *Gardener's World* magazine gave away packets of the seeds. Despite having never sown an evening primrose in my life, almost without fail every year one has turned up in the numerous gardens and vegetable plots I have cultivated.

PREPARATION AND USE

The flowers have a very delicate, buttery flavour. They are too delicate to be cooked but the buds, or unfurled flowers, can be added towards the end of a stir-fry.

NIGELLA, LOVE-IN-A-MIST
Nigella damascena

Season for picking: summer to autumn
Where to find them: flower borders, garden weeds, edgeland
Main identifying feature: shaggy blue flowers and rattling seed heads
Best use: seeds in bread

Nigella plants produce lovely, delicate, shaggy-blue flowers. They're often sown in gardens but can equally find their own way in as a weed.

The seeds of the nigella flower can be used as a spice in the same way as those of its close relative, *Nigella sativa*, often referred to as black cumin or black caraway.

PREPARATION AND USE

After the plant flowers it forms a rattling head full of the spicy seeds. Cut the top from the flower with a pair of scissors and pour the seeds onto a sheet of paper. The paper can be folded and the seeds poured into a jar.

In Hindi these seeds are called *kalonji*. They're sometimes added to naan bread, or are dry roasted as part of a mix of spicy seeds which is then used to add flavour to pickles. In Iran they are used to top sambuseh (Persian samosas).

YUCCA
Yucca spp.

Season for picking: summer
Where to find them: gardens
Main identifying feature: large white bell-shaped flowers, tough sword-like leaves
Best use: roasted root
Not to be mistaken for: dracaena

Yuccas are a slightly kitsch garden plant often found in seaside towns and caravan parks. They have a spray of sword-like green leaves and send up a large flowering spike (1–3 metres, or 3–10 feet, tall) of white, bell-shaped flowers, each the size of a golf ball in the summer.

The plant is native to North and Central America. In precolonial America the Tewa-speaking Pueblos, the Native American people of New Mexico, made use of almost every part of the plant. The roots would be bruised and steeped and then lathered up as soap for washing clothes and hair. Cord was also made from the leaves; this was woven into baskets and there is even some evidence to suggest it was used to make sandals. The fruit of the yucca was eaten raw or baked until the skin and fibre could be removed, then boiled until it formed a paste which was dried and stored.

PREPARATION AND USE
Most yuccas are edible but outside of their native habitat they don't always set fruit and some years do not even flower. When they do flower, they are edible and good in salads or cooked. They have quite rigid petals, with a more vegetable-like texture than most flowers. They can be rather bitter – adding a little honey and lemon dressing normally remedies this. If you can bring yourself to remove it before it flowers, the flowering spike, which looks like an enormous asparagus, can be peeled and boiled.

FUCHSIA
Fuchsia spp.

Season for picking: summer to autumn
Where to find them: garden borders, often by the sea
Main identifying feature: earring-like flowers, often purple and pink with long stamen
Best use: berries as a snack

Fuchsias are popular garden plants originating mostly from South America, with one or two occurring in New Zealand and Central America. Their flowers are distinctive, pagoda- or earring-like blooms, often numerous and lasting up until the winter.

The edible flowers are useful for decoration, thrown in a salad or adorning the top of a cake. They are mainly for show, as the flavour is bland at best and astringent at worst.

After they flower, fuchsias bear long, lozenge-shaped berries, which are succulent and fruity. As they are normally pollinated by hummingbirds in their native South America, when grown elsewhere a few of the garden species do not bear fruit. In my experience, the darker-flowered fuchsias (especially those with purple and red flowers) tend to be fruit bearing and the lighter colours do not.

As not all varieties bear fruit, choose hardy varieties which will more reliably produce the sweet berry, such as *F. magellanica*, *F. coccinea*, *F. splendens*, *F.* 'Pink Fizz' or the self-explanatory, half-hardy *F.* 'Fuchsiaberry'. Of this list, *F. splendens* and Fuchsiaberry are the most recommended for edible use.

PREPARATION AND USE
The fruits are sweet and juicy and my children like to eat them straight from the plant. They can act as a substitute for blueberries in muffins or pancakes. Or pop them into a smoothie along with other soft fruit, like bananas or kiwis, to add a little colour.

HIMALAYAN HONEYSUCKLE, PHEASANT BERRY, TOFFEE BERRY
Leycesteria formosa

Season for picking: summer to autumn
Where to find them: gardens, woodlands, edgeland
Main identifying feature: hanging clusters of white flowers with purple sepals. Purple and black berries follow flowers
Best use: berries as snack or on desserts
Not to be mistaken for: honeysuckle berries

Himalayan honeysuckle has a habit of turning up uninvited into gardens and occasionally escaping into the wild. It can grow in the most unusual places and if left unchecked it can become very substantial and almost impossible to weed out. It's also known as 'toffee berry', as its small berries have a delicious burnt toffee taste when they are completely ripe. The berries form and ripen at different times after the plant flowers and it is not unusual to see both flowers and fruits on the plant at the same time.

PREPARATION AND USE
The berries don't all ripen at the same time, so you'll find only a few ripe ones at once. They can be used as a snack or frozen to build up enough to use as a topping for a cheesecake or added to ice-cream.

FORAGER'S TIP
The toffee-like taste will be present only when the berries are perfectly ripe. This means a deep, purply-black berry with a dark-brown calyx (the stalky bit at the bottom, like the top of a tomato). Any that have purple calyxes, instead of dark brown, are far too bitter and inedible.

STAGHORN SUMAC
Rhus typhina

Season for picking: summer to autumn
Where to find them: gardens or wasteland/edgeland backing onto gardens
Main identifying feature: furry branches and flame-like drupes
Best use: drupes to make a lemonade
Not to be mistaken for: poison sumac

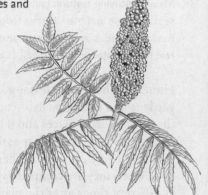

Staghorn sumac grows wild in its native landscape of the north-western United States and southern Canada. Elsewhere in the world it adorns gardens with its autumnal kaleidoscope leaves, which change from green to oranges, reds and yellows. This large shrub (or small tree) gets its name from its furry branches, which resemble the antlers of a stag.

The flame-like purple drupes can remain on the tree well into the following year.

On the end of the branches are clusters of berries that seem to form a shape like a candle flame. These clusters, or 'drupes', become conspicuous at the end of summer and remain on the leafless shrub throughout the winter.

PREPARATION AND USE
The drupes can be broken off and pushed through a sieve, forming a powder with a mild lemony flavour, which is widely used in Middle Eastern cooking. Use the powder on hummus or in yoghurt dips. To make za'atar, the popular Middle Eastern spice mix, use equal amounts of dried thyme, marjoram and oregano with a base of roasted ground sesame seeds and a generous pinch of salt.

The easiest way to use sumac is to make a lemonade. Simply squeeze the drupes in cold water and leave to steep overnight. This will create a beautiful pink liquid, lemony in flavour, which can be sweetened or drunk as it is.

FORAGER'S TIP

In North America, smooth sumac (*Rhus glabra*) grows wild across the north-eastern US and southern Canada. It also has maroon-coloured drupes, but it lacks the hairy antler-like branches. This species can be used in exactly the same way as staghorn sumac. However, it is important not to mistake either of these non-toxic plants for poison sumac, *Toxicodendron vernix*, which has white drupes, or for tree of heaven, *Ailanthus altissima*, which has clusters of drooping seeds.

DAHLIA
Dahlia spp.

Season for picking: autumn
Where to find them: flower borders
Main identifying feature: large gaudy flowers
Best use: bulbs as potatoes
Not to be mistaken for: zinnias

The bright, firework-like blooms of dahlias are some of the most diverse and spectacular garden flowers around. But as well putting on a fine display, the flowers, along with the tuberous roots, of all dahlia species are thought to be edible. The plant is rich in inulin, a type of carbohydrate which promotes the growth of good bacteria and inhibits bad, and may also help improve blood sugar levels for diabetics.

The Aztecs grew the flowers in their pleasure gardens and they were thought to have been worn by Emperor Moctezuma (c.1466–1520) as a symbol of the sun. With over 20,000 cultivars, dahlia tubers vary in taste and size as much as the flowers, ranging from spindly and bitter to swollen and good to eat. With so many to choose from, you should approach any unknown cultivars with caution, eating a little at a time to see how your body responds. The tubers are high in inulin, and for an unfortunate few this can have somewhat explosive results (and, very rarely, can trigger an anaphylactic response). The body may slowly adjust to inulin, but it may not be easy to convince someone of this after a night of painful wind!

PREPARATION AND USE

To cook, remove the bitter peel and boil a little longer than you would a potato. The tubers remain somewhat hard, rather like a water chestnut. Alternatively, they can be grated and used in place of carrots or courgette in cakes or mixed with eggs, flour and seasoned to use in place of potatoes in a rosti.

All varieties are edible but 'Yellow Gem', 'Inland Dynasty', 'Kennedy' and 'Hoamatland' are said to be among the best to eat.

JAPANESE FLOWERING QUINCE
Chaenomeles japonica

Season for picking: autumn
Where to find them: shrubby borders and hedges
Main identifying feature: red-pink spring blossoms, round hard yellow fruit
Best use: quince jelly or roasted quince

When I was growing up my family had a flowering quince in the garden and for years my mother had no idea what it was. One year, when it had not been vigorously pruned by my sometimes over-enthusiastic father, it produced a single, hard, apple-like fruit. We split it open to reveal the pips, which confused us even more: was this some sort of crab apple? I pored over the family's gardening books until I eventually worked out what it was. I can still recall my excitement at this discovery.

Chaenomeles quinces are grown for their orangey-red or pinky spring blossoms. In an over-cultivated garden, the shrub is shaped and cut back after it flowers, which removes any prospect of the faded blooms swelling into fruit. If they are pruned to the flower, rather than beyond it, they will retain the current season's fruit and produce more the following year.

PREPARATION AND USE

The hard fruits have a citrus flavour, somewhere between lemon and apple. They cannot be eaten raw and are cooked in the same way as a pear quince to make a jam or jelly.

They can also be roasted. Halve them and remove the tough skin around the seed, then put them on a baking tray with about 2 cm (1 inch) of apple juice and sugar or undiluted cordial (such as elderberry). Cover and roast at 150°C (300°F) for 1–2 hours or until soft. Serve with ice cream.

To make a refreshing lemonade, simply grate the quince fruits, add water and sugar, leave overnight, strain and serve. Since quinces can lose their flavour if harvested late, add the juice of a lemon or some sumac (see page 58) to enhance the lemony flavour.

ORNAMENTAL CRAB APPLE

Season for picking: late summer to autumn
Where to find them: gardens and parks, municipal planting schemes
Main identifying feature: small apple-like fruit
Best use: crab apple jelly

In the mountains of Kazakhstan there are entire forests of apple trees. Such is the genetic diversity of this bountiful woodland that the apples can vary in size from a tiny 2.5 cm (1 inch) to the same size as a domesticated apple, or bigger. The taste varies too, from sweet, complex and nutty to sour, dry and astringent.

Having worked as a gardener for many years, I have found the taste of a crab apple can vary almost as much as that of a wild Kazakhstani forest apple. All crab apples are edible and there really is only one way to find out if the variety in your garden is good to eat.

The seeds contain cyanide, which in large amounts (around 150 seeds) can be lethal. However, if left unchewed, these will pass right through you without doing any harm. As the seeds are not only toxic but bitter, most recipes will call for the fruit mixture to be sieved free of seeds, stalks and other inedible material.

PREPARATION AND USE

Crab apples can be gently simmered in a little water or apple juice (2–3 tablespoons in a pan, adding more if the apples dry out) until they break down into a pulp. Push the pulp through a sieve to remove the seeds and stalks. It can then be sweetened if necessary by adding one or more of the following: sugar, a mashed banana, dates, stevia, honey, sweet cicely leaf, cinnamon, or birch or maple syrup.

Crab apple pulp can be used to make jams, apple sauce, the basis of a ketchup or spread out on parchment paper and dehydrated to make fruit leather. Adding blackberries, raspberries, cooked rose hip flesh or even fennel seeds adds to the complex flavour of the fruit leather.

....

Common garden weeds

Weeds are a bane to gardeners but a boon to foragers. And time spent uprooting dandelion roots for coffee, hoeing chickweed and bittercress for salad or chopping nettles for a smoothie becomes a harvest rather than a decluttering chore.

This list brings together some of the most common garden invaders and the best way to eat or drink them. Many of the weeds below are also looked at in more detail in other chapters.

	Name	Scientific name	Use
	Chickweed	*Stellaria media*	In salads, has a fresh taste
	Dandelion	*Taraxacum*	Tea. Use in salads before it flowers or as a green vegetable
	Greater plantain and spear plantain	*Plantago* spp.	Can be cooked like a vegetable. Or chew and place on stings
	Ground elder	*Aegopodium podagraria*	As a herb (tastes like carrot mixed with parsley). Good in pesto or as a wilted green with other spring greens (such as nettle)

	Name	Scientific name	Use
	Hairy bittercress	*Cardamine hirsuta*	Salad green, tastes like watercress. Has pinnate leaves and exploding seeds
	Lamb's quarters/ goosefoot	*Chenipodium album*	Like spinach but has a superior taste
	Nettle	*Urtica dioica*	More vitamin- and mineral-rich than spinach. Good in teas. Use as you would spinach
	Wood avens/herb bennet	*Geum urbanum*	Use leaves as a cooked vegetable. Roots are like cloves

CHAPTER TWO

Urban Parks and Public Spaces

D
URING SHORT SPELLS of living in London, I would seek out any scrap of green I could find. I would examine my A–Z map to plan the greenest walking routes possible; I would spend my lunch breaks in pocket parks and weekends in the larger royal and city parks.

The plants in these environments are born survivors, refugees from distant lands. Little of the urban environment is there by chance; almost every inch has been scrupulously planned out by landscape architects, gardeners and planners. Many of these plants are not native but have been grown in nurseries and chosen for their decorative foliage and blossom or their ability to grow in the shade, which can give them an advantage over native plants.

This means they often come with a deep cultural history in their countries of origin. Mahonias, for instance, with their striking yellow winter blossoms, grow quite happily just across the road from my local cinema. I've picked them after watching a film so I can mix them in with porridge the following morning. Of course, these shrubs didn't evolve in a Somerset town centre, but are native to the Douglas fir forests of North America. Historically, Native American and First Nation foragers from the eastern Pacific seaboard would have been as familiar with them as Europeans are with blackberries. The fruits would have been dried and sometimes mixed with other foods, such as sweeter berries or meat, to help sustain the population through the harsh winter.

Similarly, the medlar is not native to the Devon churchyards or Welsh public gardens where I have found it growing. The medlar's strange, ancient-looking fruits evolved in the beautiful upland forests of the Alborz Mountains in northern Iran. In some parts of Iran, festivals still take place during which people turn the fruits into a syrup in large cauldrons over an outdoor fire. And tourists can trek up the mountains to find medlar fruits, which still grow in abundance throughout the woods.

By its very nature, the urban landscape can't hope to resemble the wild mountain forests of Iran or the conifer woodlands of North America. In cities and towns, an adaptation which allows a plant to grow in dense woodland can be put to use in the shade of an office block or an adaptation to drought in a supermarket carpark. But thanks to their wild origins, these plants are already adapted to harsh environments and are equipped to deal with the unnatural conditions presented by our city streets. For the forager, these nursery-grown plants can be unlikely yet abundant sources of wild food.

Foraging in most (but not all) public places is legal and sometimes even actively encouraged. But this is not always the case, and discretion should be exercised. Trudging through a flower bed to reach a fruit tree or stripping the blossoms from an ornamental cherry in a grand public garden may be more than a little frowned upon. Observe the laws in your own region, only take what you need, and try to leave ornamental displays complete. You may feel a little self-conscious picking things in public places. If people stare, I normally smile and wave, and it is amazing how quickly they avert their eyes. More often than not people are curious; they ask what you are doing and are genuinely interested to hear you can eat those berries or that blossom.

Avoid foraging in areas likely to be very polluted, such as by the sides of busy roads. It helps if there is some form of barrier between the road and what you are foraging – even a narrow hedge or fence will mean the wild foods on the other side take up much lower amounts of airborne pollutants.

BAY
Laurus nobilis

Season for picking: all year
Where to find them: outside pubs and restaurants, in gardens and parks
Main identifying feature: glossy aromatic leaves
Best use: in soups or stocks
Not to be mistaken for: bay laurel

Before I had one in my garden, I would regularly pull the odd leaf from a bay tree overhanging onto the pavement on my way home. In warmer regions they grow in parks and gardens, forming large trees and hedges. They can also be found growing in pots outside of hotels and restaurants as a single-stemmed ornamental tree, often clipped into a pom-pom shape.

PREPARATION AND USE
Bays have aromatic, glossy green, pointed ovoid leaves. These leaves are used for flavouring soups and stews and are normally removed before serving. I like to use them in vegetable stocks with cleavers, nettles, leek and carrot tops, onion, herbs and seasoning. They're also great in cream sauces and court bouillon. A local cafe owner I know uses the leaves to flavour rice, adding a good handful to the cooking pot.

ROSEMARY
Salvia rosmarinus, syn. *Rosmarinus officinalis*

Season for picking: all year
Where to find them: outside supermarkets and in car parks, parks and gardens
Main identifying feature: shrub with aromatic, spiky leaves and purple flowers
Best use: as a herb

Rosemary grows in abundance outside many supermarkets, so it's beyond me why people still buy a few sprigs in packets from inside the store. As a native of the Mediterranean it is a tough, cold-hardy, drought-tolerant plant as happy in the rocky hills of Greece and Italy as it is in a shopping centre car park in the English Midlands.

It is easy to spot. Just rub your fingers up the needle-like leaves and you will smell the familiar floral, oily, pine-like scent.

PREPARATION AND USE
Rosemary can be made into a tea, which is said to enhance memory. As a herb it is commonly used with roast meats like lamb or beef and I normally throw a few sprigs in when roasting potatoes or mixed vegetables.

CAMPFIRE OR BARBECUE VEGGIES

1. Coat chopped root vegetables or Mediterranean vegetables in olive oil.
2. Wrap the vegetables in a foil parcel along with 5–6 rosemary sprigs and 2–3 cloves of garlic (or a handful of wild garlic leaves).
3. Cook for 20 minutes, or until soft and delicious, on the coals of a barbecue or campfire.

LIME TREE, LINDEN TREE
Tilia × europaea, T. cordata, T. platyphyllos, T. americana

Season for picking: leaves in spring, blossom late spring
Where to find them: parks, leafy avenues
Main identifying feature: large sometimes sticky heart-shaped leaves, fragrant blossoms
Best use: leaves in tea

At university I would regularly drink lime blossom tea as I found it helped with the low-level stress from exams and assignments. Part of me wonders if the soothing effect of the blossom is in part thanks to the act of picking it. It always comes during the late spring and early summer, when the days are warm and long. I've picked it from village greens on long cycle rides and in church-yards with my son on my shoulders. And I have a very happy memory of gathering it from a row of trees on Tooting Common, during the early days of my relationship with my partner.

From the Mesolithic period (9600–4500 BC) to Saxon times (AD 410–1066), the lime tree dominated the woodlands of England from the Midlands down to the southern shoreline. Fragments of these woods survive, including a small collection close to the village of Barney in Lincolnshire. Time it right and you'll be overwhelmed by the smell of the pollen and the deafening sound of the hundreds if not thousands of bees struggling to pollinate so many trees.

Although they share their name with the citrus fruit, the lime trees of the *Tilia* genus actually get their name from *lynde*, the Middle English word for the tree, whereas the word for a citrus lime stems from the Arabic word *lima*. There are various wild and hybrid species in Europe and North America, growing between 20 metres (66 feet) and 40 metres (132 feet) tall. They are easy to spot, with a rounded triangular silhouette. Their leaves are heart shaped, and sometimes sticky with aphid secretion, and their flowers are whitish yellow and fragrant. They were popular with Victorian landscapers, who liked to use them as a parkland and avenue tree, and they can still be found in many urban parks.

The small-leaved lime, *T. cordata*, has smaller leaves whereas the blossoms of the basswood, *T. americana*, are slightly larger and tend to come into flower a couple of weeks later. Although when it comes to gathering blossom all are used in the same way.

PREPARATION AND USE

The tree comes into its own during the spring when the leaves are just coming out and are a near-translucent shade of light green. Until they darken later in the spring, the leaves are good to eat. The flavour is like a mealier mild lettuce, and the leaves make a perfect base for a salad.

The trees sometimes send out masses of shoots from the trunk, which are cut back by diligent park keepers. Tender young leaves regrow from these shoots, giving a second flush later in the season. They produce an abundance of leaves that can be picked in relatively substantial amounts with little harm to the tree. As they will not keep for very long, they are best eaten fresh, although they can be dried to make savoury lime flakes (see the instructions below).

Following the leaves, blossoms appear in mid-to-late spring and can be used to make a relaxing tea. After graduating, I spent a very pleasurable six months working as a postman as I contemplated my next move. Before I got used to the early nights and early mornings I mixed lime blossom with lemon balm and valerian to bring on sleep. The blossoms of the larger basswood keep the best and, in my opinion, have the finest flavour for tea.

SAVOURY LIME FLAKES

1. Clean the leaves.
2. Brush with a little soy sauce or liquid aminos.
3. Dehydrate in an oven on a low temperature or in a dehydrator, checking every half-hour or so for about 2–3 hours. The leaves are ready when they flake apart easily in the hands.
4. Use as a garnish or as an alternative to added salt.

MAHONIA
Mahonia × media, M. nervosa and *M. aquifolium*

Season for picking: early spring
Where to find them: gardens, parks, municipal planting; outside gyms and shopping centres
Main identifying feature: yellow winter-flowering spike, pinnate holly-like leaves, purple berries
Best use: berries in jam
Not to be mistaken for: holly

M. aquifolium is a low-growing shrub naturally found in the understory of the expansive woodlands of the Pacific Northwest. Most species thrive in shade, including the most commonly found hybrid *M. × media*, which is sometimes referred to as the Japanese mahonia (even though it was developed in Northern Ireland). This aversion to full sun makes them useful in all kinds of municipal

Mahonias grow well in partial shade, so are often employed as an urban landscaping plant.

landscaping where buildings, walls and large trees stand in for their native Douglas fir canopy. Look for them in the beds outside shopping centres, gyms and multi-storey car parks, as well as in urban parks and gardens.

All commonly planted species of mahonia have glossy, spiny, holly-like leaves and bright-yellow sprays of flowers which bloom in the winter. Sometimes referred to as the Oregon grape, *M. aquifolium* and the similar species *M. nervosa* were eaten by indigenous tribes in the Pacific Northwest, who mixed the tart berries with sweeter tasting fruits like dried salal – you can use raspberries or blackberries. However, the taste can get a little lost when mixed with dominating flavours.

PREPARATION AND USE
Although industrial amounts of sugar are needed to sweeten the tart mahonia berries, their flavour is rich, like a complex blueberry, and well worth the effort. They make an excellent jam (page 19) or a vividly coloured cordial (page 25), which is delicious mixed with a cooled spruce-tip tea. The berries also make a good full-bodied red wine.

It is possible that eating the berries in large quantities may cause an upset stomach, but that is also true of plums! The flowers are also edible, adding a little colour to salads in the winter.

JELLY BEAN BUSH
Elaeagnus × submacrophylla (formerly *E. × ebbingei*)

Season for picking: early to mid spring
Where to find them: city-centre planting schemes, ornamental hedgerows, coastal hedgerows, gardens
Main identifying feature: gold-and-green or dusty-green lance-to-oval-shaped leaves with silver scales. Jelly bean-shaped fruits
Best use: jams and jellies

The *Elaeagnus × submacrophylla* or 'jelly bean bush' is a common urban landscaping plant with edible berries. It is a cross between two East Asian shrubs, *E. macrophylla* and *E. pungens*, two plants that make their homes on windy hillsides and thickets across China and Japan. Evolving in sometimes harsh landscapes, this tough hybrid can cope with all kinds of punishment, so you will find it on roadsides, on central reservations, in supermarket car parks and in busy town centres. I've found it growing quite happily on a windswept hillside in coastal Lyme Regis and I picked my first fruit from a soulless urban planting scheme in Plymouth city centre.

Although easily overlooked, the *Elaeagnus* is an attractive shrub with variegated gold-and-green or dusty-green leaves, which are lance or oval shaped and have silver scales underneath. In the autumn, small discreet clusters of white bell-shaped flowers bloom on the plant, which give way to speckled jelly bean-shaped fruits from late winter to mid-spring.

The autumn olive, or Japanese silverberry, *E. umbellata*, can also be found in urban parks. It grows as a small shrub, or on occasion a tree of around five metres in height. The young leaves are silver, becoming green as they age but retaining their silver underside. Sprays of bell-shaped flowers give way to circular, red-speckled berries, which are among the most aesthetically pleasing fruit I've ever come across. These are used in the same way as those of the jelly bean bush. In warm climates they can be seen as a bit of a pest, growing wild in waste ground and neglected areas.

Nearly all *Elaeagnus* species provide edible berries and fibrous but equally edible seeds. You might find deciduous or evergreen species grown as specimen plants or hedging.

PREPARATION AND USE
Berries do not develop consistently on this plant, and in some years you'll only find a handful at best. They are simultaneously sour and sweet and particularly good to eat raw as long as they are fully ripe (they can be astringent before this). If you are lucky enough to find them in abundance, you can use them to make fruit leathers or jam, or as a syrup for a martini.

JAPANESE BLOSSOMING CHERRY
Prunus serrulata and *Prunus* spp.

Season for picking: spring
Where to find them: parks, streets and avenues, civic centres
Main identifying feature: bright-pink blossom
Best use: salted cherry blossom

There are few urban spectacles to compete with the floral pink canopy of spring cherry blossom, also know as sakura. In Japan the coming of the spring blossom is deeply symbolic and there are cherry blossom festivals to celebrate the arrival of the blooms. This tradition has been adopted by Seattle and Washington DC, following the gift of blossoming cherry trees from Japan in the early 1900s. Generations later, the Japanese repeated this act of generosity when in 1990 a Japanese TV company raised money to donate cherry trees to the newly reunified Berlin, as a symbol of renewal.

PREPARATION AND USE

All deciduous species of cherry have edible blossoms, but the double blooms of the flowering pink or white ornamental cherries are the best to cook with. They can be used in cookies, cakes, shortbread, pastry and rice dishes, imparting a delicate pink colour and subtle floral flavour.

To make syrup to use as a mixer or a cordial, or to drizzle on desserts, cover the blossoms in hot water and leave to steep for 24 hours. Strain the liquid and dissolve an equal weight of sugar in it.

Many of the species of cherry selected for their blossom produce fruits of little value. Some, however, are good to eat as a passing snack or used to make drinks such as cherry brandy. For more uses of edible cherries see page 114.

SALTED CHERRY BLOSSOM

In Japan they preserve the sakura blossom to make salted cherry blossom. This is eaten with steamed rice or as a garnish, or used in marinades.

1. Wash the blossoms and remove any that have wilted or become discoloured.
2. Place blossoms in a bowl layered with plenty of salt.
3. Cover with cling film or a saucer weighted down with something heavy. Store in the refrigerator for 2 days.
4. Drain off the brine.
5. At this stage you can either dry the petals for a day or dehydrate the blossoms and store.
6. Alternatively, to preserve the colour and add extra flavour, submerge the blossoms in ume plum vinegar for 3 days before dehydrating. Pack the dried blossoms in salt and store in a jar.
7. You can use as suggested above or you can wash the salt from the blossoms to make into a refreshing tea.

LAVENDER
Lavandula spp.

Season for picking: summer
Where to find them: park and garden borders, lining paths
Main identifying feature: floral scent and purple-blue flowers
Best use: flowers sparingly in biscuits

Grown in decorative borders of parks and gardens, lavender is best foraged when it starts to flop – this is when it is due a prune so it will not be missed.

PREPARATION AND USE
Both French and English lavender are edible in moderation. Add a few sprinkles to cakes, ice cream or teas. They work particularly well melted into chocolate, but only use a little at a time – a pinch or two is ample for a 100 g (3½ oz) bar.

BLACK MULBERRY
Morus nigra

Season for picking: summer
Where to find them: parks and gardens
Main identifying feature: long, blackberry/raspberry-like fruits
Best use: fruits eaten raw

In the town where I live, mulberry season is announced each year by mauve-red patches of splattered fruit below the large tree which grows on my way to the train station. Although the berries resemble a cross between a raspberry and a blackberry they are not related to either. When fully ripe, they have a melt-in-the-mouth quality, sweet with a note of acid-sour, and are delicious. As when gathering wild bilberries, their sticky juice oozes out when picked, staining the hands.

The black mulberry is rare to find in the wild outside of southern Europe, and in the US the native red mulberry *M. rubra* is more common. However, black mulberries are widely cultivated and I've found them on riverside paths, in the grounds of stately homes and hanging over into the street from private gardens. The park I played in as a child has a mulberry tree which is said to have grown from a cutting taken from a tree in William Shakespeare's garden.

PREPARATION AND USE

The fruits arrive in mid-to-late summer and are best when allowed to fall onto soft grass rather than when plucked from the tree. This also helps when foraging in public places, as they can be gathered from the ground and little or no permission is needed.

As the berries don't keep well, and are easily bruised and bumped in the process of transporting, they are best eaten on site. If they survive the journey home, they are good mixed with yoghurt as well as in pies, muffins, as sorbet or added as flavour to ice cream. Traditionally dried in their native Iran, they are incorporated into flour to make a sweet tasting bread, mixed with crushed walnuts for a snack or cooked with sugar, strained and cooled. Dried mulberries make a delicious addition to breakfast cereals such as muesli and granola.

SHARAB EL TOOT

Just as many northern European gardens have an apple tree, many Lebanese families have a mulberry. This recipe for traditional Lebanese sharab el toot, or mulberry syrup, makes around 500 ml (2 cups) of juice, using 1 kg (2 lb 4 oz) of gathered fruit, but it can be scaled up or down accordingly.

METHOD:

1. Blend 1 kg (2 lb 4 oz) of berries in a blender without water. Do this in batches if you have a small blender.
2. Squeeze each batch of blended berries into a bowl through a muslin bag.
3. Add 400 g (14 oz) of sugar for every 500 ml (2 cups) of liquid.
4. Simmer on a low heat, stirring constantly until the sugar is dissolved.
5. Squeeze in the juice of half a lemon.
6. Use the end result as a cordial. It will keep for a couple of weeks in the fridge, after which it may start to ferment. Serve on ice cream or with Pimm's, gin and lemon juice as a late-summer cocktail.

FIG
Ficus carica

Season for picking: summer, second crop sometimes in autumn
Where to find them: overhanging from gardens, in suntraps, up against walls
Main identifying feature: large lobed leaves
Best use: raw fruit

In warm regions, such as southern Europe and the American South, the fig grows easily and in abundance, producing two or more crops in a year. In cooler regions, fig trees only produce one crop a year. In Britain, they normally ripen in the second week of August, although climate change has brought this forward.

As figs thrive in warm conditions they do well in towns and cities, thanks to the 'urban island effect' – a phenomenon of increased urban temperature due to sun-absorbing concrete and tarmac surfaces. Look for them in parks and hanging over into the street from gardens. The heat from engines helps the trees flourish in car parks and they will also thrive in suntraps, like south-facing walls.

When picked 'wild' the fruits range from the small purple-black variety, known as 'Brown Turkey', that you find squeezed into a plastic containers in British supermarkets, to big pendulous green or yellow figs, such as the Atreano or Melanzana varieties.

PREPARATION AND USE
Figs can be dried for later use or mixed with a little vanilla essence to make a jam, which is excellent on pancakes. Try them baked with a soft cheese (blue cheeses, goat's cheese and rind cheeses all work well) and something sweet, such as sycamore syrup, honey, balsamic vinegar or dark sugar.

CHINESE AND NEPALESE RASPBERRIES
Rubus tricolor and *R. nepalensis*

Season for picking: summer
Where to find them: verges, car parks
Main identifying feature: ground-cover plant with prickly stems
Best use: as a snack

As plants that evolved in the forests of China and Nepal, these ground-cover raspberries are shade tolerant and have a creeping, prostrate (or flat-growing) nature. We might recognise them in the West as they are often used to keep the weeds down and deter adventurous children on steep verges, roadsides and the fringes of car parks. I always notice a large mat of them on the sloping verge of a housing estate near a friend's house – in the summer we often turn up on their doorstep with a small offering of raspberry-like berries.

All creeping or ground-cover raspberries are part of the *Rubus* genus, flowering plants that include raspberries and blackberries. *R. nepalensis*, the Nepalese raspberry, and *R. tricolor*, the Chinese bramble, are the most commonly planted, resembling a prostrate raspberry and bramble respectively. Both plants have small thorns or spines running across the stems and yield small but tasty fruit, which looks like the top end of a raspberry. The flavour is sweet, somewhere between raspberry and blackberry, and it can be used in place of either in recipes. However, as the plant rarely yields more than a handful at a time, I tend to prefer to eat what I can on site.

The orange-berried creeping raspberry, or *R. pentalobus* (sometimes *R. calycinoides*), can be found in the same places.

JUNEBERRY, SERVICEBERRY, SASKATOON
Amelanchier alnifolia, A. grandiflora and *Amelanchier* spp.

Season for picking: summer
Where to find them: supermarket car parks, central reservations, public parks and gardens
Main identifying features: striking white spring blossom and round early-summer fruits
Best use: fruits as a snack

Although the juneberry or Saskatoon is a well-known fruit tree that grows both wild and cultivated in Canada and the US, in most of Europe, including the UK, it is far less familiar. In the UK these trees tend to go unnoticed, but I often find them along the strips of land separating one car park from another, especially in retail parks. They are beautiful shrubby trees and used to brighten up the outside areas of offices, hospitals, parks and gardens.

They are at their most conspicuous in the spring when they send out sprays of brilliant white-to-light-pink blossom, followed by bronze or pinky-orange leaves. At the end of the growing season, the mature leaves turn a dramatic shade of red. They are less showy when they come into fruit, looking much like countless other shrubby, green-leafed trees, which is perhaps why they are so often overlooked. When they are at their most flamboyant and easy to spot, even from a passing car, I make a mental note of their location and come back in late June or early July, hoping to beat the birds.

Historically, indigenous groups across North America prized amelanchier trees for their wood and fruit. The wood was used to make arrows and the fruit was used as an ingredient in pemmican, a mix of rendered fat, dried meat and ground-down berries. Pemmican has an incredibly long shelf life. In 1924 a storage container from John Franklin's ill-fated expedition to the Northwest Passage was found, containing still-edible pemmican dating from eighty years previously.

PREPARATION AND USE

Amelanchier grandiflora, *A. lamarckii* and *A. canadensis* can all be eaten. The 'true' Saskatoon, *A. alnifolia*, has larger fruits but is less common in landscaping.

The reddish-purple fruits are similar in appearance to a blueberry, despite being more closely related to the apple. They taste sweet, like a mix between a blueberry and a raisin with strong notes of almond. Underripe berries have a much stronger almond taste due to the presence of cyanide, although this is in much lower quantities than in almonds. Even so, underripe berries should not be eaten in large quantities.

I normally eat the fruits straight from the tree as they spoil quickly. When they do make it home, I'll eat them within a day or two or else cook or freeze them. To use them fresh, add to any recipe which calls for blueberries. Infuse them in gin or vodka (see sloe gin, page 178) or make into a cordial.

As the berries have a large seed it can be tricky to dry them and as the fruits are often small, it's barely worth the bother. However, the pulped fruit can be dried, making a fruit leather for winter use (see page 26).

To protect soft fruit from the hungry beaks of birds, gardeners often net their soft fruit. Whilst it would be impractical to net entire urban fruit trees (not to mention dangerous to birdlife), a plastic bag tied over a fruiting branch will do the same job. Just make sure you remember to return and remove the bag!

WALNUT
Juglans regia

Season for picking: late summer
Where to find them: parks, countryside
Main identifying features: strong-scented leaves and round fruits which open to release the nut
Best use: toasted in salads

While on holiday in France one sunny September, my partner and I repurposed our youngest child's pushchair as a foraging shopping trolley, filling the under-seat storage compartment with fresh figs, apples, salad leaves and countless ripe walnuts.

I eagerly gathered up armfuls of the nut, saving them from the crunch of passing cars along the dusty French lanes. The air was so dry, many of the cases had already fallen away. We ate these nuts each evening in salads, risottos or as a snack washed down with cool beer. We brought home all we could carry, much to the amusement of an airport security guard. At Christmas that year I baked all that remained in a nut roast.

There are ninety-two aromatic compounds responsible for the walnut tree's distinctive resinous aroma. Once you are familiar with the scent it is impossible to mistake the tree for anything else. They are usually no bigger than a large apple tree, but can grow a little taller. The Persian or European walnut, *Juglans regia*, has between five and nine pairs of long, oval, pinnate leaflets (pairs of small leaflets on a central stalk), while the American black walnut, *J. nigra*, has slightly more.

The European walnut is native to the region between the Balkan Peninsula and the Himalayas, and it grows throughout southern Europe. Generations of squirrels have spread it throughout northern Europe, but outside of France I've rarely found more than two or three trees at a time growing wild. However, I have reliably picked large numbers of windfalls from the grand parklands of stately homes or in urban parks.

FORAGER'S TIP

A study in Berkeley, California, found that squirrels bury caches of similar nuts in different locations: walnuts in one, hazelnuts in another. So, if when looking for walnuts in the wild, you find nothing but hazels, move on – you may have better luck elsewhere.

PREPARATION AND USE

Harvested ripe as 'wet walnuts' they have a sweet, aromatic flavour and a vegetable-like crunch. They are best for pesto or desserts such as ice cream or baklava. One word of warning: the black-brown pigment released from ripe and immature walnuts when preparing can stain not only your hands but clothes, carpets, dogs and the containers they are prepared in. From experience I would advise you to wear gloves, and don't prepare them in containers anyone in your household is fond of.

Alternatively you can avoid the staining by waiting until the green cases have dried, turned black and dropped away. I normally put them on a few sheets of newspaper on a windowsill for a couple of weeks, picking off the driest cases from time to time until they have all fallen away.

Cooked walnuts have a melt-in-the-mouth richness, soaking up flavours around them while retaining much of their own. I like to add them to risottos and soups, especially those with broccoli or Brussels sprouts and blue cheese. Alternatively, I'll simply toast them and add them to salads. In breads they give extra flavour and nutrition, and I also pop them in a coffee grinder and use the flour with grated vegetables in veggie burgers. You can also crush and mix the nuts with fruit puree for tasty energy balls.

PICKLED WALNUTS

If you can't wait for ripe walnuts you can pick immature walnuts for pickling around the first day of summer. These should be green and around the size of a golf ball or slightly smaller. If the shell has started to develop they are too ripe to pickle – check by digging a pin into the fruit and seeing if it is met with any resistance.

Once processed, pickled immature walnuts resemble oversized olives, but have a soft crumbly texture and a unique, aromatic flavour if pickled well. Over time the flavours become more complex and the walnuts can be eaten years after they are pickled.

METHOD:

1. Pick the immature fruits around the first day of summer.
2. Prick them with a fork and place in a container. Cover in 1 part salt to 6 parts water/brine solution.
3. Cover the container and put in a dark cupboard.
4. Stir daily to stop mould from forming.
5. Change the brine after 7 days and store for another week, stirring daily again.
6. Drain the brine and spread the nuts carefully on a tray to dry for 48 hours.
7. When the nuts are dry, pack the walnuts in clean jars.
8. Make a solution of 50 per cent vinegar, 50 per cent dark sugar, flavoured with about a teaspoon of pickling spices.
9. Warm the solution on the hob to dissolve the sugar but do not boil.
10. Cover the walnuts with the solution and seal the jars.

QUINCE
Cydonia oblonga

Season for picking: late summer
Where to find them: grand gardens, specialist orchards, occasionally as a street tree
Main identifying feature: hard, pear-shaped fruits
Best use: slow roasted

Quinces are deciduous ornamental trees, grown for their blossoms and hard, pear-shaped fruit. When slow roasted, the fruit is sweet and fragrant with a butter-like texture. Part of my training as a gardener took place in the gardens of a grand hall where they had a beautiful set of quince trees. On the day the quinces came into fruit they were fenced off to prevent keen foragers, including myself, from eating them. I returned home downhearted only to find more growing by the roadside in the nearby village.

The trees are rare in Britain but you can very occasionally find them growing as ornamental trees in public areas such as the outside of office buildings and hospitals, as well as in car parks and streets. More commonly they grow in grand public gardens or orchards where windfall fruits can be gathered from manicured lawns.

PREPARATION AND USE
The fruit is far superior to the more easy-to-find Japanese quince (*Chaenomeles* spp.), and should be slow roasted to really be appreciated. You can add a single roasted fruit to give apple pies a mellow, aromatic quality. The fruit can be used in the same way as that of the Japanese flowering quince: in jams, jellies and 'cheeses', or as a lemonade-type drink (see Japanese quince, page 60).

CHILLI-ROASTED QUINCE

When slow roasted with sugar at a low temperature for an extended period, quinces go through an almost alchemical change from a hard, pale fruit to a soft, sweet, deep burgundy delight. The chilli here lends itself to the sweetness of the sugar and rich perfume of the fruit.

YOU WILL NEED:

- 1–2 quinces
- 2 generous tbsp honey
- 2 tbsp dark-brown sugar
- A large glass of red wine or apple juice
- Generous pinch of chilli flakes

METHOD:

1. Preheat the oven to 150°C (300°F).
2. Halve the quinces and remove the seeds.
3. Place in a baking tray just large enough to accommodate them.
4. Spoon the honey into the craters made by removing the seeds.
5. Mix the sugar with the wine or apple juice and pour into the baking tray.
6. Sprinkle the chilli flakes onto the quinces.
7. Cover with foil and bake in the oven for 2 to 3 hours, checking to see if the quinces have softened.
8. Serve with a dollop of whipped double cream or vegan ice cream.

YEW TREE
Taxus baccata

Season for picking: late summer and autumn
Where to find them: churchyards, parks, woodlands, especially in the south of England
Main identifying feature: conifer with red berries
Best use: edible fruit

Warning: do not eat any part of the yew tree except the red flesh of its 'berry' or cone. The leaves, leaf buds, inner bark and seeds must not be eaten as they are all highly toxic.

EAT ONLY THE FLESH

ALWAYS SPIT OUT THE SEED

Yews are a remarkably long-living tree, with an average lifespan of between 400 and 600 years. In exceptional circumstances they can reach as much as 2,000 or even 3,000 years old. I have visited many of the ancient yews across Britain and it is a humbling experience to be in the presence of a living organism that predates the Roman conquest. Many of those in British churchyards may have marked pre-Christian religious sites or trading posts on long-distance paths. These days you can find them in woodlands, especially in the south of England, grand gardens and churchyards.

Almost every part of the yew is poisonous. The leaves, the leaf buds, the seeds and the inner bark are all potentially fatal if ingested.

However, the fleshy red berries (or technically the aril surrounding the deadly poisonous seeds) are edible, sweet and, despite being a little glutinous, good to eat.

When teaching I've seen cautious students squeeze the aril away from the seed, which can be a gooey affair, while the more gung-ho ones simply spit the seed out.

JAPANESE ROSE, RUGGED ROSE
Rosa rugosa

Season for picking: summer to autumn
Where to find them: housing estates, supermarket car parks, municipal planting schemes
Main identifying feature: thorns, fruits like flattened tomatoes
Best use: as a syrup

The Japanese rose has vicious thorns, so landscape architects use them to both to brighten up areas and deter trespassing. I regularly pass a stand of them in the carpark of a large discount hardware shop. If not a glamorous place to forage, it is reliable: the flowers always come up here in the late spring and the hips follow on in the summer.

I've also reliably found them on new-build housing estates, especially those built in the 1990s, which makes me wonder if nurseries were selling them off cheaply during this time. As soon as you get an eye in for them, you'll start to see them everywhere, so look for them around doctors' surgeries, gyms, shopping centres and other typical urban planting schemes. Native to eastern Asia, they can be found growing wild along the coast and occasionally inland across Europe and North America.

They are easy to identify, living up to the name of 'rugged rose' with much more pronounced thorns than a domesticated rose and stronger, more robust-looking stems. The flowers are a dark pink, with an open form more like a wild rose than a cultivated one. After flowering they produce large hips, which bear a resemblance to a flattened tomato.

PREPARATION AND USE

Unlike the hips of the diminutive dog rose, it is quite easy to eat the flesh of the Japanese rose while completely avoiding the irritant hairs. You simply bite down, taking only half a centimetre or so of the juicy flesh, stopping when you see the seeds. They have a sweet but mildly tangy taste which is hard to describe, but is a little like a persimmon mixed with a tomato.

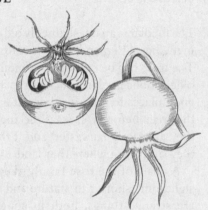

Rosa rugosa hips make a good nibble – just be sure to avoid the seeds!

The hips can be used in the same way as the European native dog rose *R. canina* (see page 168). They have the added advantage of being larger and more succulent, so it is far easier to gather the fruit in big quantities.

You can use the hips to make rose hip syrup, in jams or jellies, fruit leathers (see page 26) or even as an extra flavour for soups (they are particularly good in beetroot soup). In all cases the fruit should be stewed then passed through a fine muslin cloth.

MEDLAR
Mespilus germanica

Season for picking: autumn
Where to find them: churchyards, old public gardens, parks, private gardens
Main identifying feature: flattened, brown, apple-like fruits
Best use: in desserts

The medlar is an unashamedly old-fashioned fruit, more at home in medieval England or ancient Rome than in the modern world. The trees can be rare but community orchards, churchyards and older public gardens, such as those around stately homes, are all good places to look for them. It is worth finding out who owns the trees before you start picking. However, in my experience they are rarely harvested and if the windfalls are not removed, they simply rot where they land.

As part of the rose family, they resemble apple trees at first sight, only shorter in stature and with bigger leaves. The fruits are strange things, both in appearance and in how they are prepared. They have a large calyx, much bigger than that of an apple or tomato, and this spreads out to show convex seed tubes separated by a five-pointed star. This strange display gives rise to its French name of *cul de chien*, which translates as 'dog's arse'.

As the fruit doesn't fully ripen in temperate climates like Britain, northern Europe and much of North America, it must be either bletted or put in the freezer overnight. Freezing is the easier option, softening the fruit and releasing the sugars to give it a sweet, apple-like flavour. Bletting – allowing the fruit to partially rot before it is good to eat – is also straightforward but takes a little longer. I simply gather the fruits in a cardboard box, put them away out of direct sunlight to reduce spoilage, and check on them a couple of times a week until they have darkened, softened and sweetened. I discard any that smell alcoholic or have started to fizz.

PREPARATION AND USE

Once bletted or frozen and thawed, the fruit is excellent either raw or cooked. It tastes a little like apple but with hints of fig: sweet yet slightly mealy.

The Victorians were known for having an irrepressible sweet tooth and would make a paste or 'cheese' from the sweetened berry pulp, leaving it to set in tin-lined copper moulds, very much like jelly moulds. These set pastes originated in Tudor times when they were given the prefix 'charde' – a quince cheese became a 'chardequince', and a medlar cheese would be a 'chardemedlar'. The Victorians also liked to stew the fruits and serve them with fresh cream, or make pots of medlar jam or jelly.

One of my favourite things to do with medlars is to make a kind of coconut milk ice cream, which is suitable for vegans. I take 2 fruits, which have been allowed to freeze and thaw, push them through a sieve to remove the flesh and seeds, then mix this with a tin of coconut milk, 4 dates and a couple of drops of vanilla. Then I whizz it all up in blender and pop it in the ice cream maker.

MEDLAR CHEESECAKE

Another way to make the most of the creamy yet fruity quality of medlars is to make them into a topping for a cheesecake.

YOU WILL NEED:

- 120 g (4 oz) digestive biscuits or graham crackers
- 60 g (2 oz) melted butter
- The pulp of 6 medlars (freeze and thaw them then push through a sieve)
- 3 tsp cocoa powder
- 90 ml (3 fl oz) cream cheese
- 1 tbsp sugar or 8 dates
- 90 ml (3 fl oz) plain set Greek yoghurt

METHOD:

1. Crush or crumble the biscuits into a powder and mix them together with the melted butter.
2. Press this down in a 20–25 cm (8–10 inch) flan dish to form a flat base – put this in the fridge for 1 hour to set.
3. In a food processor, mix the yoghurt and the pitted dates or sugar. Spoon this into a bowl and combine with the remaining ingredients.
4. Work the mixture until it forms a smooth homogenous paste.
5. Remove the biscuit base from the fridge and spoon on the mixture, smoothing it down with the back of a spoon.
6. Refrigerate for at least 1 hour and serve.

CHINESE OR JAPANESE DOGWOOD
Cornus kousa

Season for picking: autumn
Where to find them: public parks
Main identifying feature: knobbly red fruits
Best use: as a passing nibble
Not to be mistaken for: European dogwoods

Found growing in parks throughout Europe and North America, Chinese or Japanese dogwoods are best spotted in the spring when their huge white or pink blossoms coat the entire tree. On closer inspection you'll notice the 'petals' are ovoid, with a point, and ribbed, like a plantain leaf. These are in fact bracts or modified leaves; the true flower is just the knobbly little ball in the centre. The bracts drop away and the flower forms into an equally knobbly red berry during mid-to-late autumn when most other fruits are past their best. The fruits resemble a strawberry with a hard skin and a bad case of acne. Although not thought to be toxic, it is best to avoid the black fruits of other dogwoods.

PREPARATION AND USE

For some, the skins of the fruits are said to cause contact dermatitis, but I've never found this to be the case. Once you have navigated around the skin and the many seeds, the fruits have a superb flavour, a bit like a custard apple. They can be used in the usual ways: in jams, jellies and fruit leathers (see pages 19 and 26), but are perhaps best as a passing nibble.

CHAPTER THREE

Paths, Cycle Paths and Roadsides

A FEW YEARS AGO, when fewer responsibilities meant I could set off anywhere on a whim, I hopped on my bike and set off for the Dorset coast. The journey took me through the rolling Somerset and Dorset hills, down single-track lanes with humpbacked bridges, past ancient woodland and summer meadows. The rain stayed away and a cool summer breeze seemed to guide me on my way. I packed oats for breakfast and noodles and miso for lunch and dinner, with the intention of finding more ingredients en route. There was more than enough to eat on the way with field mushrooms, puffballs and jelly ears aplenty along with plantain, nettles and mallow. The fields were alive with the sounds of grasshoppers and I spotted fireflies as I pitched my tent in the fading evening light.

Each morning I added a few foraged blackberries to my porridge. Then when I reached the coast, accompanied by a salty breeze, I found rock samphire, sea beet and wild cabbage on coastal cliffs, far above the endless blue of the sea. I can't remember going hungry at all or spending a single penny on food.

Travellers throughout human history have been similarly sustained by what they could find in the wild. One famous example is the ancient 'Iceman' who was found, his body almost perfectly preserved for over 5,000 years, in the Ötztal Alps on the border of Austria. Recent analysis of his hair and stomach found that he subsisted on preserved meat and fruit along with bread made of einkorn, barley and seeds. Further evidence suggests he added roots, grains, berries and herbs to his diet, most of which he must have picked in the lowlands prior to reaching the alps.[4]

This age-old tradition of travellers eating wayside plants is reflected in their old names or nicknames. Plantain (*Plantago major*) for instance is a very common weed which favours land that has been compacted by feet, and the word plantain comes from the Middle English *planta*, meaning 'sole of the foot'. Plantain was called *wagbreed* in Anglo-Saxon England, but this was later corrupted into 'waybread' as it was a staple of travellers looking for sustenance.

Journeys by car have undoubtedly taken away some of this tradition of wayside foraging, yet they may have also helped distribute the plants themselves. Seeds travel in the treads of car tyres. Fruits sold in lay-bys for motorists have self-seeded, and discarded cores and pips from roadside picnics have seen traditional hedgerow fruits like crab apple, sloe, hawthorn and wild pear joined by apples, domestic pears and occasionally a stray cherry or apricot. I have found a good proportion of giant puffballs by the side of the road, after their many spores have been dragged on the slipstream of passing vehicles.

Foraging on a road can sound unappealing. I tend to favour less polluted country roads or quieter, residential streets for my wayside foraging. To be on the safe side, I nearly always soak any roadside bounty in salty water before I eat it, just in case dog walkers have passed through on the same route.

PLANTAIN
Plantago major

Season for picking: all year
Where to find them: meadows, pathsides, parks, lawns
Main identifying features: round leaves and a long seed head
Best use: as a cure for nettle rash

Greater plantain, *Plantago major*, is an unassuming herbaceous plant with round, ribbed leaves and a long, upright, flowering stalk. Most people associate the name plantain with *Musa × paradisiaca*, the starchy banana plantain fruit. Although spelt identically, the two words are as unrelated as the plants. The first gets its name from the Middle English word *planta*, meaning 'sole of the foot', the second from the Carib word *palatana*, meaning 'banana'.

FORAGER'S TIP

Greater plantain loves to grow on compacted land, favouring the edges of paths and tracks where people diverge from the main thoroughfare. It spreads easily as a weed and Native Americans called it 'Englishman's foot', as it tended to sprout on the paths taken by white settlers. But plantain doesn't only grow on ground compacted by human traffic; the next time you open a gate to a cattle field, look down and you will inevitably find plantain growing.

PREPARATION AND USE

Bizarrely the leaves taste like mushrooms and are far more effective than dock (which may only act as a placebo) in helping to reduce hives caused by a nettle sting. Simply squeeze the juice from the leaf and apply to the affected area. I chew the leaf to break up the cell walls and get the juices running before applying.

In terms of eating, plantain is at its best when the young leaves are about the size of the head of a spoon. Older leaves are very bitter and contain tough ribs, a little like celery, though these can be removed and salt, lemon and vinegar all temper the bitterness.

The seeds are more reliably good to eat. They are best from overgrown plants, such as those found on farm tracks and open woodland, with 10–20-cm-long seed heads. The seeds can be gathered by running your hand up the long stem, gently pulling off the seeds and chaff into your hand. Once gathered, rub them through a sieve until the chaff and the seeds are separated. Use a tablespoon of the seed in a small loaf of bread for added texture and a nutty flavour (a little like poppy seeds).

You can also toast the stalks on an open fire then pull the seeds off with your teeth – this way they taste rather like rye-crackers.

PLANTAIN CRISPS

1. Wash the leaves and cut out any large ribs.
2. Dress with a splash of soy sauce or liquid aminos and a little oil.
3. Bake in the oven at a moderate temperature for around 10 minutes, until browned and crispy.

ROSEBAY WILLOWHERB, FIREWEED, BOMBWEED
Chamaenerion angustifolium

Season for picking: late spring and summer
Where to find them: roadsides
Main identifying features: pointed leaves and pink-purple flowers
Best use: Ivan's tea
Not to be mistaken for: foxgloves

Rosebay willowherb is a plant that loves to announce its presence. During the summer, its bright pink blooms brighten up the banks of roads and lanes everywhere. As temperatures cool they send out their wispy wish-fulfilling seeds in vast numbers.

You'll find great rows of the pink flower spike on a stem around a metre or more tall, with lance-shaped leaves jutting out in a spiral. Before it flowers, the plant can resemble other willowherbs, although they generally have leaves on branching stems and can be smaller. Don't confuse rosebay willowherb with the poisonous foxglove, which generally appears earlier and has bell-shaped flowers and large leaves.

As a colonising plant, willowherb favours areas which have been previously cleared, so look for it on roadsides, waste ground, edgeland or anywhere which has recently been cleared by fire – hence the alternative name 'fireweed'. Historically it was found on bombsites, leading to another popular name: 'bombweed'.

PREPARATION AND USE

There are many references to the new shoots being cooked like asparagus, with a mild pea-pod taste. Quite when these delicately flavoured willowherbs grow has always escaped me as I have never found them to be anything other than bitter and unpalatable. However, the flowers can be infused in sugar solution of various strengths to make a vivid pink cordial or sugar syrup.

My favoured use for the plant is in the preparation of Ivan's tea, or Koporye tea. Unlike so many other herbal teas, including ordinary black tea, it is not diuretic. It has a satisfying flavour, mildly bitter like a black tea but with a better texture and mouthfeel. In the early nineteenth century, enterprising crooks used the naturally abundant leaves to adulterate imported tea leaves. A parliamentary investigation in 1835 found that over four million pounds in weight of 'fictitious tea' had been sold in Britain, much of it coming from rosebay willowherb and sloe.[5]

IVAN'S OR KOPORYE TEA

As you may have guessed from the name, Ivan's tea is a popular drink in Russia. It is thought to have originated sometime in the twelfth or thirteenth century in the village of Koporye around sixty miles west of St Petersburg. It is quite unlike the herbal teas you might be used to from tea bags, with a flavour closer to green tea than one made with nettle or peppermint. It is naturally free of caffeine, so can be drunk at any time of day.

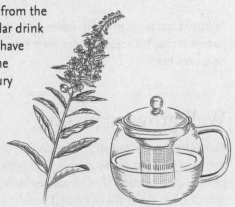

Ivan's tea is a refreshing caffeine-free alternative to black tea.

1. Remove the leaves from the plant by pulling your hand down the stem, gathering fistfuls as you go – this can be done at home or with the plant in situ to ensure it still goes to seed.
2. Wash the leaves, then pat them dry and lay them out on a sheet outside to wilt for 4–5 hours if sunny, 12 hours if cloudy.
3. Roll the leaves, 2–4 at a time, into little balls then put them into a ceramic bowl.
4. Cover the bowl with a tea towel or saucer and leave to ferment for at least 6 hours, or as long as 4 days. Longer ferments produce a more complex flavour.
5. Once fermented, the leaves will have a floral smell and will have lost their grass-like scent.
6. Dry in a dehydrator or on the lowest heat in an oven for 4–12 hours, checking until the leaves feel dry.

7. Store and use as you would black tea, with or without a milk of your choice.

In Russia, rather than being rolled by hand, the leaves are often passed through a meat grinder then either dried or baked on a low heat until black.

....

Wall-growing plants

Plants have amazing strategies to survive in man-made environments. I've seen ferns clinging to light fittings in deep underground quarries and shrubs such as buddleia, elder and hawthorn sprout from the walls of ruined buildings.

The plants in this section have all adapted to urban environments and are able to grow in the tiniest cracks within a man-made wall, thriving for years on end on what seems to be nothing but bricks and mortar.

Growing high above the leg of a passing dog, these plants avoid contamination and as they have little competition, their identification is often simpler than that of their ground-growing relatives.

WALL PENNYWORT, NAVELWORT, PENNY-PIES
Umbilicus rupestris

Season for picking: spring to autumn
Where to find them: walls and trees, especially in areas of high rainfall
Main identifying features: fleshy leaves the size of an old penny
Best use: salads

On my way home from horticultural college on a warm day, I would pluck pennywort from an old, shaded wall as a refreshing snack. It is a European native, favouring cool, damp areas

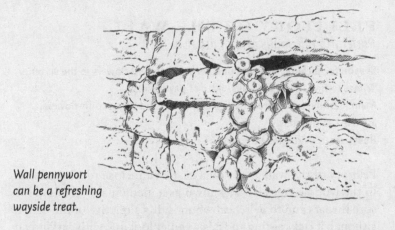

Wall pennywort can be a refreshing wayside treat.

such as the dark side of trees and, more commonly, stone walls. It tends to prefer rural locations and thrives in wetter climates, like Wales and the south-west of England. It is called pennywort as the fleshy leaves grow to the size of an old penny.

Although plants known as marsh pennywort or dollar weed (*Hydrocotyle* spp.) look remarkably similar to the wall pennywort, they are completely unrelated. Marsh pennywort grows in wetlands, woods and lawns across Europe, Asia and the USA. It is equally edible and sometimes juiced and sold as a drink.

FORAGER'S TIP

Pennywort is at its most succulent after rainfall, and becomes thin and bitter after prolonged periods of dry, sunny weather – so aim to pick after periods of heavy rain.

PREPARATION AND USE

The leaves have a mild, cucumber-like taste. Indeed, pennywort can take the place of cucumber in a cheese sandwich or a traditional salad with lettuce and tomato. You can also try it in East Asian dishes such as an aromatic stir-fry. Alternatively, serve with seafood and a creamy tarragon dressing.

PELLITORY OF THE WALL
Parietaria officinalis and *P. judaica*

Season for picking: all year, but at its best before it flowers in the summer
Where to find them: old walls, sides of pavements
Main identifying features: dark-green leaves and tiny, scruffy flowers attached to the stem
Best use: in mixed wilted greens

Pellitory of the wall grows on a castle ruin close to where I live. In the Middle Ages it was known as a medicinal herb, used for sore throats and to help heal wounds. It's a relative of the nettle, although it lacks a sting and it is weedier looking, with dark-green leaves and an often reddish stem with tiny flowers attached. A native to the dry rocky areas of the Mediterranean, it is found growing on old walls in southern Britain and throughout Europe. It has naturalised in parts of the US where it grows alongside similar tasting and looking native plants of the same species.

PREPARATION AND USE
With a pleasant nutty flavour, pellitory of the wall is one of my favourite wild plants to cook with. I use the chopped leaves, cooked in butter with spring onions and a little balsamic vinegar, as a side dish. It is at its best before it flowers in the summer and, as it's an invasive weed (in Britain and America at least), you can pick as much as you like without much worry. Use it in recipes that call for nettles or spinach. Also see base recipes (page 12) for more ideas.

IVY-LEAVED TOADFLAX, KENILWORTH IVY, OXFORD IVY
Cymbalaria muralis

Season for picking: all year
Where to find them: cracks in walls
Main identifying features: lilac flowers with yellow bulges
Best use: in salads or as a garnish

With its delicate, lilac, snapdragon-like flowers with two yellow-ish bulges, the ivy-leaved toadflax is a common sight on brick and stone walls. In its native habitat of southern Europe, it grows out of cracks in rocky surfaces, colonising areas other plants struggle to reach. Two adaptations allow the plant to do this: firstly the flower is phototropic, meaning it likes sunlight and actively moves toward it. However, once pollinated, the seed-containing head of the plant becomes photophobic, meaning it shies away from light. To avoid the sun's rays, like a tiny hand carrying the seeds, the flower stalk pushes itself into dark crevices where it can germinate.

The leaves are edible when young but can be bitter, especially after flowering. They act best as a garnish rather than the focus of a dish.

ROCK VALERIAN
Centranthus ruber

Season for picking: spring
Where to find them: walls, old ruins, coastal gardens
Main identifying features: white pink or red flowers, slightly fleshy leaves
Best use: young stems, blanched

A red, sometimes white or pink, flowered plant with slightly fleshy pointy leaves and a fleshy stem, rock valerian can grow in abundance, bringing colour to ruined churches and railway sidings.

The very young stems have a pleasant taste with a slight hint of bitterness which can be reduced with cooking. However, the older stems are about as pleasant to eat as coffee grounds and should be left alone.

SHAGGY INK CAP
Coprinus comatus

Season for picking: late spring to autumn
Where to find them: roadsides, paths, in woodchip
Main identifying features: shaggy dome-shaped cap
Best use: fried with butter
Not to be mistaken for: Magpie fungus

Whenever I see shaggy ink caps pop up along the cycle path close to where I live, I always think they should be called yeti's fingers. When young, they are roughly the girth of the fingers in a baseball glove and anything from 15 to 40 cm (6 to 16 inches) tall. The stubby white fingers are the caps, which grow upwards to slowly reveal the stalks beneath. Each cap then opens to resemble a half-put-up umbrella with a mottled black fringe or, as my youngest son puts it, a woman in a dirty skirt.

Be careful not to confuse with the magpie fungus *Coprinopsis picacea*, a poisonous mushroom that looks similar but has white spots on a dark cap.

PREPARATION AND USE
As an excited young forager, I remember finding a good-sized haul of these mushrooms early one morning on my way to work. I packed them in an empty lunchbox, which I then shoved into my backpack. When I returned home that night the mushrooms had reduced to an inky black mess.

If transported home quickly, younger mushrooms will keep a little longer than this, especially if kept in the fridge with the stalks complete. (Older specimens have a tendency to leak their ink over anything else they share a pan with and don't always have the best flavour.) They are best cooked soon after picking, preferably in a pan with a little butter, a stone's throw from where you found them. I especially like them fried but you can also make them into soup.

WILD STRAWBERRY
Fragaria vesca

Season for picking: summer, normally June–July
Where to find them: pathsides, woodland fringes
Main identifying features: tiny strawberry fruits
Best use: as a snack
Not to be mistaken for: false strawberry

Before the 'discovery' of the New World, the only strawberries in Europe were the pea-sized fruits of the wild or alpine strawberry, *Fragaria vesca*. The larger garden strawberry, *F.* × *ananassa*, came about much later as the result of French botanists crossing two species found growing in the Americas: *F. virginiana*, which still grows wild in the US and Canada, and the larger *F. chiloensis*, which grows in coastal Chile.

There is much confusion over the origin of the word 'strawberry', as no equivalent exists in any other European language. The name may derive from the plant's habit of straying or sending out runners and could be a corruption of 'stray berry'. Another explanation is that the seeds are distributed or 'strewed' by birds, or that the seeds themselves resemble flecks of straw. However, the most common, but etymologically least likely, explanation is the fact that straw is used as a mulch around the plant to protect from slug damage.

Wild strawberries like to grow by the side of cycle paths, especially those on former railway lines, right across the length and breadth of Britain. I've found them in the cracks of old stone steps, along footpaths, in open woodland and in parks and gardens. They have tiny five-petalled white blooms with yellow centres. The leaves are trefoil and serrated. Their appearance is very much like their domestic cousin's, only much smaller.

FORAGER'S TIP

Despite being bright red, the fruits can be hard to spot as they have a tendency to hide under a tangle of runners. So it is easy to miss them, especially when cycling past at speed. They are more conspicuous when in flower in the spring to early summer, so make a note of where you've seen them and return around June–July when they are in fruit (hoping no one else does the same).

The flowers of the wild strawberry are more easily spotted; find these first before returning for the berries.

PREPARATION AND USE

What the diminutive wild strawberry lacks in size, it more than makes up for in flavour. The tiny fruits are sweeter and lack the pineapple notes of a larger strawberry, and seldom make it home after a foraging expedition.

If you do manage to save some, they make an excellent Scottish dessert called cranachan. Roughly chop the fruit into a glass and add a layer of whipped cream mixed with whisky. Next add alternative layers of honey then butter-toasted oatmeal, crumbled flapjack or granola. Repeat the layering until the glass is half full (or half empty depending on your outlook).

To make a liquor, create alternate layers of wild strawberries and sugar in a jar and top with enough vodka to fill the jar. Shake it once or twice a week for at least a month. Strain and store. It's best served when you have little to do the following day.

In Italy, wild strawberries are called *fragoline* and are sold in local markets. They are made into jams, or into *fragoline di bosco al balsamico* (strawberries with balsamic vinegar). To make the latter, coat around 500 g (1 lb 2 oz) of strawberries in 100–150 g (3.5–5½ oz) of sugar – preferably caster sugar – and leave them for up to an hour. Then mix them with 2–4 tbsp of a good balsamic vinegar and a few sprigs of mint.

HORSERADISH
Armoracia rusticana

Season for picking: all year
Where to find them: roadsides, allotments, gardens
Main identifying features: large dock-like leaves
Best use: horseradish sauce
Not to be mistaken for: dock

The leaves of a horseradish plant tower a metre or so high, so they are big enough to be spotted from a passing car. Closely resembling dock, their large size and habit of becoming lobed or toothed when older makes them easily distinguishable. As a member of the cabbage family they have white, cross-shaped flowers and grow as a common roadside weed throughout Europe, Russia and eastern USA.

This large leafy herb is best known for its fiery-tasting root, which can grow to the size of a child's arm. Both root and leaf release volatile oils when their cells are crushed. These oils, or isothiocyanates, stimulate nerve endings and send pain messages to the brain. This is enough to put off most herbivores but for us masochistic humans it is the main reason we eat horseradish. Some theories suggest we like spicy foods because they release pain-relieving chemicals into the blood, giving us a warm woozy feeling when the pain subsides.

It is illegal to dig up the root in the UK without the landowner's permission. However, as the plant can become invasive, gardeners and allotment holders over-run with the weed may be all too grateful to have some of the roots removed if you ask them. You will need a spade and perhaps a fork to liberate the roots from the soil. And keep your diary empty that afternoon as in my experience they really can take some digging out.

PREPARATION AND USE

Always clean the roots with a scrubbing brush to remove any dirt. Once cleaned, the roots keep for a couple of weeks in the fridge but are better stored in the freezer, allowing you to grate off small amounts when you need to. This preserves the root for far longer and reduces the amount of eye-watering isothiocyanates given off.

To make horseradish sauce, grate the root, add vinegar and a little salt to taste. The root also works well grated and mixed into mayonnaise or cottage cheese as an accompaniment to fish dishes, or dolloped on lentil stew. Grate it into dishes towards the end of cooking, as adding it too early diminishes the flavour.

The vast majority of wasabi paste sold outside of Japan is actually made from horseradish with added green dye. To make this imitation wasabi paste, grate the root and dehydrate it in an oven on the lowest setting, or in a dehydrator, for anything up to 8 hours. The pulverised stem of the plant can be added for colour, or mix instead with a little food colouring if that sounds too much like hard work. You may also need to add a little oil to make dried root into a paste.

The leaves make an edible but bitter salad green – the flavour is strong so only a small amount is needed. Add no more than 1 chopped leaf to a pan of milder more abundant leaves, such as spinach, fat hen or nettle.

GOOSEBERRY
Ribes uva-crispa

Season for picking: summer
Where to find them: cycle paths, hedgerows, roadsides, woodland thickets, open woodland, gardens, allotments
Main identifying features: small shrub with prickly branch and hairy green fruits
Best use: gooseberry fool

If you ask me, I think the term 'wild goose chase' must be a corruption of 'wild gooseberry chase' as the bush can be almost impossible to find by anything other than chance – even though it is apparently a fairly common plant. I've stumbled across them growing in hedgerows, by the side of the path in old woodlands and growing close to allotment sites. They also grow in bushes alongside roads and cycle paths. They look and taste almost exactly like their domestic cousins but with a slightly tarter flavour.

In France they are given the name *groseillier à maquereau*, or mackerel berry, as they are often served as a sauce to accompany the fish. In Britain the favoured dish is gooseberry fool, a mixture of cream and sugar, sometimes with added elderflower cordial, served as a dessert.

FERMENTED GOOSEBERRIES

Fermented gooseberries make a delicious snack or canapé. I like them best pureed into a sauce and served with masa corn tortillas, avocado, refried black beans and spicy tomatoes.

1. Wash your gooseberries and pack them into a jar, leaving a 2.5 cm (1 inch) gap above the berries.
2. Top the jar with whey or the liquid from strained yoghurt.
3. Ferment for 2 days, then tip out the liquid and exchange for brine.
4. Stir in a teaspoon of Korean red pepper or chilli powder.
5. Store in the fridge. The flavour will improve with age.

APPLE SEEDLINGS
Malus spp.

Season for picking: late summer and early autumn
Where to find them: roadsides, abandoned railway routes, cycle paths, hedgerows
Main identifying features: round red or green fruit
Best use: apple pie

I used to regularly visit an old quarry with my son when he was a toddler. I recently returned to the spot with him just before his ninth birthday and found a straggly apple seedling tree in the very spot where we would eat our lunch. We sat in the same place, now with his younger brother, eating the juicy, crisp red apples.

Commercial apple trees are never propagated by seed. Instead, they are the results of branch grafted onto existing rootstock. Seedling trees tend to be genetically unpredictable and the fruits cross-pollinate with any wild or domestic apple within range of the local bee population (which can be anything up to four miles).[6] Trees grown from discarded Granny Smiths, for example, will never grow into another Granny Smith apple tree. But just as my father and I both tell terrible, corny jokes to strangers, the apple trees may share some of their parent's characteristics. A Golden Delicious seedling, for instance, might be the same colour but half the size of the parent tree, or russet seedlings might be russet coloured but as tart as a Bramley.

PREPARATION AND USE
As the tastes of these seedling apples can vary so much, they are worthy of some experimentation. A tart cider apple can make an excellent juice (or of course cider), whereas crisp, cox-like seedlings are great raw or thrown into a salad with dry or wet walnuts. Apples too sour to eat raw can be cooked with sweeter varieties or sweetened with sugar in pies, crumbles and tarts. I love them baked with wood avens roots and honey, or I'll stew them and top with a mix of oats, nuts and seeds toasted in butter with a pinch of cinnamon.

Apples can be an important food for local birdlife, so try and pick from the lower branches, leaving the higher ones for them. Also see crab apples (page 61).

OPIUM POPPY
Papaver somniferum

Season for picking: mid to late summer
Where to find them: roadsides, paths, gardens
Main identifying features: white, pink or red flower with
greyish-green leaves
Best use: seeds in bread

The opium poppy is a common garden escapee and wayside weed. The leaves point upwards on the plant and are either semi or fully lobed. The entire plant is a light greyish-green and the wide-open flowers range from white, through pink to red and sometimes, but rarely, black. They are much larger than the diminutive Flanders poppy, the Welsh poppy and the Californian poppy and produce a large, oval rattling seed head full of edible seeds in mid to late summer.

It is from this species of poppy that opium is harvested. Although the seeds do not contain any opium and do not have a narcotic effect, eating them can give a false positive in a drugs test. In 2017, English television presenter Angela Rippon, then age 72, tested positive for opiates in a routine drug test after eating poppy seed bread.

PREPARATION AND USE
It's best to harvest when the seed heads are completely dry and the seeds rattle around in the case. Snip the stalk at ground level, upturn the seed head and knock the seeds onto a sheet of paper. Once all the seeds are removed, fold the paper in half and pour the seeds into a spice jar for later use.

The seeds can be used in baking, especially biscuits, bread and cakes. They also add an extra texture to salads and slaws.

CHERRY PLUM, MYROBALAN PLUM
Prunus cerasifera

Season for picking: summer
Where to find them: pathsides, roadsides, hedgerows
Main identifying features: red and yellow fruits
Best use: in a plum sauce

Cherry plums are so named as their size, flavour and picking times sit between the wild cherry and the wild plum. They are one of the earliest of all the *Prunus* spp. or plum relatives to come into blossom, beating even the early-spring blooms of the black-thorn. The trees can grow between 5 metres and 8 metres tall and are native to the Balkan Peninsula and Iran and Iraq. They have naturalised in temperate regions across the world, including much of eastern and northern Europe, Britain, scattered states within America and even parts of Australia and New Zealand, where they have become an invasive weed tree.

The fruits are red, yellow or a mixture of the two, golf ball sized and absolutely delicious. Hybrid varieties such as the purple-leaved sand-cherry, *P.* × *cistena*, are popular in British gardens or as ornamental street trees. The dark leaves cunningly hide purple fruits from all but the keenest eye, and the fruits only become visible when they drop. Another closely related species, the beech plum or *P. maritima*, grows mostly in US coastal regions from Virginia to Maine.

PREPARATION AND USE
The harvests for a row of trees can be considerable, producing more fruits than you could possibly carry, with plenty left over for visiting birds and mammals. When growing above long grass they make a good windfall fruit and sometimes you'll find more on the ground than you will on the tree.

They are as versatile as cherries or plums, making good jams, pies and desserts of all kinds. They can also be used in place of cherries in a cherry plum clafoutis.

CHERRY PLUM SAUCE

Cherry plums are naturally sweet with just enough tartness to make a delicious sauce. You can use the sauce to dip spring rolls, as a stir-fry sauce or as a dressing for cooked tofu dishes or cooked meats such as duck.

YOU WILL NEED:

- 600 g (1 lb 5 oz) deseeded plums
- 1 tsp dried wild garlic flakes or 1 clove crushed garlic
- 1 tsp soy sauce
- 1 tsp chilli powder (half this if you don't like it spicy – double if you do!)
- 1 tsp five spice powder
- 60 ml (2 fl oz) rice wine vinegar
- 140 g (5 oz) sugar
- Salt to taste

METHOD:

1. Simmer the plums in a large pan on a low heat with the vinegar.
2. When they start to break up add the soy sauce, chilli powder, five spice powder and garlic or wild garlic flakes.
3. Add the sugar and continuously stir until the mixture is completely broken down into a jam-like sauce.
4. Check for flavour and add salt if necessary.
5. Keep in the fridge if using quickly or store in heat-sterilised jars.

CHAPTER FOUR
Edgeland

OST OF US don't live in areas that we would describe as 'wild'. More than half the world's population live in urban areas, so as much as we might love to spend every day roaming the wilderness, we often find ourselves confined to the jungle of brick, concrete and steel. It is safe to say that city centres, supermarket car parks and urban parks lack the romance of a wind-swept moor, hillside forest or coastal bay. But close to our urban doorsteps, there are half-wildernesses to explore – spaces that are known as the 'edgelands'.

Edgelands are the areas at the periphery of towns and cities, the forgotten hinterland between urban streets and rolling countryside. Here, disused railway tracks, pylon-lined wastelands and self-sown patches of woodland on the fringes of housing and industrial estates can be a rich and surprising kind of wilderness. Often unloved, uncared for and overgrown, these places always remind me that if humans were to disappear overnight, nature would simply take over and carry on without us.

I spent much of my childhood exploring these in-between places: cycling to find minnows in concrete drainage streams, picking blackberries behind large retail estates and playing tag in garage-lined alleyways. Later, these edgelands became my foraging grounds, where I learnt to identify pineapple weed, plantain and nipplewort growing in the cracks of worn-out paths, or picked elderberries, haws and cherry plums in copses on the edges of housing estates. There is an abundance of plants that grow in these areas and, roaming around them, I found I was able to tick off most of the plant species in my field guides and foraging books.

Centuries of human activity interspersed with neglect produce diverse, mosaic habitats full of opportunistic and resilient pioneers, thuggish invasive species and garden escapees. Decaying concrete and tarmac create an environment that is not so different to the rocky land formed by retreating glaciers or cooled lava flows. Deposited here by the wind, weeds such as dandelions, willowherbs or prickly lettuce will exploit the tiniest scrap of earth in the cracks. Eventually these first weeds, or 'primary pioneer species', decompose, forming enough soil for larger secondary pioneer shrubs and trees to grow. In a natural environment, this process of ecological succession would continue and over tens or hundreds of years would eventually settle as a climax community of hardwood trees, like beech and oak.

In edgelands, though, this natural development is often disrupted by man-made interactions such as seeds carried in by cars or blown along rail tracks by fast-moving trains. In some areas, illegally dumped garden waste or plants like bamboo and sumac sneak out from under fences. Passing birds will drop seeds, adding cotoneaster and Himalayan honeysuckle to the list of species. In parts of Cornwall the flowers of fuchsia, crocosmia and *Rosa rugosa* are as common a sight among the mining and clay work ruins as those of native species. Occasionally, a more thuggish non-native like Japanese knotweed will muscle in too. Originating from the cooled lava flows of Japan, this infamous pest has tremendously strong roots, which can tear through concrete.

This edgeland mishmash can create fascinatingly dynamic environments. I have seen signs of otters among thickets of Japanese knotweed, bees gathering nectar from late-blooming Himalayan balsam and caterpillars consuming Oxford ragwort originating from the slopes of Mount Etna. Wild strawberries, vetches, primroses, cowslips and poppies poke their pretty flowers up from the ballast of abandoned railways. Horseradish, wild lettuce, nettle, cleavers and rosebay will colonise the broken glass, tarmac and concrete of wasteland.

In the edgelands of Bristol I have discovered hawthorn, sloe, bramble and seedling apples growing on the land around abandoned Second World War gun turrets, and I've found raspberries, sumac and currants fleeing cultivation just beyond gardens and allotments. The trick is to keep your eyes open while you walk. Change your regular routes, always asking 'What's behind there?' and 'What's up there?' Look for alleyways, old railways, riversides and cut-throughs you had not considered before. Find the empty places on maps and cross-reference with Google Street View. Although some may be fenced off and dangerous to visit, there is a surprising amount of disused land criss-crossed with public and permissible footpaths. If you keep your eyes and your mind open, you will soon be returning with plenty of edgeland bounty for the kitchen table.

BIRCH
Betula spp.

Season for picking: late winter
Where to find them: abandoned or disused ground, edges of paths, fringes of woodland
Main identifying features: white/silver trunks with dark horizontal lines
Best use: twigs as a tea, sap reduced to make syrup

I once spent the night in a caravan on the site of a semi-demolished print works. I was filling in for a friend as a night watchman because the landowner feared the site would be ransacked for scrap metal. Signs of spring were just coming: early primroses flowered by the potholed roadside and coltsfoot sent up its bright-yellow daisy-like flowers through cracks in the concrete.

The buds of the birch trees looked swollen, so I tested the trees by drilling a small hole into some of the trunks and found the sap was rising too. That evening, before the light failed, I got to work setting up taps on the trees. I cut holes with my penknife and inserted cut-down plastic tubes and collected the sap in recycled plastic tubs, all of which was salvaged from the site. The following afternoon my friend returned to relieve me of duty and we sat in the sun of an unusually warm afternoon drinking the cool, slightly sweet sap while taking pot shots at cans with his air rifle.

It was hard to say if the birches had been intentionally sown at the site of the ruined building or if they had arrived themselves from seed. Birches are a pioneer species, meaning they are one of the first trees to move in to colonise land. They are the only domestic tree of Iceland, a country so challenging that people there refer to themselves as living 'on' the country rather than in it.

Outside of Iceland, birch trees often grow exposed outside the cover of a woodland. To cope with this exposure, the tree has evolved its own sunscreen – its white or silvery trunk reflects the sun's rays rather than absorbing them, as a darker tree trunk would in a forest. Young birches have dark horizontal lines called lenticels which help with gas exchange. As the trees mature these morph into dark triangular shapes on the trunk. As the tree ages further and its neighbours grow tall around it, it no longer needs its white trunk as sunscreen so the bark darkens and becomes rough.

PREPARATION AND USE

Although you can eat the young triangular birch leaves, they can stick in the back of the throat. They work best in a mix of greens for a springtime salad.

A simple tea can be made from the young twigs along with their buds. Gather a few twigs and peel the bark with a sharp knife or potato peeler. Loosely fill a bowl or large jar with the twigs and peelings and top with hot water. Leave to infuse for a few hours, and try cold or reheat as tea. It has a pleasant, unusual taste: fresh and almost minty.

However, the most delicious part of the tree by far is the sap. The hardest part of tapping for sap is timing. Traditionally the best time to tap is when the snow begins to melt but with increasingly snow-free winters this isn't a reliable gauge. Depending on where you live, the sap can be ready as early as late February or as late as early April, but it normally coincides with when the first celandines or early daffodils are in flower. When the sap is ready the buds on the tips of the branches start to swell. This can be difficult to spot if you are not in regular contact with the trees so to be sure, cut off a piece of branch and see if a tear-like trickle of sap oozes out.

Only tap older trees – if you can clasp your hands around the trunk and touch your fingers and thumbs it is much too young. However, if there is at least a 10 cm (4 inch) gap between your fingers and thumbs you are good to go.

There are many different ways to tap a birch, but it is best to do it on the side of the tree facing away from anyone who might interfere with the tap. When I lived in Bristol, my perfect spot was on a group of trees growing on a downward slope, away from a cycle path. Only the tops of the trees were visible to passers-by, so my taps were always completely hidden. Some foragers actually climb the tree to insert their tap way up in the branches where no one is likely to disturb it.

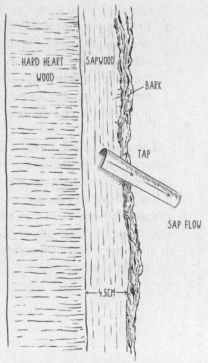

The sap flows through vascular bundles under the bark, in the living tissue of the tree.

There are two main approaches to tapping a birch tree:

1. **Traditional tap:** Twist in a knife or drill an inch-deep hole into the main trunk, just beneath the layer of bark, stopping when it becomes wet. Drill the hole at an upwards angle so the sap will drip downwards. Insert either a tap or hollow dowel to which you can attach a plastic tube or insert the plastic tube directly. Put a container below the tube (a container that will hold 4 litres (1 gallon) or more is best) and leave to fill up – this can take 12–24 hours. For larger trees you can refill the container 2–3 times.
2. **Low-impact method:** Cut the ends of a branch with a pair of secateurs. Tie the branch to the trunk so it bends downward, and the branch should start dripping sap. Secure a bottle over the branch using tape or place a container below the drip. You can also put a plastic tube over the branch and place a bottle underneath.

The resulting sap tastes a little like a slightly sweet mineral water and it's the best cure for a hangover I have ever found. It can be drunk straight away or simmered (but not boiled) until it has reduced to produce a sticky syrup which can be used to sweeten desserts. This can be done on campfire coals or in a slow cooker. Around 98 per cent of the liquid needs to evaporate to make the syrup, or for a sweet birch drink reduce by around 60–70 per cent.

JAPANESE KNOTWEED
Reynoutria japonica, syn. *Fallopia japonica* and *Polygonum cuspidatum*

Season for picking: spring
Where to find them: wasteland and disused land, riversides, near railways, in the gardens of unhappy homeowners
Main identifying features: green bamboo-like shoots
Best use: like rhubarb in pies or crumbles

Warning: always wash thoroughly and do not harvest if there are signs of spraying.

I must have been seven or eight when my grandfather bemoaned the Japanese knotweed he had growing in his Berkshire garden. 'They grow a foot a day!' he said.[7] I was excited by this and sat watching the plant, expecting it to move like the triffids I'd seen on TV.

The triffids are an easy comparison but I think it even more likely that H. G. Wells was thinking about Japanese knotweed when he came up with the red weed in *War of the Worlds*. Few plants look as alien as the towering, bamboo-like Japanese knotweed. They have speckled stems, sometimes predominantly red, sometimes green. The leaf stalks are also red while the leaves are green and shaped to a point. When they come into bloom in the summer they send out threads of tiny white flowers.

Knotweed is a born survivor. In its native Japan, its long roots burrow down beneath lava flows thriving in the sulphur dioxide environment where no other plant can. Elsewhere in the world this ability to grow in areas that are inhospitable to other plant life has made it one of the most noxious, hated weeds of the urban environment. So pernicious is the weed that planting it is a criminal offence. It has been known to grow through cracks in the road, through brickwork and along streams and railway embankments where it blocks out native plants. It can even push its way into buildings.

Knotweed can grow from a single piece of the stem weighing no more than 0.7 grams. More often than not, however, it spreads by the rhizomes or root system, thriving in newly built or derelict land. In Swansea, the knotweed thrives where no other plant could: in the ruins of the declining copper industry. Over time it has well and truly colonised the city and the local council still employs a Japanese knotweed officer responsible for its control and eradication.

PREPARATION AND USE

Despite all the bad press knotweed receives, its shoots are one of the best wild foods you can harvest in the city. The new shoots look like asparagus from another planet; they are fleshy and hollow with distinctive nodes or rings around the stem and a pointed bunch of leaves on the top. They come in around mid-spring, between the blooms of the primrose and the elderflower. They should be harvested when the plant is still young, no more than a foot or two high. Cut the shoots with a sharp knife at soil level or just above.

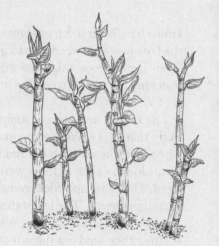

Rather surprisingly, Japanese knotweed tastes just like rhubarb.

Japanese knotweed shoots have an unusual taste, sour but with an earthiness to them, not at all dissimilar to rhubarb – I once cooked a knotweed and apple crumble for friends who all assumed it was rhubarb. Knotweed therefore lends itself well to any rhubarb recipe and is one of my favourite chutney ingredients, too. Aside from pies, crumbles and jams, it also can be cooked as a vegetable to be paired with strong East Asian flavours like coriander, chilli, soy sauce and sesame oil.

FORAGER'S TIP
A little care needs to be taken harvesting knotweed as it is often sprayed by local authorities. This is normally very obvious as the plants look sick but you should avoid anything with wilted, brown, dropping or shrivelled-up leaves, or anything painted or marked in any way. Watch out for any plants containing injection holes and of course any growing in areas that have been cordoned off. Always soak the shoots in salty water and wash thoroughly before consumption. If in doubt, call your local council to find out their knotweed strategy.

As the plant can grow from even just a finger-sized piece of stem, I advise not putting any left-over plant matter in compost, but instead either burning it or leaving it somewhere to completely dry out and shrivel before disposing of it bagged up in a landfill dustbin.

Plants with dandelion-like flowers

Dandelions and their relatives are some of the most successful flowers on earth. Their bright-yellow flowers, some of the first to bloom in the year, are never short of pollinators. In a relatively short amount of time the flowers are transformed into the feather-like 'clocks' that are so familiar to children. Each seed is equipped with its own means of propulsion, a tiny Mary Poppins-like umbrella frame capable of sending the seeds hurtling through the air on the slightest breeze. They seem to germinate wherever they land, turning up between cracks in the pavement, and on scraps of wasteland.

However, not every plant that appears to be a dandelion is in fact a dandelion. Look closely and you'll see many differences. The leaves may be rougher, smoother or hairier; the flowers may be on a solitary stalk or on multiple branched stems. Though they are often overlooked, the taste of these wayside weeds can be superior to that of the dandelion.

DANDELION
Taraxacum officinale or *Taraxacum officinale* agg.

Season for picking: all year
Where to find them: edgeland, lawns, grassy banks, gardens, parks, waste ground, field margins
Main identifying features: toothed leaves
Best use: salads

The dandelion is one of the most common self-sown plants on earth and although it originated in Europe, it has spread to every continent except Antarctica. Its success is partly due to its tenacity; each plant produces up to 300 seeds, grows throughout the year and takes just nine weeks to go from germination to a seed-producing dandelion clock.

Dandelions get their common English name from the French *dent de lion* or 'tooth of lion', because of their jagged, tooth-like leaves. The plant has orange-yellow flower heads made up of countless petals and a long hollow stem. If you're looking for something to do on a sunny day, you can cut this stem off, remove the flower, put a 2 cm (1 inch) horizontal split in it and blow through it to get a rasping sound like a clarinet. You won't get it every time but it is great fun when you finally do!

In the 1930s a new species of dandelion called *Taraxacum kok-saghyz* (TDK or Russian dandelion for short) was found in

Kazakhstan, then part of the Soviet Union. Amazingly, the Russian dandelion was found to be a good source of rubber, so when rubber supplies from South-east Asia were threatened during the Second World War, this species of dandelion became an emergency source of the material. More recently, its economic value has been recognised by the tyre manufacturer Continental, who have used it to produce rubber for both bicycle and car tyres. One benefit of using dandelion is that it takes only six months to produce a viable crop, whereas a rubber plant takes seven years.

The roots are an important source of inulin, a naturally occurring sugar that acts as a probiotic.

PREPARATION AND USE

Dandelions have a unique flavour – fresh and earthy at first, followed by a bitterness. Because of this bitterness, raw dandelion leaves are best used sparingly in mixed salads. I tend to mix them with sweeter flavours such as apple, carrot and raisins. You could also try dandelion leaves with tomatoes, cucumber and sour sorrel leaves, or a lemon dressing. To my taste they are much better cooked and have been a welcome extra green in curries, soups and even pasta sauces, especially at times when I've lacked a garden or money has been tight. My children both eat the petals from the flowers as a passing snack and I sometimes cut these off with a pair of scissors and sprinkle them over a salad.

The flower heads are useful too. I like to simmer them in a sugar and honey solution to make a bright-yellow syrup which is good on ice cream. The petals of the flowers can be cut from the head and tossed into salads to give a little extra colour. Country wines have also been made from dandelion flowers although more for novelty and colour, as they do not seem to have much of a flavour.

The roots can be eaten as a vegetable but the best way to use them is as a coffee (see below).

DANDELION BHAJIS

YOU WILL NEED:

- 20–25 fresh dandelion flower heads
- 100 g (3½ oz) gram flour
- 100 ml (3½ fl oz) cold water
- ½ tsp baking powder
- ½ tsp ground coriander
- ½ tsp turmeric
- A generous pinch of chilli powder or chilli flakes
- A drizzle of vegetable oil

METHOD:

1. Mix the flour, spices and baking powder together in a bowl.
2. Add the cold water, a little at a time until it makes a stiff batter.
3. Heat the oil in a pan to 180°C (350°F). If you don't have a thermometer, drop a little of the batter into the pan and if it sizzles and browns within a minute or so it is hot enough to cook.
4. Stir the dandelion heads into the mixture in the bowl.
5. Using a dessert spoon, drop dollops of the bhaji mix into the hot oil.
6. Cook until they brown, then serve hot with a yoghurt dip such as sorrel (page 234) or chickweed (page 223).

DANDELION COFFEE

It takes 10–15 good-sized dandelion roots to make each cup of coffee, so I would advise digging up enough for at least 4 cups to make the practice worth your while.

1. Harvest and thoroughly wash the roots.
2. Cut them into 2 cm (½ in) pieces, discarding any thin straggly bits.
3. Pop them on a baking tray and place into a warm oven set to 180°C (350°F). Heat for about 40 minutes or until the roots are a dark brown (though not black).

4. For each cup of coffee grind approximately 1 tbsp of the root. Boil the ground roots for 10 minutes, using a coffee cup and a quarter of water for each person (the extra is to compensate for evaporation). Add flavourings such as cinnamon or cardamom if you wish. You can also mix with regular coffee, chicory or coffee substitutes such as Barley Cup.

NIPPLEWORT
Lapsana communis

Season for picking: spring
Where to find them: urban areas, roadsides, pathsides, hedgerows, field edges
Main identifying features: small dandelion-like flowers, shovel-shaped leaves
Best use: salads

Nipplewort is a common street-side plant with a hairy stem and yellow dandelion-like flowers. It has rosette-forming leaves which, when young, have a shovel-like leaflet at the tip and smaller sections either side of a central grooved vein. The leaves change once the plant flowers, sending out pointed, almost heart-shaped leaves. Growing in many of the same environments as the dandelion (apart from the side of pavements), nipplewort is a common garden weed and hedgerow plant. The leaves make a more passable salad green than those of the dandelion. They can be cooked and prepared the same way as any other wild green leaf (see base recipes, page 12).

PRICKLY AND WILD LETTUCE
Lactuca serriola, L. virosa

Season for picking: spring to autumn
Where to find them: urban areas, roadsides, pathsides
Main identifying features: dandelion-like flowers, prickly midribs
Best use: salads

Wild lettuce was among the first edgeland plants I learnt to identify – not because I wanted to eat it, but because as a rebellious teenager I wanted to smoke it. I had read the plant would produce a high, a little like marijuana only a lot more accessible to a suburban teen. Although wild lettuce is used as a sedative and a pain reliever, a kind of a non-addictive opium, it is very mild and I didn't bother seeking it out again!

Prickly lettuce is more of a matt green in colour and has prickly leaves with small spines along the back rib. Wild lettuce lacks the prickles and is a more 'dandelion' green. They both have oval leaves with the latter sometimes breaking into lobes, like an oak-leaf lettuce. They begin life as a rosette, sending up the flowering stalk with its many small flowers, followed by wispy seeds. Both plants grow up through gaps in the pavement and during a warm June it is not unusual to see prickly lettuce growing to head height or more.

PREPARATION AND USE
Both prickly and wild lettuces are better in the rosette form when they can be used as a bitter but nonetheless palatable salad green. It's worth adding a bit of flavouring to the leaves – try lemon, olive oil and a good white wine. The bitterness can be masked with homegrown or frozen peas in a soup or pesto, giving a refreshing flavour. For prickly lettuce you will have to cut away the midrib, but this still leaves more than enough edible material.

GOAT'S BEARD,
JACK-GO-TO-BED-AT-NOON
Tragopogon pratensis

Season for picking: spring
Where to find them: urban areas, roadsides, pathsides, fields and meadows
Main identifying features: flowers close around midday
Best use: blanched stems

When it has gone to seed, goat's beard looks like a rather more flamboyant dandelion. The seed head is around twice the size of a dandelion's, with a diameter more comparable with a tennis ball than a golf ball. I like to think of goat's beards as natural fireworks.

The plant's alternative name, Jack-go-to-bed-at-noon, is beautifully evocative – it describes the plant's habit of closing its yellow, star-shaped flower around lunchtime. When I worked as a postman, I would pass this plant fully open at the start of my shift only to see it closed by the time I walked home.

Jack-go-to-bed-at-noon really does close its large flower head around noon.

PREPARATION AND USE
As a member of the *Tragopogon* genus, goat's beard root has a flavour that strongly resembles that of its close relation salsify.

The root tastes mild and almost sweet, every bit the antidote to its bitter cousin the dandelion. It is good dressed in butter and lemon or spiced as a side vegetable. Or you can use it in a medley of roasted roots, with a light lemon and tahini dressing along with a sprinkle of toasted nuts.

The young stem is good to eat, as are the flowering buds, which have been likened to a sweeter asparagus. The leaves are also good but, again, they need to be harvested when still young. As the plant is more distinctive when in bloom, it may be best to identify it one year and return the next, to see if any new plants have taken root around the parent plant.

CAT'S EAR, FALSE DANDELION
Hypochaeris radicata

Season for picking: spring to summer
Where to find them: lawns, under lamp posts
Main identifying features: shaggy dandelion-like flower
Best use: salads

The flower head of cat's ear has fewer petals than a dandelion and has distinctive scales at its base. Coupled with its smaller, often rough-toothed leaves, this gives the plant an overall far shaggier appearance. It crops up on lawns everywhere, including my own. I find it useful as an extra leaf in the winter to counter all those with more mustardy flavours which seem to be around at that time. It can be bitter, but far less so than the dandelion and even after it flowers the leaves still taste good in moderation.

ROUGH HAWKBIT
Leontodon hispidus

Season for picking: spring to autumn
Where to find them: wasteland and edgeland
Main identifying features: dandelion-like flowers
Best use: salads

Looking very much like a dandelion, only with a hairy green stem and smaller flowers, rough hawkbit is a tough survivor of a plant. It tends to favour environments with little water and poor nutrients, such as chalk or limestone soils, old quarries and the fringes of car parks. It can be bitter, especially raw, but with all the usual tricks of lemon juice, honey balsamic or a mild white vinegar the taste can be improved. Unless you are surrounded by it, hawkbit is more useful as a passing rather than a go-to wild green.

SOW THISTLES
Sonchus oleraceus, S. asper, S. arvensis

Season for picking: spring to summer
Where to find them: wasteland, pathsides, fields and meadows
Main identifying features: dandelion-like thistle
Best use: salads

There are three kinds of sow thistle: the smooth or common sow thistle (*Sonchus oleraceus*), the perennial sow thistle (*S. arvensis*) and the prickly sow thistle (*S. asper*). Depending on their growing conditions they can have as little as two or as many as twenty bright-yellow flowers. They are best described as a dandelion-like thistle, with either glossy or matt lobed leaves growing in a rosette when young, and up the stalk as they flower.

Younger specimens found in the spring or autumn don't yet have spines on their leaves – these are best to eat. When they age, they grow the spines for protection and to deter predators, unlike many other plants that deter pests by having bitter leaves. Sow thistles have a pleasant, mild taste with leaves that are higher in iron than spinach. All varieties of sow thistle are good in salads or as a cooked green leaf.

SHEPHERD'S PURSE
Capsella bursa-pastoris

Season for picking: late winter to spring
Where to find them: grassy patches, meadows, pasture, edgeland
Main identifying features: upward-pointing lobes on leaves
Best use: salads

You will find shepherd's purse as a farm weed, on pastureland, in gardens and in wasteland or edgeland. Before it flowers the leaves of a shepherd's purse look like those of a diminutive dandelion – they are jagged and grow in a central rosette. Apart from the size, the difference lies in the direction of the lobes on the leaves: they point upwards on a shepherd's purse and down on a dandelion. Shepherd's purse also has a small, white four-petalled flower. Its name comes from its many heart-shaped seed pods or 'purses'. Harvest from late winter to early spring before the plant comes into flower.

FORAGER'S TIP
As shepherd's purse likes to grow on disturbed land, it can grow on patches of grass churned up by vehicles, bicycles and mowers. Look for a different shade of green on grassy banks close to paths and roads.

PREPARATION AND USE

As a member of the cabbage or mustard family, the leaves have a mild mustard flavour and make a useful salad green or pot-herb. The root can also be used; it is small but has a pleasant radish-like flavour.

In Korea shepherd's purse is used to make musubi, a spring-time dish in which the whole plant, leaves and roots, is blanched in saltwater, chopped, and mixed with sushi rice. The rice is rolled up in a nori sheet, sandwiched either side of a light egg omelette and spread with bean paste. The whole thing is served with spicy cabbage tempura.

PINEAPPLE WEED

Season for picking: spring to summer
Where to find them: cracks in paths, field edges, waste ground
Main identifying features: feathery leaves and pineapple scent
Best use: as a tea

Pineapple weed has an itinerant past. It is thought to have travelled to America on the feet of prehistoric settlers' dogs, via the land bridge that once existed between north-east Asia and North America. It still grows as a common weed on farmland through North America.

In 1869 it was brought to the famous Kew Gardens of London and within two years it had escaped cultivation and started to spread around the surrounding area. By the early twentieth century it was all over the country, transported far and wide in the tyres of motor cars.

At first glance it resembles a small mayweed or camomile plant, only without petals. Once you crush the leaves a little in your hand and take a sniff, however, the sweet, pineapple-like smell should make it unmistakable. I most commonly find it on cracked farm paths and lanes, but once you begin to look you will find it everywhere; poking up in cracks in pavements, on waste ground and on the edges of fields.

PREPARATION AND USE

I tend to use it as a tea and, whether or not because of association, I find it has similar properties to the soothing effects of camomile. It can also be used to give sorbets and baked goods a pineapple-like flavour.

THREE-CORNERED LEEK, ONION WEED, STINKING ONION
Allium triquetrum

Season for picking: spring to autumn
Where to find them: verges, scraps of land
Main identifying features: triangular stem, garlic scent, bluebell-like flowers
Best use: in soups and stews

Some people refer to the three-cornered leek simply as 'wild garlic', categorising it by flavour rather than worrying about botanical definitions. Though it is technically not wild garlic, it is an allium, so part of the onion family and related to true wild garlic, *Allium ursinum*.

The three-cornered leek is a distinctive-looking plant with white, bluebell-like flowers. It has long green lance-shaped leaves, each with a central ridge that forms a shallow 'v', and a distinctive three-cornered flower stalk. Like other alliums, it has a strong garlic scent when crushed, making it easy to identify from any similar-looking flower.

Native to the Mediterranean, it has slowly crept northwards into Britain and Ireland. The flavour is much more pungent than a leek and although garlicky it is far less so than true wild garlic. I have found it on the verges leading to a train station in Bristol and growing by the side of the pavement elsewhere. For urbanites, it can be easier to find than true wild garlic. The season is much longer too, starting in the late winter and running right up until the autumn.

PREPARATION AND USE
The leaves are good fresh in soup, stews and curries or dried and used as a garlic sprinkle for year-round use. Alternatively use fresh leaves mixed up with chopped ripe tomatoes, capers and plenty of olive oil. The flowers make a perfect edible garnish and the bulbs can be peeled and pickled like tiny onions.

The beauty of the three-cornered leek in foraging terms is that, as an invasive weed, it can be harvested in great quantity without any worries about damaging the environment. The more you pick, the more native plants can thrive.

NETTLE
Urtica dioica, U. urens

Season for picking: all year
Where to find them: waste ground, overgrown gardens, parks, fields
Main identifying features: toothed leaves and irritating sting
Best use: cooked like spinach

Many of us can recount traumatic childhood incidents involving nettles, so the plant needs little introduction here. However, it is not found the world over. I was reminded of this recently when, leading a group of garden volunteers, I spotted a Brazilian woman poised to rip up a particularly brutal looking nettle with her bare hands.

The nettle has pairs of toothed leaves that increase in size as you move down the stem. The tiny flowers form green clusters which distinguish it from the large, orchid-like flowers of the white dead-nettle and the pinky-red of the red dead-nettle.

The nettle's liking for potassium- and nitrogen-rich soils means it thrives near human habitation, colonising wasteland and edgeland areas near towns and cities. An omnipresent plant, it can also be found in hedgerows, parks, gardens and on road-sides, and seems to especially favour areas where you have just dropped your car keys.

Its painful sting is administered by hollow hairs which act like miniature hypodermic needles, injecting any would-be herbi-vorous predator with a potent mix of chemicals. Histamine, sero-tonin and acetylcholine (and to a lesser extent the small amounts of formic acid) cause the pain, swelling and itching. Tartaric and oxalic acid, in a sadistic twist of evolution, ensure that the pain lin-gers so that even an animal with a short-term memory will leave it alone.

The sting puts most people off foraging the nettle and I am often asked why I am not stung when I cook it. The simple answer is that the stinging hairs become limp once the plant is cooked or dried. The nettle will still contain the compounds responsible for the sting, but it has no way of administering it.

Perhaps the reason it puts up such a defence is that it is one of the most useful and nutritious plants around. Just 100 g (3½ oz) of blanched nettle provides all your daily requirement of vitamin K and almost half that of calcium, a mineral often hard to include in a vegan diet. It also has significant amounts of iron and pro-vitamin A.

HOW TO PICK NETTLES

Gardening gloves provide reliable protection against the sting but I have also successfully improvised with a thick plastic bag double-wrapped around my hand. A pair of sharp scissors or secateurs also help a great deal.

The phrase 'grasping the nettle' means to tackle a challenge with courage and determination. And picking nettle tops firmly at the stem before swiftly placing them into an open bag does minimise the chances of getting stung. The theory is the sting is pressed upward rather than into the skin. It's an acquired skill, usually mastered after many painful thumbs and fingers.

To eat a raw nettle can be another mastered skill. The underside of the leaves do not sting. So if you pluck one from the plant, pinch it from underneath, folding it in on itself in half, and half again keeping the underside of the leaf always on top. Pop it in your back molars and chew. It has a fresh nutty taste, like a substantial salad green.

PREPARATION AND USE

As it gets older, a nettle's larger leaves take on a gritty flavour so it is best to harvest the younger leaves or just the top six or so. Although this normally means a spring harvest, new growth following a recent strimming is also particularly good to eat.

In my opinion the flavour of a cooked nettle is far superior to spinach, chard or any other cultivated leaf. Often described as nutty, the flavour is full and satisfying, lacking any of the bitterness or heat of the cabbage family.

Nettles can be used in any recipe that requires cooked spinach. I particularly like them mixed with a rich cream sauce oozing out of a homemade cannelloni, or trapped in parcels of ravioli with ricotta. It was perhaps the first wild food I cooked as a child, when I would put it in a soup topped with crème fraiche – a recipe I still make to this day (see base recipes, page 15). My children like it as a pesto made after a light blanching to remove the sting.

Nettle crisps are a delicious snack and taste a little like crispy seaweed. They are easy to make: simply mix a little oil and perhaps salt or liquid aminos, toss this over the leaves and toast them in a hot oven until they go crispy and brown.

For a healthy spring tonic drink, pick fresh young nettles, push them into a blender and top with a glass of water. Blitz this up until the leaves are completely macerated, then pass this through a sieve and drink on its own or in a smoothie with kiwi, avocado and cucumber – and perhaps with a little fresh mint.

The leaves can be blanched and frozen for later use, or dehydrated into a powder and sprinkled into dishes for an added bit of nutrition and flavour. Nettles also make a very passable beer and there are plenty of recipes online if you're interested in trying it out.

NETTLE SEEDS

Nettle seeds contain significant amounts of linoleic acid, a polyunsaturated omega-6 fatty acid that is also found in sesame seeds, almonds, walnuts and sunflower seeds.

To harvest, wait until the clusters of green flowers begin to droop and slightly darken. The seeds form on the female plant and look like tiny bishops' hats clustered together; on the male flowers though they don't droop and look more like small hot cross buns. You can remove the seeds by cutting the plant, hanging it upside down and gathering the seeds on a newspaper as they fall – or simply harvest the seeds while still in their green cases.

The flavour of the seeds is very subtle. They can be added to smoothies and breads or mixed with dried herbs and added to dishes for extra texture and nutrition.

PERENNIAL WALL ROCKET, WILD ROCKET
Diplotaxis tenuifolia

Season for picking: all year
Where to find them: wasteland, close to rivers
Main identifying features: heavily lobed leaves, mustard-like scent
Best use: salads

Several years ago, I grew wild rocket while volunteering in a community garden in a rundown city suburb. It soon self-seeded and, although the community garden vanished, many years later I would find it growing all over the surrounding area.

Perennial wall rocket is a spicy, yellow-flowered plant with heavily lobed leaves that grows readily in clumps along waste ground, especially in ports and on land close to abandoned industry. If you crush the leaves you should smell the plant's mustard-like scent. It looks and tastes very much like cultivated rocket, *Eruca vesicaria*, but with smaller leaves and a hotter flavour. The 'wild rocket' you buy in the shops can be either *Eruca vesicaria or Diplotaxis tenuifolia*. The latter has cross-shaped flowers and long, thin green seed pods, which help identify it as part of the cabbage family. Although the flavour is fiery it is far more interesting than other hot-tasting leaves and it isn't hard to see why it is more commonly sold than mustard greens.

PREPARATION AND USE
The plant can become bitter after it flowers so the younger leaves are best to eat. The flavour also improves if the plant is well watered, so do not be put off if you try it for the first time during a period of dry weather.

My favourite way of using rocket is in the Italian style, thrown on top of a thin-crust pizza just after cooking so the residual heat wilts but does not cook the leaves. It tastes great folded into pasta with olive oil, parmesan and lemon juice. It's also good as a pesto ingredient, in sandwiches, in quiche and wilted in soups – but the classic way to eat it is as a salad green. Being on the peppery side, it works well mixed with neutral-tasting leaves such as lime (*Tilia* spp.) and lettuce.

RURAL

CHAPTER FIVE

Hedgerows and Farmland

A FEW YEARS AGO, I was studying horticulture in south Devon and rented a house that backed onto farmland on the outskirts of the picturesque town of Totnes. The house was set back from the road, under a canopy of birch trees from which an owl would hoot into dark nights that shone with thousands of stars.

To the side of the house was a particularly old and species-rich hedgerow, which provided food for me and the local wildlife all year round, offering up new treats with each season. In the spring the first pollinators would arrive; bumble bees would warm their wings inside the tubulous blooms of daffodils and the diminutive narcissus. Delicate primroses, violets and stitchwort opened to the sun's rays. I would bring the sunshine-yellow primroses into the kitchen, serving up couscous salad with raisins and finely chopped hawthorn shoots worked through the grain, like the leaves of parsley. Nettle tops and goosegrass shoots would find their way into the blender for a nutrient-rich springtime tonic, or as an addition to breakfast smoothies.

As the days warmed, the delicate whites of enchanter's nightshade, the spikes of bistort and pinky-purple campion peppered the hedgerow like confetti. When the sun returned in full force, the creamy, frothy blooms of rowan and elderflower burst open marking the start of summer. I gathered the elderflower in great armfuls, returning to my country kitchen to make light, aromatic muffins, indulgent elderflower ice cream with birch syrup, and savoury bhaji-like fritters. I would only harvest from the lower branches, leaving the berries at the top for the panicked clouds of finches that moved from tree to tree as I wandered the lanes.

As the days cooled, hazelnuts dropped and rolled their way down the lane. Aware that the nuts were as much for the tiny nuthatches, with their Adam Ant eye stripes, the energetic squirrels and tiny dormice, I'd take only what I needed, sometimes spreading the harvest over many miles. Haws, sloes and crab apples provided food for robins, starlings, blackbirds, wasps and all kinds of invertebrates. In my kitchen I gathered together the haws and crab apples to make a deliciously thick, blood-red ketchup, which I have done every year since. The sloes of course went into sloe gin, which I gave away as Christmas presents to friends and family.

The success of these ancient hedgerows, some of which can support close to 300 different species of plant, is down to years of successful management. Trees and shrubs are regularly coppiced, which let light through to small herbs and flowers. The margins of the fields do not receive any fertiliser so nutrient-hungry weeds like nettle and goosegrass do not muscle in and push out more delicate native plants. This particular lane was unsuitable for vehicles, so the plants were left to grow undisturbed.

The hedgerow is often seen as a purely British invention, yet any satellite image will show you distinctive lines of trees and shrubs surrounding fields everywhere from Ukraine to Mexico. Some satellite images show a continuous line of trees emanating from an old woodland, either the result of forest clearance or self-seeded trees, marching year on year along a perimeter. Over time these can develop into ecosystems as complex as any British hedgerow.

Not all hedges are spontaneous like this though. The first planted hedges are probably as old as farming itself. It is believed that Neolithic farmers (4500–2500 BC) used thorny sloe and hawthorn as a kind of prehistoric barbed-wire fence to prevent cattle from straying and keep would-be rustlers at bay. In Cornwall, throughout the Neolithic Age and the Bronze Age (2500–800 BC), farmers banked up earth, faced it in stone and allowed shrubs to grow on top, just as they still do today. Some of these Bronze Age hedges can still be found criss-crossing the Cornish countryside, older than the pyramids at Giza.

In the post-war period in Britain, many ancient hedgerows were removed in an effort to make the country self-sufficient in food by increasing the size of fields, allowing heavy farm machinery to work the land. Even more recently, in the years between 1984 and 1990, England saw a 20 per cent decline in hedgerows and in Wales 25 per cent were lost. Only now are we beginning to recognise their ecological significance, and many of Europe's hedgerows are now protected under environmental law.

Fertile farmland can provide rich pickings for the forager. Charlock and wild mustards grow all year along field margins, providing nutrient-rich greens for the kitchen table. The banks and fringes yield even more goodness and goosegrass, hedge mustard, hogweed, ground ivy and nettles are gathered for refreshing herbal teas, hearty soups and crispy tempura.

PRIMROSE
Primula vulgaris and *Primula* spp.

Season for picking: spring
Where to find them: hedges, grassy banks, garden borders
Main identifying features: yellow flowers with a darker yellow centre
Best use: salads or cake decoration

During the early spring, when the nights are still cold but the days are warming up, the first flowers of the season open their petals to bees waking from their winter hibernation. Wild primroses are one of the earliest spring flowers to show. They have lovely pale-yellow flowers about the size of a fifty-pence piece and a rosette of dark-green crinkly leaves. The centre of the flower is a darker yellow and has a pinhole opening, which may or may not contain a stamen depending on the sex of the flower.

Their name derives from the Latin *prima rosa*, meaning the 'first rose' of the spring. They are in full flower by March but can be spotted as early as January – or in rare cases, November.

Among cultivated flower beds, primroses display their neat little flowers in almost all the colours of the rainbow. Most of these garden varieties are non-toxic, but can have irritant leaves.

PREPARATION AND USE

Only the flower head itself is good to eat so it should be gently plucked from its green calyx. This also ensures the seeds still develop in the remaining ovary.

Their flavour is delicate and can be easily overwhelmed in a dish so mix it with mild flavours if you want the taste to really shine.

They make a good wayside nibble or I use them as a garnish in salads or couscous. They also serve as a decoration for cakes to add a pop of colour, and contrast well with the rich brown of chocolate icing. They have a mild but detectable sweetness and slight floral notes.

WILD MUSTARDS
Sinapis and *Brassica* spp.

Season for picking: all year, best in early spring
Where to find them: banks of hedges, farmland, wasteland
Main identifying features: yellow cross-shaped flowers and serrated leaves
Best use: steamed or boiled mixed greens

During late spring and early summer, you will catch glimpses of yellow mustard flowers towering above low-growing crops or nestled in hedgerows. As the season moves on, these flowers give way to skinny green fruits, which mature into pods containing mustard seeds. Mustards love disturbed land so can be found anywhere people have been, like hedgerows, waste ground, footpaths and edgeland.

White mustard, charlock, black mustard and other plants in the *Brassica* and *Sinapis* families all regularly mutate and interbreed. They're so close in appearance and use that, for convenience, I've grouped them all together as wild mustards. Most are annual but they can be biennial and perennial. Mustards are related to cabbages, radishes and broccoli, so anyone familiar with these plants should quickly recognise the overall look of a wild mustard. Charlock and other wild mustards can have rough, hairy, dark-green leaves. Others begin life with smoother, lighter green leaves, which can grow to 30 cm (12 inches) or more and are often jagged. They will have that wasabi/mustard-like scent when crushed.

In form but not colour, the immature flower heads look like sparse purple sprouting broccoli and they mature into clusters of cross-shaped yellow flowers. The seeds grow one above the other in rows within a slender pod with a point at the end. As the plant goes to flower, the leaves on the stalk change shape and size, shrinking down to around 5 cm (2 inches).

PREPARATION AND USE

Depending on the species, the flavour of the leaves varies from a mild pepperiness to an eye-watering heat. This means the young leaves can make an excellent salad green, but the older leaves need blanching, boiling or steaming, adding a good balsamic vinegar, plenty of butter, and soy or salt to temper the bitterness. Lemon juice also works well with the older leaves, as does mixing with something milder tasting, such as nettle.

Lacto-fermentation is another great way to temper the bitterness in mustard greens, and those which are too fiery to eat raw can be quite palatable as kimchi (see page 24). Adding a little miso and sugar to the kimchi also helps and there is no need for chilli as the leaves pack enough heat on their own.

In the early summer, it is possible to gather great armfuls of the straggly, seed-bearing plants in next to no time. However, hulling the pods and grinding the seed is a labour of love. See the entry for garlic mustard (page 156) for how to separate the seed and make a mustard paste. For wholegrain mustard, separate the seed and steep the whole grain in a vinegar of your choice (I find cider vinegar works best).

I like to munch on the flowers and flowering buds as a wayside nibble, sometimes taking the latter home to steam and serve with a dollop of butter and squeeze of lemon.

GROUND IVY, CREEPING CHARLIE, GILL-OVER-THE-GROUND
Glechoma hederacea

Season for picking: all year, but can be absent in winter
Where to find them: banks of hedges, woodland, grassy verges, under trees in parks and gardens
Main identifying features: purple flower and hoof-shaped, serrated leaves
Best use: steamed or boiled mixed greens

I often find ground ivy quite by mistake when foraging for mushrooms, as it makes its home in the shade under hedgerows on the woodland floor. Often it is the plant's scent which first alerts me to its presence, as it sends up a musky perfume when crushed under foot. The smell alone is enough to distinguish it from other plants – it has an earthy, floral, spicy scent which is difficult to describe but unmistakable once correctly identified.

Ground ivy plants have hoof-shaped, serrated leaves about the size of a large coin. During the late spring they announce their presence with little purple flowers. The plant's alternative names, creeping Charlie and Gill-over-the-ground, describe the way it grows prostrate or horizontally across the ground. However, when it comes into flower this form changes and it stands to attention, raising up its dead-nettle-like blooms to attract pollinators. Its heart-shaped leaves, with scalloped edges, begin life a dark-green colour and turn lighter as the year progresses. The plant is also slightly hairy and, as a member of the mint family, has a square stem.

Historically it has been used for a range of purposes: as a poultice for sore eyes or to heal wounds, as a tea for stomach ulcers, as an additive to snuff, or juiced and squeezed in the ear to help alleviate tinnitus (although it is doubtful this was effective). Long before hops were introduced into Britain the herb was used to clarify and flavour beer. I've been lucky enough to try ground ivy ale and would recommend it to any skilled home brewer.

PREPARATION AND USE

Ground ivy is my partner's favourite wild tea. It has a mellow, musky flavour to it, rather like a mint plant that has started smoking cheroots, listening to jazz and reading beat poetry. To make a mug of tea, grab a loose palmful of the leaves, cover in boiling water and drink when it has cooled slightly.

I like to use the rich, earthy flavour of the leaves in baba ghanoush as it marries well with the smoky flavours of the grilled aubergine. Traditionally, the plant was used as a stuffing for roast pork. It would be chopped like parsley and mixed with sweated onions, herbs, breadcrumbs and butter before being baked with the meat.

DEAD-NETTLE
Lamium album, L. purpureum

Season for picking: spring to autumn
Where to find them: grassy hedgerow banks, edgeland, open woodland
Main identifying features: yellow flowers with a darker yellow centre
Best use: salads or cake decoration

Dead-nettle is not actually a nettle at all but, like ground ivy, is a member of the mint family. It is easily recognised by its square stem, nettle-like leaves and distinct lack of sting. The name *Lamium* comes from the Greek *laimos*, meaning 'throat', due to the hollow petal tubes of the orchid-like flowers.

You will come across two main kinds of dead-nettle: one with white flowers and one with red. There are also various closely related species, such as henbit with its upright purple flowers and yellow archangel, a mostly woodland plant with yellow blooms.

FORAGER'S TIP
With all variations of the dead-nettle you can pluck the flowers and suck out the nectar. This is best done on a bright sunny day, when the nectar is sweetest. White dead-nettle is by far the sweetest to try and eating three or four flowers at a time packs a nectar-rich punch.

PREPARATION AND USE
The leaves have a mild grassy flavour, working well as a cooked green along with other leaves in season. They can also be eaten raw. My children and I include dead-nettle as part of our 'mouth salads', a combination of whatever comes to hand in the hedgerow. We try to select only the most succulent tips and mix them in the mouth while wandering country paths and lanes. Our favourite 'mouth salad' includes dead-nettle tips, primrose flowers, goosegrass shoots and a little Jack-by-the-hedge to give it some garlicky flavour.

HOGWEED
Heracleum sphondylium

Season for picking: spring to autumn
Where to find them: grassy hedgerow banks, edgeland, open woodland
Main identifying features: white umbel flower
Best use: deep-fried shoots in batter
Not to be mistaken for: giant hogweed, *Heracleum mantegazzianum*

Warning: only the shoots, flower buds and seeds of hogweed should ever be eaten and it should be cooked to avoid the toxic sap, most present in the adult plant. Hands should be washed thoroughly when preparing.

Hogweed is a common British native plant found in hedgerows, edgeland and by the side of rivers and canals. During the spring and summer its tall flowers are the most likely to be those obscuring road signs as you drive or cycle through the countryside. Growing between waist and head height (usually the lower of the two) it has a hollow, hairy stem, pinnate lower leaves that are around 60 cm (2 feet) in length and produces umbels of white flowers the size of your open hand.

It can be mistaken for its toxic close cousin giant hogweed, *Heracleum mantegazzianum*, but the giant variety practically screams 'Don't touch!' The leaves of giant hogweed have bristles underneath and have a far spikier appearance than the rounded leaves of hogweed. The stems can be blotchy (or sometimes continuous) purple and also have sharp bristles. As the name suggests, giant hogweed is also much bigger, sometimes towering up to 5 metres (16 feet) tall with a flower head that can reach up to 80 cm (2.5 feet) across.

Both plants come with a warning though. Their sap contains toxins called furanocoumarins which can be photoreactive, becoming active when exposed to sunlight and causing welts and burns on the skin. The burns from the giant hogweed are far worse, sometimes requiring hospitalisation. As a child I was warned about this plant as my parents had read stories in the news of children who used the hollow stems as peashooters and ended up with a nasty ring of burns around their mouths.

Despite the risks, hogweed shoots, which emerge in early to mid-spring, are one of the most prized spring plants among foragers. Their flavour could be described as somewhere in between spinach and asparagus but this doesn't really do it justice – there is a fullness to the flavour with aromatic notes.

A similar tasting and looking species, the cow parsnip, *Heracleum maximum*, is common throughout North America. Historically, the Nlaka'pamux (formerly known as the Thompson River Indians), a first nation group indigenous to British Columbia and Washington, would peel and cook the young leaf and flower shoots just as foragers do today with the European hogweed.

PREPARATION AND USE

As a gardener I was all too aware of the toxic sap of hogweed and it put me off the plant as a forager for many years. Eventually I discovered the sap was only a problem in the mature plant. I bit the bullet and harvested the broccoli-like immature flower heads, still wrapped inside their veiny light green bracts, and plucked fresh new shoots before the leaves had properly unfurled. Blanched for around ten minutes they had a melt-in-the-mouth taste which was utterly unique and totally delicious.

Hogweed shoots –
a forager's favourite.

You can use both the leaf and flower shoots in this way – they soak up butter and lemon and make a perfect springtime side dish. However, they really come into their own in dishes of tempura or battered blossoms. I like these dipped in the previous year's hawthorn ketchup, but they work equally well with a satay or sweet plum sauce.

TEMPURA HOGWEED BLOSSOMS

You can taste the spring in this dish; the crispy crunch of the batter, the tender bite of the hogweed blooms. I've found even the harshest wild food critics love this dish so it is a great one for keen foragers to die-hard sceptics – even my meat-and-two-veg parents asked for more.

YOU WILL NEED:
- 1 bowl immature hogweed blossoms
- 100 g (3½ oz) white flour
- 1 tsp baking powder
- 1 tsp dried wild garlic flakes or handful of fresh coriander leaves
- 100 ml (3½ fl oz) cold water (or alternatively you can use sparkling water and omit the baking powder)

METHOD:
1. Wash the blossoms and inspect for insects.
2. Sieve the flour into a bowl and add the baking powder (if using).
3. Slowly pour the water into the mix, whisking until the lumps are gone and it forms a light batter.
4. Heat the oil to 160–180°C (320–350°F). To test without a thermometer, dip a wooden spoon handle into the oil and watch for a steady bubble around the edges of the wood (a vigorous bubble means it is too hot).

5. Chop the coriander and sprinkle into the batter, or sprinkle in your wild garlic flakes.
6. Dip the hogweed blooms into the batter and shake off any excess.
7. Deep-fry until golden brown.
8. Serve with hawthorn ketchup (page 176) or cherry plum sauce (page 114).

FAT HEN, LAMB'S QUARTERS, PIGWEED, GOOSEFOOT
Chenopodium album

Season for picking: late spring to autumn
Where to find them: farms, waste ground, vegetable plots
Main identifying features: grey-green leaves shaped like a goose's foot
Best use: as spinach
Not to be mistaken for: orache

One summer, while on a camping trip with friends, the children were playing particularly boisterously and all the adults were desperate to find them something to do. A nearby field had been allowed to go fallow and I had noticed the grey-green leaves of goosefoot were growing prolifically. I put the kids to work and they each came back with big handfuls of this leafy, spinach-like plant. We cooked them up alongside mushrooms in a little butter with a twist of pepper and served it on top of pasta for lunch. The kids lapped up the food in near silence. That night they harvested more and it went in a black bean curry. Then the next morning we had all that was left worked into scrambled eggs. It was remarkably easy to get the children to eat this green once they'd invested a bit and time and effort themselves.

Goosefoot, or fat hen, is a common farmland weed which thrives in fertile soil. It likes ground that has been disturbed, so you will also see it pop up on allotments, in gardens, in parks and on waste ground. I've found it growing in abundance on the land around new-build properties too. As it prefers fertile soil, follow field boundaries looking for areas where the crops (such as corn or maize) are at their highest – as long as the land hasn't been sprayed or weeded, you should find it.

Goosefoot is sometimes grown as a crop in India and I once picked escaped plants growing by the roadside close to the mountain town of Shimla. I've also seen a relative of the plant, *Chenopodium nuttalliae* or huauzontle, popping up through cracks in the pavement in Mérida, Mexico. Further north on the American continent goosefoot was a popular food among many Native American tribes who cooked it like spinach, dried it, made soups and stews or made the seeds into bread. In the Russian Gulag it provided an important source of nutrition for many prisoners – it was one the few plants the guards would overlook and allow to grow, considering it a worthless weed.[8]

The plant has pale-green leaves with a light-white dusting, which are slightly toothed, diamond or triangular in shape and resemble a goose's foot – hence one of its alternative names. The leaves grow in opposite pairs and the flowers are tiny green or red clusters, much like those of the nettle only more bunched and upright. It does have some lookalikes and can be mistaken for the salty tasting coastal plant orache (page 362).

PREPARATION AND USE

Use as you would spinach, though in my opinion it has a far superior flavour. I use it in pesto or cooked in olive oil with mushrooms. Follow any of the cooked leaf recipes at the start of the book or simply wilt it down in butter with a bit of nutmeg and black pepper. Although it is high in calcium and rich in vitamins the leaves should not be eaten too regularly as they contain high levels of oxalate (see page 235).

GARLIC MUSTARD, JACK-BY-THE-HEDGE, HEDGE GARLIC
Alliaria petiolata

Season for picking: spring to autumn
Where to find them: hedgerows and in shady spots within edgeland, parks and overgrown gardens
Main identifying features: large, heart-shaped, nettle-like leaves
Best use: salads and as a cooked green

Garlic mustard also goes by the name hedge garlic and the colloquial name of Jack-by-the-hedge. Plant historian Kim Walker suggested to me that the name may originate from a time when people would use popular names like 'Jack' or 'Robin' to refer to common plants that had a use for everyman.

Garlic mustard can be found almost everywhere: hedgerows, roadsides, parks, gardens, farmland, towns, cities and edgeland. However, it does live up to its alternative name and it is best to look for it under hedgerows, as it tends to do best in areas of moderate shade. It begins life as a rosette of rounded, heart-shaped, nettle-like leaves with a colour ranging from lime to dark green. As a biennial it flowers in its second year. Like mustard, the flowering buds look like a white version of purple sprouting broccoli at first, though later in the season these give way to the familiar small, cross-shaped white flowers of the cabbage and mustard family. At this

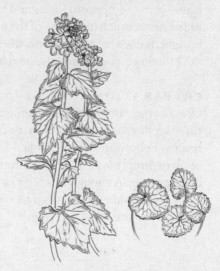

stage, the leaves become pointier, shaped more like an arrow-head than a heart.

The plant is very distinctive and seems to have no dangerous lookalikes, so it is often one of the first leaves people confidently forage. If you are in doubt, crush a leaf between the fingers – it should have a garlic or mustard-like scent.

PREPARATION AND USE

Garlic mustard leaves taste appropriately somewhere between garlic and mustard. They are mild and lack any bitterness during the spring or autumn, when they have a second flush. As ever, try a little before you pick a lot and cook any bitter leaves.

The leaves retain a lot of their flavour when cooked, and are versatile, lying somewhere between cabbage and spinach in the way they are used. When I first discovered garlic mustard, I became slightly obsessed with adding it to every meal. I would add it to salads, sauces, run it through pasta, batter and deep-fry it, make mixed greens and use it as a herb to flavour mashed potato.

The root has a mild horseradish flavour and makes for a less eye-watering substitute. One of my students cuts it up finely and uses it as a wasabi-like flavouring in sushi, with the leaves standing in for sheets of nori.

Garlic mustard seeds have been found in pottery dating to 4100-3750 BC, making them perhaps the oldest known spice. They are formed in soft pods which turn brittle as the plant dries. I normally place the stalks on a sheet of newspaper and dry them on a windowsill until the pods crack open. Some of the seeds will fall onto the newspaper and the rest can be separated by rubbing the pods on the wire mesh of a sieve.

GARLIC MUSTARD ... MUSTARD

Garlic mustard does, unsurprisingly, make a great mustard. It is particularly good with a strong cheese like mature cheddar or as a spicy extra in burritos and wraps.

1. Toast the separated seeds in a dry pan for a couple of minutes to release the oils.
2. Add apple cider vinegar, a little at a time, to the pan, stirring as you do so until it forms a paste.
3. Add bought or foraged mustard seeds, prepared in the same way, to bulk up the mix if necessary.

GARLIC MUSTARD DOLMADES

Garlic mustard leaves make a delicious alternative to vine leaves for stuffed dolmades.

FOR THE FILLING:
1. Cook a little rice or couscous.
2. Work in finely chopped vegetables, such as tomato or cucumber.
3. Add herbs, like parsley and thyme.
4. Add lemon, sumac and salt and pepper to taste.

FOR THE LEAVES:
1. Blanch the leaves for a couple of minutes.
2. Using a teaspoon, add a little of the filling mixture to the centre of each leaf.
3. Roll the leaves up into stubby cigar-shaped tubes, tucking in the ends to seal.
4. Drizzle with olive oil and a squeeze of lemon and serve as a starter or snack.

HOPS
Humulus lupulus

Season for picking: spring
Where to find them: hedgerows, gardens
Main identifying features: climbing shoots with pointed tips
Best use: cooked like asparagus
Not to be mistaken for: bindweed or the poisonous bryony

Hops are famous as the integral flavouring for beer and this is most people's only encounter with their bitter, floral flavour. However, hop shoots are also delicious to eat and something I look forward to every spring. You should find them if you walk a length of hedgerow during early to mid-spring, normally a couple of weeks after the first primrose flowers have bloomed.

Look out for the tell-tale snaking shoots; they can be woven into the hedge poking out at random angles or seen reaching for the light right at the top, standing upright like a mob of meerkats.

The tips are pointed, with very small, upward-facing leaves, cupped around the shoot at regular nodes. Follow these down and you should see the somewhat rough, toothed, five-sectioned larger leaves below. For the uninitiated, the plant could be mistaken for bindweed or the poisonous bryony, both of which have far glossier leaves.

Hop shoots can tangle into themselves so do take care not to gather any which have tangled around poisonous shoots. For young shoots, take the top 25 cm (10 inches) or so, and half of this for older shoots. This

Hop shoots can snake above a small hedge.

does not damage the plant as it will send out two shoots for each one taken.

PREPARATION AND USE

Hop shoots wilt very quickly and it is best to eat them on the day of picking. However, they will keep in a glass of water, like a bunch of cut flowers, if stored in the fridge for a day or two. They can be slightly coarse but have a delicious, slightly bitter yet aromatic flavour which can be lost when served with anything too strong-tasting. I use them as a green vegetable in stir-fries or serve them like asparagus with butter and lemon. They go well with cheese, tofu, poached eggs or in a quiche or frittata.

GOOSEGRASS, CLEAVERS, STICKYWEED
Galium aparine

Season for picking: spring to summer
Where to find them: hedgerows, overgrown gardens, agricultural land
Main identifying features: sticky leaves and stems arranged in whorls
Best use: seeds as coffee
Not to be mistaken for: hedge bedstraw

For most of us, our first encounter with 'stickyweed' is in the school playground. I can clearly remember, aged five or six, naughtily sniggering as the green stalks stuck miraculously to my classmate's back – and later crying when it had to be disentangled from my hair. Its ability to stick to fur, woollen jumpers and even skin has given birth to countless nicknames: 'kiss the girl' in Bristol, 'sticky Willie' in Scotland, 'sweethearts' in Hampshire and, in parts of Spain and Portugal, *amor de hortelano* – which roughly translates as 'gardener's love'.

Goosegrass, or cleavers, grows abundantly in hedgerows, gardens, waste ground, parks or anywhere it can get a foothold.

With lance-shaped leaves arranged in whorls around a central stem, it clumps together to form great tangled mats. It owes its stickiness to tiny hook-like hairs all over the stem, leaves and tiny circular seeds, which are said to be the inspiration for Velcro. Dog owners who have pulled the round ball-like seeds (called 'priest's lice' in Wales) from their pet's fur will appreciate how effective the seeds are at transporting the plant far from its home.

Hedge bedstraw, *Galium mollugo*, looks just like goosegrass but it lacks the sticky hooks on the leaves and buds. It tastes much the same as its relative: sweet when young, becoming a little bitter after flowering.

PREPARATION AND USE

The shoots or tips of the plant are good as an occasional nibble in the spring, before they get a chance to fully develop those nasty hooks. The plant has a mild, grassy, slightly sweet flavour. My partner likes to squeeze as much as she can into a cafetière, mixing it with nettles and other spring herbs for a refreshing herbal tea. Try the whole plant in a vegetable stock with vegetable scraps and herbs like bay leaves, thyme, rosemary and wild garlic.

CLEAVER SEED COFFEE

Cleaver seed coffee lacks caffeine but shares the bitterness and full flavour of coffee. It can be time consuming to pick the requisite amount of seeds from a plant but it isn't an onerous task, especially on a warm day. The coffee is satisfyingly smoky, which makes up for the fiddly effort of preparing it. It's good on camping trips if you can work out a way of grinding the seeds – the base of a jar in a mess tin works pretty well.

1. Roast about a tablespoon of the seeds in a dry pan on a moderate heat.

2. Use a coffee grinder or pestle and mortar to work the toasted seeds into a rough powder.
3. Top with hot water in a cafetière or cup.
4. Add spices such as cinnamon, (washed) wood avens roots, nutmeg or allspice.
5. Brew for a few minutes and drink black or with milk. Sweeten with sugar or honey.

SWEET CICELY
Myrrhis odorata

Season for picking: spring to autumn
Where to find them: grassy banks and hedgerows, especially in colder regions
Main identifying features: feathery aniseed-scented leaf
Best use: salads
Not to be mistaken for: hemlock

Sweet cicely is commonly found in misty Scottish glens and parts of northern England. I have found it in the remote Eden Valley and on the verges around Pendragon Castle, the supposed home of the fabled King Arthur. It has feathery, fern-like fronds and during the summer when bees buzz from one of its open flowers to another it is easy to picture it in its native home, the mountain regions of southern and central Europe.

The fruits of sweet cicely are very distinctive but its leaves can resemble poison hemlock.

Sweet cicely is widespread in places that experience cold winters. It is rare in North America but by a strange twist of convergent evolution, another aniseed-flavoured plant which Americans also call sweet cicely (or mountain sweet cicely), *Osmorhiza berteroi*, grows throughout mountain regions of the continent.

Sweet cicely is a member of the carrot family and has white umbel flowers and fern-like leaves, similar to those of wild parsley, Queen Anne's Lace and, more worryingly, the deadly poisonous hemlock. There are key differences between it and these other plants, most notably the strong aniseed scent released when its leaves are crushed. Sweet cicely's fruits are also much bigger than those of most other plants of the carrot family, around 2 cm (1 inch) tall and 3 mm broad. They are flame shaped, pointed at the top and have distinct grooves. The fruits start off green and are edible at this early stage, like little aniseed sweets, but they quickly turn brown and then black.

The plant is slightly hairy and the leaf stems can turn purple at the base, unlike hemlock which is hairless and has purple blotches as if someone has flicked paint at it. Avoid any plants growing by or in water and if you have any doubt in your mind, do not pick – there are always easier options.

PREPARATION AND USE

The leaves of sweet cicely have a fresh, sweet, aniseed flavour and make an unusual but pleasant addition to a salad. They are on the stringy side so it is best to cut them finely as they can get caught in the throat. Children seem to really love the taste, no doubt because of its sweetness. They make a very pleasant cordial, with or without the addition of mint. This works well as a mixer with clear spirits like white rum or vodka.

The roots are like a cross between parsnip and fennel, with the texture of the former and flavour of the latter. These can be roasted or boiled. The seeds, which are best picked in the summer when they are bright green, are like little aniseed-flavoured snacks. The stems are useful as a straw for kids' soft drinks or adults' cocktails, imparting a little of the distinctive flavour as you drink.

ELDER
Sambucus nigra

Season for picking: start and end of summer
Where to find them: hedgerows, edgeland, woodland fringes, gardens, parks
Main identifying features: clusters of purple-red fruit or white blossoms, scented bark when scratched
Best use: desserts
Not to be mistaken for: rowan or mountain ash

If you run a fingernail down the bark of an elder during the growing season, you'll find a lime-green inner layer which has a distinctive scent. I would describe it as a mixture of cut grass, almonds and cat's urine. The smell takes me back to building dens among thickets of elder, so I find it quite pleasant – but I may be in a minority.

The young trunk of an elder is green to light brown and somewhat knobbly or warty. As the tree ages this turns a lighter grey-brown and the surface of the bark breaks up becoming more cork-like, with grooves or furrows. The leaves comprise pinnate leaflets arranged in pairs and the flowers and fruit form on umbels. It is hard to mistake elders for anything else, but they are occasionally confused with rowan or mountain ash which also has white umbel blossoms. The rowan blossom is larger, denser and shaggier, normally standing upright. The scent of the elderflower should be enough to give it away, quite pleasant on a sunny day and closer to cat's urine on a wet one.

In medieval Europe superstitious beliefs circulated about the elder, and people were afraid to cut them down. Farm workers would sometimes leave elder trees intact while cutting down everything else around them. In Denmark, the Hyldemoer, or 'Elder Mother', was said to live in the tree and would avenge the death of anyone who harmed her. In Germany they would pray to 'Frau Ellhorn' before cutting the wood; and in England, burning the wood in the hearth was said to bring bad luck. Where did these superstitions come from? They can all be tied together with a little scientific knowledge. The elder contains cyanide in its sap wood and burning the tree in the hearth would release cyanide gas. When the population of Europe moved from ventilated huts to stone-built houses they must have noticed an increase in cyanide poisoning when elder was burnt, and believed it to be enchanted.

PREPARATION AND USE
Elderflowers
The blossoms of the elder, or elderflowers, start to bloom between mid-spring and early summer. They are great added to baked goods or made into a syrup and used as a mixer for fruit juices or gin. For elder fritters, use the tempura batter recipe listed under hogweed and substitute the herbs for a good pinch of cinnamon. Serve with runny honey or a drizzling of elder syrup solution.

To make elder vinegar, useful for preserving or as a salad dressing, simply fill a small bottle with elderflowers (stalks removed) and top with a white vinegar.

APPLE AND ELDERFLOWER CORDIAL

Elderflower cordial recipes usually call for tooth-rotting amounts of sugar. I have tried various ways of reducing this and come up with an alternative using half the amount of sugar, using apple juice concentrate in its place. Stevia granules also work if you want to reduce the sugar content further, but the cordial won't keep as long.

YOU WILL NEED:

- 20–30 elderflower heads
- 1.5 l (1/2 gallon) boiling water
- 450 g (1 lb) sugar
- 300 ml (10 fl oz) apple juice concentrate
- 50 g (2 oz) citric acid
- 3 unwaxed lemons

METHOD:

1. Bring the water to the boil, dissolve the sugar and pour in the concentrate. Leave to cool.
2. Slice the lemons, give them a quick squeeze into the mix and then throw them in.
3. Stir in the cleaned, bug-free flower heads, trying to remove as much of the stalk as possible.
4. Add the citric acid.
5. Leave the mix overnight or for 24 hours if possible.
6. Strain through a muslin cloth into heat-sterilised bottles.

The cordial should keep for a month or two, and sometimes longer, but it can start to ferment in as little as two weeks, especially when the weather is warm. It's therefore best to store it in the fridge or a cool cupboard. You can mix it with still or sparkling water and it works well as a mixer for gin- or vodka-based cocktails.

Elderberry

Raw elderberries are unpleasant to eat and can also be highly poisonous, as they contain significant amounts of cyanide. Cooking the berries not only improves the flavour it also eliminates any cyanide, which evaporates when heated.

The flavour of cooked elderberries is excellent – if you imagine a blackberry after a few Christmas drinks you'll be somewhere close. Added to berry mixes it gives a layer of flavouring that is distinctly autumnal and fruity without being overpowering. Sweetened with sugar or maple syrup, the flavour of elderberries is floral, fruity, rich and moreish. My favourite way to prepare it is to make a jam or jelly, using an apple for pectin (see base recipes, page 19). Alternatively add a couple of handfuls to haws simmering in vinegar, spices and sugar to make a delicious ketchup.

JELLY EAR, WOOD EAR
Auricularia auricula-judae

Season for picking: all year
Where to find them: mostly on elder trees
Main identifying features: like a small brown gelatinous ear
Best use: as soft-centred chocolates

If you find an elder tree, you might well also discover the brown, fleshy, ear-like fungus known as a jelly ear mushroom, which likes to grow on the trunk and branches. It is also occasionally found on beech, sycamore, ash and spindle.

PREPARATION AND USE
The jelly-like flesh and slightly crunchy texture of a raw wood ear mushroom can give you the rather curious sensation that you might be eating an actual ear. Frying it is a bit of a horror show, too; it spits and can pop right out of the pan, scalding the unfortunate cook. The best way to cook it is to boil it – it has an uncanny ability to soak up any flavours it is cooked with.

The mushroom is especially good in soups with East Asian flavours such as soy sauce, miso and chilli. You can dry the mushrooms in a dehydrator or simply by leaving them on a windowsill for a couple of days. I regularly use the dried mushroom as an ingredient for noodle soup and find it great to pack on camping trips as it weighs almost nothing and takes up almost no space. By far the most delicious use I have found for the dried jelly ear is to reconstitute it with a fruit juice, sweet cordial or liqueur, such as apple juice, elderflower cordial or Cointreau, then dip it in chocolate.

During a hot, dry summer, jelly ear dries to a dark-brown crinkly fungus on elder trees. This can be easily plucked off and is ready to store and rehydrate at a later date.

DOG ROSE
Rosa canina

Season for picking: summer to autumn
Where to find them: hedgerows, edgeland, verges and roadsides
Main identifying features: thorns and red fruits called hips
Best use: rose hip syrup

Dog roses are native to Europe and are so named as they were said to cure the bite of a mad dog. I often feel them before I see them, the thorns snagging my jumper as I lean in to pick something from a hedgerow. They grow as solitary bushes or as a hedgerow plant with thorny branches and pinnate leaves, very much like their domesticated counterparts. The flowers are open, fragrant and blushed in different tones of pink and white. Once pollinated the base or ovule slowly swells to form the fruit: the scarlet hips which appear in the summer and sometimes last through to the frosts of winter. In parts of rural Portugal children are told by their parents to suck on rose hips to extract the vitamins.

For a forager the hips have both advantages and disadvantages. They are abundant and extremely high in vitamin C, but the thorns and irritant hairs can make them hard to pick and prepare. However, the rose hips do stay on the plant right until the first frosts turn them to mush and they will keep for a long time. This long shelf life means they can be picked little by little rather than all at once. As the summer comes to a close but the cold and wet of autumn is yet to arrive, I like to spend a week or so building up my cache, taking a little from here, a little from there, until I have a good, workable amount. Apart from hedgerows you will also find them along paths, on roadsides and in edgeland.

PREPARATION AND USE

You can make a tea from fresh or dried rose hips without the need to remove the hairy seeds, as you infuse only the outer casing of the fruit. Simply cover the hips with boiling water and allow to infuse. The taste is mild so you'll need to use at least a tablespoon of hips per cup. Add thyme, lemon and cinnamon for extra flavour.

The petals are a very underused wild food, but they can be dried or used fresh to add a piquancy to salads or sweet dishes, such as in a chocolate and rose petal panna cotta (see page 364).

ROSE HIP SYRUP

Rose hip syrup can be used as a drink on its own, added to fruit juices, mixed with lemon as a cold remedy or served on ice cream. To make the syrup, use 3 parts rose hip to 2 parts water to 1 part sugar. For example, use 300 g (10½ oz) rose hip, 200 ml (7 fl oz) water and 100 g (3½ oz) sugar.

1. Roughly chop the hips and remove any seeds you can (don't worry too much about this as you will strain them later).
2. Bring the rose hips to the boil then simmer on a low heat for about 20 minutes.
3. Strain through a fine jelly bag or muslin cloth.
4. Put the rose hip pulp back in the pan and cover once again with the strained water. Simmer again for about 10 minutes.
5. Strain this liquid twice through a jelly bag to remove the last of the hairy seeds.
6. Return to the pan and add the sugar, stirring until all the sugar has dissolved.
7. Bottle and store for later use – it keeps for up to a year.

BULLACE AND DAMSON
Prunus domestica

Season for picking: late summer into autumn
Where to find them: hedges, orchards
Main identifying features: round, plum-like fruit
Best use: eaten straight from tree

Finding a juicy, fat bullace in a hedgerow is a real treat. After a long walk up and down steep, chalky downs in the rolling Sussex countryside one sticky September day, my friends and I descended into a lovely, secluded valley. All along the path were hedges full of bullaces. We were heading to a quaint little cafe which promised the best cakes in Sussex, but when we found the cafe was closed we instead quenched our thirst with great armfuls of the sweet, juicy fruits.

Although damson and sloes look alike, they are two completely different species. The sloe has small dark fruit and long thorns, whereas the damson tree lacks thorns and has decidedly larger, more plum-like fruit. The differences between a damson and a bullace however get a bit more blurred; some argue they are essentially variations of the same fruit. I've laid out all three for comparison in the table opposite.

	Sloe	Bullace	Damson
Name	*Prunus spinosa*	*P. domestica* subsp. *insititia* Var. *nigra*	*P. domestica* subsp. *insititia* Sometimes *P. damascena*
Flavour	Very astringent	Astringent before ripe then sweet, sometimes with a hint of sharpness	Sweet
Season	Late summer to early winter	Late summer to early autumn	Late summer to early autumn
Shape	Round	Round	Round to plum shaped
Size	Pea to marble size	Between damson and sloe size	Like a small plum
Seed	Lacking furrow	Lacking furrow	Furrowed stone

PREPARATION AND USE

Bullaces and damsons are essentially wild plums so can be used in the same way, either raw or cooked. They can be made into jams, jellies, pies and desserts. One of my favourite ways to prepare them is to slice them in two, remove the seed, fill this hole with honey and sprigs of thyme and then bake until softened.

Damsons also lend themselves very well to being made into anything alcoholic. Damson or bullace wine is a particularly good rich, red wine especially when made with the addition of elderberries. Damsons and bullaces also make exceptionally good gin, prepared in the same way as sloe gin, a recipe for which appears later in this chapter (page 178). You can also mix them with apples to make a delicious crumble.

GUELDER ROSE
Viburnum opulus

Season for picking: autumn
Where to find them: hedgerows, woodland fringes
Main identifying features: bright-red fruits
Best use: jelly
Not to be mistaken for: bryony or woody nightshade

Guelder rose is a common hedgerow tree that favours wet ground. The scarlet to blood-red umbels of fruit hang down from the tree in great clusters, adding a splash of colour to pathsides and hedgerows across Europe.

The red berries can resemble those of poisonous bryony (a vine) and woody nightshade (a herbaceous plant), so pick with caution. The leaves of the guelder rose are similar to those of the maple but with three lobes and a channel running down the centre of the leaf stalk. You'll find the plant in hedgerows, fens, parks and gardens, and along rivers.

In North America you are more likely to find the similar-looking and superior-tasting highbush cranberry, or squashberry (*Viburnum edule*). In Europe these are park and garden trees but they regularly seed outside of these environments. The most effective way of telling these trees apart are small differences in the blossom rather than any visible difference in the fruit, so identification between species can be confusing.

PREPARATION AND USE

The berries of guelder rose are incredibly bitter and although they have a pleasant first bite they have a nasty aftertaste so need to be sweetened. Most recipes call for mixing with orange juice or citrus to make a jelly. I would recommend making a jelly with orange zest, a little orange juice, apple and sugar, which has a delicious Christmassy marmalade flavour.

The berries of guelder rose can cause an upset stomach if eaten raw, so they should always be cooked, and a minority of people are allergic so consume small amounts at first to test.

HAWTHORN
Crataegus spp

Season for picking: leaves in spring, fruits in late summer/autumn
Where to find them: hedgerows, parks, gardens, edgeland
Main identifying features: red berries
Best use: ketchup
Not to be mistaken for: bryony or woody nightshade

Many believe that the crown of thorns on Jesus's head was made from the wood of a hawthorn. Legend has it that Joseph of Arimathea, the keeper of Jesus's tomb, brought the first hawthorn to England and planted it at Glastonbury Abbey where it is said to flower on Christmas Day. However the 'hawthorn' at Glastonbury was actually most likely some species of winter blossoming viburnum, as the hawthorn is one of Britain's few truly native trees. But why let the truth get in the way of a good story?

In Ireland lone hawthorn trees were called 'fairy thorns' and it was thought that anyone who cut a branch off one would be cursed. Fallen branches were sometimes tied back on to the tree. Even to this day, while leading foraging walks, I have had people insist I ask the tree's permission before taking the fruit.

The blossom of the common hawthorn has a beautiful scent when it comes out in May, unlike the midland hawthorn, *C. laevigata*, which has a really unpleasant smell. The latter grew near my school as a child and we would call it the 'stink bush', daring each other to go into the thicket (no one ever did).

Common hawthorn blossom has rounded white-petalled flowers (or pinky-white for cultivars and hybrids). Hawthorns can be clipped into a hedge or left to grow as adult trees, reaching

15 metres (50 feet) or more. The bark is brown-grey and the branches have distinctive thorns. Although these thorns are not as tough or large as those of the blackthorn, you know when you've been scratched by one. Unlike sloe, hawthorn leaf buds break before the blossom to form lobed, toothed 6 cm (2 inch) leaves. Later in the year the trees are covered in red edible berries. A midland hawthorn berry will have two seeds and the common hawthorn one seed. The berries of the fleshy hawthorn, C. *succulenta*, are excellent raw, whereas the C. *crus-galli* and the hybrid C. × *persimilis* can have much drier flesh and are better cooked or made into a jelly.

PREPARATION AND USE

Hawthorn berries, or haws, are perhaps the most abundant of all British native fruits and the fruit stones have been found on archaeological sites throughout the British Isles. My eldest son and I love to snack on haws, picking the ripest, chewing off the flesh and spitting out the stones. He likes to eat three or four of them before popping in a sloe, as the haws coat the inside of the mouth and reduce the tartness of the astringent sloe.

As summer moves into autumn, when the evenings are still light and the leaves are yet to fall, I like to take a walk from my house to pick haws. I look for the plumpest berries (which are often near water), returning home with a great carrier bag of haws to make ketchup.

FORAGER'S TIP

As most recipes call for the pulp of hawthorn it doesn't matter so much if you pick the stalks along with the fruit as these will be sieved out later. This can make harvesting a lot easier as handfuls can be plucked from the tree at a time.

Leaves

The first bright-green shoots of the hawthorn can be eaten as a green in early spring but the season can be short. As spring really starts to kick off, the leaves become dark green and bitter and are no longer good to eat, raw or cooked. While still in season they are good in salads or as a passing snack. I like to incorporate them into couscous, drizzled in olive oil and lemon.

Berries

Hawthorn berries can be eaten raw but the stones mean they provide no more than a passing nibble. You can work them into a puree with your hands, squeezing great handfuls at a time. If they are too dry, add apple juice or water to aid the process, picking out the stones as you go. Although this can be gooey fun, I've found it simpler to simmer them in water, vinegar or apple juice (depending on what you intend to do with them) to loosen the flesh from the stones. Then pass the flesh through a strong metal sieve, pushing with the back of a wooden spoon. You'll find yourself scraping the goo from the bottom of the sieve and it can take a bit of pushing, but it is worth it. The pulp can be mixed with dates and nuts to make energy balls.

To make a fruit leather, simmer this pulp on its own or with apples and perhaps a little sugar, then spread thinly on the tray of a dehydrator (see page 8). Chinese supermarkets stock hawthorn fruit leathers sold in discs or rolled-up strips, but these come from a slightly different species of hawthorn.

The fruit pulp can also be used to make jams and chutney. Or the whole fruits can be steeped in vodka with sugar and lemon to make a hawthorn liqueur.

HAWTHORN KETCHUP

By far my favourite use for haws is to make a hawthorn ketchup.
You can follow the recipe below, adding extra chilli for a chilli sauce,
five spice for a 'haw sin' sauce or an apple or two for a thick haw and
apple salsa.

YOU WILL NEED:

- At least 500 g (1 lb 2 oz) haws
- At least 300 ml (10 fl oz) cider
  vinegar or white malt/distilled
  vinegar
- Brown sugar
- Coriander powder
- Chilli powder
- Cumin
- Water

METHOD:

1. Weigh your haws and place in a pan. For every 100 g (3½ oz)
   of haws, top with 60 ml (2 fl oz) of water and 60 ml (2 fl oz) of
   vinegar.
2. Simmer until the berries are softened and come away from the
   seeds easily when pressed with a wooden spoon.
3. Allow to cool a little and push the berries through a sieve into
   another pan, along with the water and vinegar. The berry pulp
   will stick to the bottom of the sieve and you'll need to scrape it
   off with a butter knife and add to the pan. It's sticky work but
   worth it in the end.
4. Add 30 g (1 oz) of dark-brown sugar for every 100 g (3½ oz)
   of haws, along with a good pinch each of coriander, chilli and
   cumin powder.
5. Simmer until the sauce starts to thicken and the sugar is
   dissolved.
6. Store in sterilised bottles.

SLOE, BLACKTHORN
Prunus spinosa

Season for picking: late summer to autumn
Where to find them: hedgerows and edgeland
Main identifying features: thorns and marble-sized purple fruits
Best use: sloe gin

One of my favourite walks begins and ends with a long row of blackthorn or sloe trees on a Somerset hillside. They burst into blossom in March, declaring that spring is well and truly on its way. In this part of the world folklore dictates that a period of cold weather following the blossom, 'a blackthorn winter' as it is known, is a bad omen and can lead to a spoilt summer.

The tree also has deep roots in folklore and links to the supernatural in other parts of the world. In Sussex the flowers were said to foretell the death of a family member. In the Balkans, stakes made of blackthorn wood were said to be the most effective in killing vampires. And in Ireland, apparently most witches would not be seen dead without a broom made from blackthorn.[9]

Blackthorn is a shrubby tree often planted as hedging. It has thin, serrated leaves about 5 cm (2 inches) long, with similar-sized or larger, evil-looking thorns. The thorns evolved in prehistoric Britain and were tough enough to pierce the skin of an aurochs, an ancient and hardy breed of cow that was much larger than modern breeds.

The fruits are pea- to marble-sized and are blue-black in colour, often with a dusty sheen which acts as a kind of antifreeze. You'll find them from the very late summer right through until winter. Overgrown hedgerows often yield better results than neatly clipped ones and I've found some of the most abundant sloe bushes on hedgerows close to abandoned or neglected farms. If you spot a bush but don't see any fruit at first, allow a few moments to get your eye in and examine the plant from top to bottom. If you still don't find any, move on and as always, make a note of your prize spots so you can return the following year.

PREPARATION AND USE
Sloes are best in gin. Use 1 l (4 cups) of gin, 500 g (1 lb 2 oz) of sloes and 250 g (9 oz) of sugar, mix them together and store for 3 or more months.

On their own, sloes are extremely astringent and just one bite will remove nearly all the moisture from the mouth. Yet the seed turns up again and again in the stomachs of bog bodies and in middens or prehistoric rubbish dumps. It seems that prior to the Roman invasion, when plums were introduced, sloes were a common food, which then begs the question: how did people eat them?

I decided to experiment to see if I could figure out what our ancestors might have done to make the berries more edible. I tried several techniques and combinations, with limited success. Eventually I tried fermenting the fruit, as people do with immature plums in Japan or olives in the Mediterranean, and found that immature sloes could be cured to break down the hard skin and mellow the astringency. Once cured I put them in a jar topped with olive oil and after a month or so they were plumped up and had the rich oily texture and salty flavour of an olive, with an underlying hint of something complex and floral.

SLOE OLIVES

The process of making sloe olives is a careful and considered one. The sloes need to be cured for a week at a time, tasting to see when the astringency has been removed. If white mould spots appear on the top of the liquid simply rinse the sloes and repeat the process. If the sloes themselves form mould spots you should discard the whole batch and start again. The same process can be used with underripe bullaces, damsons and plums.

1. Using a sharp knife, score a groove into each of the sloes down to the pit (trying not to cut the pit itself).
2. Prepare a brine solution of 1 part salt to 10 parts water.
3. Submerge the sloes in the brine and cover. Leave for a week and then rinse.
4. Repeat the process, curing the sloes in the brine for a week at a time, tasting each week to test if they are cured (take a small bite and work it in your mouth, biting softly – if the astringency builds and it is unpleasant to eat, spit it out and cure again).
5. Once cured, rinse the sloes again and put them in a jar.
6. Top the jar with olive oil and leave for a month or two until they plump up.

The sloes will contain their seed, so they are best served as a starter with crusty bread or as a snack with drinks.

HAZEL
Corylus avellana

Season for picking: autumn
Where to find them: hedgerows, roadsides, woodland
Main identifying features: round nut in a sheath
Best use: as a snack

Walking though the green lanes of south Devon during a hazy autumn day, I became aware of something falling from the trees onto the tarmac road with a hollow cracking sound. I looked down to see hazelnuts rolling between my feet. Nut after nut dropped to the floor until it felt as if I was wading through the little brown shells. I improvised a nutcracker with a couple of stones and tried one – it was delicious, soft and creamy, a world away from the dry nuts you get in a Christmas selection bowl.

Hazels thrive in a hedgerow as they respond well to being cut. Some coppiced hazel trees are hundreds of years old. Aside from hedgerows they grow on the edges of woodland and as an understory plant beneath oak, ash or birch.

In the spring they are covered in catkins before they come into leaf, producing an oval-shaped, toothed leaf with a point at one end. The nuts start out as white, turning brown as they ripen, and are surrounded by a sheath which goes from green to pale brown, releasing a ripe nut at the end of the season.

FORAGER'S TIP

In both rural and urban areas, wily squirrels fill their bellies with hazelnuts before we get a chance to eat a single kernel. To beat the squirrels, you can take the nuts just before they ripen, when they are still a brownish white, and ripen them at home. Squirrels also tend to avoid traffic, so trees growing on roundabouts or near busy roads can yield large numbers of the nut. Similarly, I've found hedgerows by the side of active quarries (visit at weekends when they are not blasting!) that can provide several bags full of the nut.

PREPARATION AND USE

Hazelnuts can be stored or eaten fresh, raw or cooked. I add them to risottos in the same way you might peas or beans. The dried nuts swell and soak up the stock giving a rich, creamy flavour.

They can also be ground into a flour and added to breads, or turned into milk. To make a nut milk, soak half a bowl of nuts overnight in water, discard the liquid in the morning then pop them in a blender with 1 l (4 cups) of fresh water and a couple of dates to sweeten the mix. Blend and strain through a muslin cloth.

Roasted hazelnuts make a mouth-wateringly indulgent chocolate nut spread. Skin the roasted nuts by letting them cool a little and rubbing between your hands. Next, grind the nuts in a coffee grinder, add enough oil to make a paste, add a spoonful or two of cocoa powder and sweeten to taste with maple syrup or sugar.

WILD PEAR
Pyrus communis subsp. *pyraster*, also *P. pyraster*

Season for picking: late summer to autumn
Where to find them: old hedgerows, occasionally as a street tree
Main identifying features: hard pear-like fruit
Best use: roasted in wine

Wild pears are plentiful in Germany and were once also common in Britain, though these days they are rather scarce due to loss of hedgerows and the introduction of sweeter imports replacing planted trees. I've only found them a handful of times in old or newly planted hedgerows or old woodland.

The trees rarely reach more than 4 metres (13 feet) in a hedgerow but in the wild they can grow up to 20 metres (66 feet). They have ovate, serrated leaves and white blossom, a little like apple blossom. The fruits can be pear-like or more like a stubby apple. They are much harder than domesticated pears so, like medlars, need some time to blet or partially rot. You can place them in the freezer overnight and once thawed, the flesh will soften enough to eat the pear raw.

Slow roasted, the pears are as soft as warm fudge and make a delicious dessert on a cold autumn night in front of the fire. Halve them and arrange them in a baking tray, then pour over a glass or two of red wine with some dissolved sugar. Cover with tin foil and bake for 1–2 hours on 150°C (300°F) until the fruits are soft. Serve with ice cream.

CHAPTER SIX

Chalkland and Lime-Rich Soils

S OME OF THE most dramatic landscapes around the world started life as building blocks smaller than a pinhead. Between 146 and 65 million years ago, in an area that was to become Britain and France, microscopic marine algae floated in a calm, shallow, tropical sea. When the algae died they shed microscopic plates known as coccoliths. Over an unfathomable amount of time, billions upon billions of these coccoliths compressed and coalesced. With no muddy rivers to pollute the sedimentary process, they formed a brilliant white material: chalk.

Ancient rivers carved through these chalky deposits, forming some of the most iconic landscapes of southern England and northern France. Similarly, as far back as 340 million years ago, ancient seas tossed and churned innumerable tiny microbes, fossils and sand grains in the water and particles began to form on their surfaces. These particles were then cemented in place by mud and over time grew into pebble-like forms known as ooliths, which compressed together on the sea floor to form oolithic limestone. This limestone is present across the world from the Miami basin in Florida and the Burgundy region of France, to the quarries near Bath which built the historic Georgian city.

Chalk and alkali soils such as these can have a similar nature to moorland, in that they are low-nutrient landscapes with a greatly reduced range of species compared with those growing in rich, fertile soils. This is good news for wildflowers – these landscapes are often awash with the delicate lilac, blue and bright-purple hues of orchids, harebells, vetches, wild basil and wild marjoram. Rare butterflies, like the electric-blue Adonis, flitter among flowers and lay their eggs on horseshoe vetches, a plant that is found in few other places than these fragile landscapes.

I've spent a great deal of time navigating chalk downs all over the country. In the undulating hills of Sussex, with their wide-open skies, I've watched skylarks call from overhead and hares dash from thickets. I would search the grassy banks of ancient hillforts looking for salad burnet, a small herbaceous plant with a flavour like cucumber, and for the frilly leaved yarrow. The salad burnet would return home with me for salads or cheese sandwiches made on crusty homemade bread. The yarrow would be made into a herbal tea with an aromatic, medicinal flavour.

Heading east from my home in Somerset, I often cross over into the chalky plateau of Salisbury Plain, where the sounds of buzzing insects and ground-nesting birds contrast with the loud explosions of gunfire on the British Army's vast training grounds there. There has been a military presence on Salisbury Plain since the Second World War and large areas which would otherwise have been developed have become habitats for rare marsh fritillary butterflies and birds like the great bustard and stone curlew. Footpaths crisscross the fringes of this landscape and during the spring, I'll wander the chalky paths to collect wild marjoram and wild basil.

In areas where a lime-rich rather than exclusively chalky soil dominates, the landscape can be a dramatic one. In the Yucatán Peninsula in Mexico, acidic rainwater seeps through the soil and dissolves the limestone. Over thousands of years the water has collected and formed underground caverns and great open pools called *cenotes*. Similar forces have formed caves all over Europe, like those found in the Cheddar Valley in Somerset and in the South of France. Chiselled out into the rocky, lime-rich hills, some of the earliest forms of rock art can be found at the back of these dark caverns, such as those found in the caves at Chauvet-Pont-d'Arc and Lascaux.[10]

In these lime-rich regions, plants and mushrooms that are rare elsewhere in the world can thrive. The exquisite-tasting morel mushroom can be found in woodlands where alkali soils predominate, so it favours the wooded hills and valleys of Europe and North America. Rare, edible flowers such as the cowslip and chicory also do best in these regions. Although the variety may be lower than elsewhere, what does grow in chalkland and lime-rich landscapes is highly sought after.

CORN SALAD, LAMB'S LETTUCE
Valerianella spp.

Season for picking: spring
Where to find them: grassy verges, wasteland
Main identifying features: leaves shaped like a dog's tongue
Best use: salads

When sold in shops and markets, corn salad goes by the name of lamb's lettuce. In the wild it grows on disturbed soils and, although not overly fussy, favours coastal regions and alkali soils. Growing in a rosette form, it can grow singularly but more regularly it forms clumps with other self-seeded plants. The leaves are shaped like a dog's tongue or a spatula early in the year, becoming much smaller and thinner, sometimes toothed, as the plant goes to flower. The flowers are small, white and numerous.

PREPARATION AND USE
Lamb's lettuce has a mild, sweet flavour and works particularly well in a salad. It pairs well with fresh flavours such as cucumber, apple or watermelon, perhaps with the addition of toasted sunflower seeds. As they can grow throughout the winter, these lettuces are a welcome, mild-tasting salad leaf at a time of year when fiery or bitter-flavoured leaves can dominate.

COWSLIP
Primula veris

Season for picking: spring
Where to find them: meadow banks, ditches and verges, woodland fringes
Main identifying features: little yellow tubular flowers
Best use: occasional salad green

Warning: do not pick when scarce.

Cowslips have a rosette of green, crinkly leaves resembling those of its close cousin the primrose. They flower in the spring, sending up clusters of egg-yolk-yellow tubular flowers emerging from an exaggerated light-green calyx or sepal. The flowers form clusters on a tall green stem and you often see them as a flash of yellow, reaching up through long grass as they flower in the spring. Preferring a little shade only, look for them in ditches and banks as well as the edges of woodland.

They do best on the dry, impoverished soils of chalk meadowland – an environment which is, unfortunately, becoming increasingly rare in the UK. With this in mind, it is perhaps best to leave them alone or pick only one or two as a taster where numbers of the flower are low. In mainland Europe and in parts of the US where it has been introduced, cowslip populations are much higher and they can be picked without causing any harm.

PREPARATION AND USE

Cowslip has a delicate, floral flavour, similar to the primrose, and can be used in the same way (see page 145) as a garnish or as a salad ingredient. The leaves are edible but best cooked. A minority of people are allergic to the flowers so eat in moderation at first.

The oxlip is a similar species but has light-yellow, primrose-like flowers on its tall stem. These can be cultivated or wild and the many flower heads make picking easier. Use them in the same way as the cowslip and the primrose.

SWEET WOODRUFF
Galium odoratum

Season for picking: spring
Where to find them: woodland and hedgerows with lime-rich soil
Main identifying features: whorls of leaves
Best use: vanilla-like flavour for drinks and desserts
Not to be mistaken for: goosegrass/cleavers

Warning: use in moderation as contains the anti-coagulant coumarin. Also avoid when pregnant or breastfeeding.

Sweet woodruff likes to grow in partial shade in hedgerows and the fringes of woodlands (especially beech), and favours a chalky soil. Like goosegrass (page 160), it is a member of the lady's bedstraw family and it shares much of the same characteristics, with whorls of leaves around a central stem. However, it grows as a short flower rather than a creeping plant. It has seven or eight waxy or smooth leaves, 5–7.5 cm (2–3 inches) in diameter.

It flowers from the middle of spring into the early summer, and when crushed the leaves have a distinctive, cut-grass-like scent due to a compound called coumarin. This compound intensifies when the plant is dried, giving it a vanilla-like taste, which is good for flavouring for drinks especially white wine, vodka martinis, elderflower cordial, apple juice, cider or fresh lemonades including sumac-ade. The longer you leave the leaves in a drink the more the flavour will intensify. You can also use woodruff in the same way as you would vanilla to flavour desserts such cheesecake, yoghurt or panna cotta. Note, however, that in large doses coumarin is toxic, so only use sparingly and do not consume woodruff too regularly.

MOREL MUSHROOM
Morchella spp.

Season for picking: spring
Where to find them: in well-drained or alkali soils, under trees
Main identifying features: ovoid sponge-like cap with white stem, hollow inside
Best use: in risotto
Not to be mistaken for: false morel or stinkhorn

Warning: morels are poisonous raw so must be cooked until brown.

The morel is an elusive mushroom, one I have only found a handful of times. But you'll know when you have found it as it is very distinctive; the ovoid-to-conical cap has an irregular honeycomb or sponge-like form, made up of ridges and hollow pits. They grow from the size of a finger up to the size of a stretched-out hand. Cut the mushroom in two and you'll find the cap completely hollow inside, with the stem either similarly hollow or made up of folded flesh.

The *Morchella* genus is a wide and varied one but you are mostly likely to find one of two kinds: the pale, capped, yellowish-brown or grey-brown 'yellow morel' (*M. esculenta)* and the ironically named common morel (*M. esculenta* f. *vulgaris*). These grow in well-drained, mostly alkaline soil in woodland and edgeland, and under hedges and scrub – usually next to trees like the tulip tree, poplar, apple and elm. You are very unlikely to find them under pine or oak, and both can grow in the same place for many years. The black morel is increasingly found on woodchip put down in gardens and in other public places such as the fringes of car parks. It is also said to favour sites which have been burnt.

Although distinctive, morels do have a poisonous lookalike, the false morel (*Gyromitra esculenta* and *G.* spp.), which can be deadly. The false morel tends to be a pale to dark brown or reddish brown. It also lacks the sponge-like pits of the true morel, instead having multiple folds that give it the appearance of a human brain or a screwed-up piece of paper. It can also superficially look like a stinkhorn, but these tend to come later in the season and are not poisonous.

PREPARATION AND USE

Morels have a rich, earthy flavour, making them one of the most sought-after, and expensive, mushrooms in the world.

If you are ever lucky enough to find an abundance of morels then leave the larger ones and take only the smaller ones – not only is the flavour best in smaller ones, but it's better to leave the older ones to spore. The honeycomb pits of morels make a cosy home for a myriad of mites, ants and tiny insects, so they need to be soaked in cold salted water for an hour or two prior to cooking to remove these. They should then be rinsed and patted dry with a tea towel or paper towel.

Morels cause stomach upsets when consumed raw, so need to be thoroughly cooked. Either sear them in hot oil for around 5 minutes until they are brown or boil them for 10 minutes and discard the water. Once seared, lower the heat and add a knob of butter and garlic. Cook for a further minute or two, then serve on toast.

Alternatively you can add morels to soups or risottos, or stuff them with cream cheese and crab (or mixed Mediterranean vegetables and couscous with herbs, lemon and olive oil).

OREGANO, WILD MARJORAM
Origanum vulgare

Season for picking: spring to summer
Where to find them: banks of hedges, field margins, rocky hilltops
Main identifying features: purple-pink flowers
Best use: as a herb

High on top of a little-known gorge in the Mendip Hills, a small clump of wild marjoram looks across the flat fields of the Somerset levels and down onto Glastonbury Tor. Although marjoram doesn't always cope well with cold weather, it seems to thrive up there, returning year after year.

Wild marjoram does well on most well-drained soils, especially those that are rich in lime. It can turn up on chalky down and meadowland close to housing estates, and it's also worth looking for it on field margins in areas of chalk down and at the foot of hedgerows. This is especially true when the grass is shaggy – it struggles wherever grass is regularly cut and doesn't respond well to grazing, so is largely absent from pastures.

The leaves are up to 4 cm (1.5 inches) long, 2.5 cm (1 inch) wide, light green, paired and oval-shaped. The plants purple-pink flowers give it away in the late spring and early summer, attracting all kinds of butterflies. It is best harvested before it flowers but the flavour does not change considerably, so this is not as essential as with other herbs and wild plants.

The white-flowered marjoram, *Origanum majorana*, is indigenous to the Mediterranean and western Asia and in ancient times the Romans and the Greeks would use white-flowered marjoram branches to crown married couples. In the kitchen it is used in much the same way as wild marjoram. It can be found throughout warm or sheltered areas in Europe, especially towards the south, but is rare in the northern parts of Europe. The smooth leaves are a lighter green than those of wild marjoram.

PREPARATION AND USE

Wild marjoram can be used in the same way as oregano. I use it in tomato dishes but it can also be used in salad dressings and in marinades. It's also good with roasted Mediterranean vegetables, or in place of basil in a traditional Italian pesto.

WILD BASIL
Clinopodium vulgare, syn. *Satureja vulgaris, Acinos vulgaris*

Season for picking: spring to summer
Where to find them: hedgerows, fringes of farmland, pathsides
Main identifying features: purple-pink tubular flowers and opposite leaves
Best use: as a tea

I first caught sight of wild basil while walking the chalk-rich landscape around Salisbury. It was a splash of purple among the yellows of wild mustards and the dry, clumpy alkaline soil, more reminiscent of southern France or central Spain than anywhere in England. The landscape was relatively new to me at the time but I intuitively knew this plant to be edible. Its square stem and dead-nettle-like form gave it away as a member of the mint family and, armed with the knowledge that this whole family is non-toxic, I nibbled on a leaf to try it. The first notes I found to be very mildly basil-like, but next came hints of mint and then oregano, giving an overall taste that was slightly bitter, floral and smoky.

The flowers that form on the nodes during the summer are purple-pink and tubular, like woundwort or a dead-nettle. The leaves are ovoid and hairy and you will find big clumps of it on the edges of fields, especially in chalkland and along hedgerows.

As wild basil has a strong association with lime soils, it roughly follows lines of chalkland in the subsoil. Look for it in unmanaged patches towards the edges of meadows, and either side of paths running through areas of alkaline subsoil (such as those found in southern England and northern France).

PREPARATION AND USE

Despite its name, wild basil does not really taste a lot like basil. It is much closer to oregano or marjoram, but the taste is very mild and can get lost among strong flavours. It comes into its own as a tea with a satisfying smoky taste, much like that of ground ivy. The tea is said to help reduce flatulence and, like mint, aid digestion.

Wild basil can sometimes be mistaken for its close relative basil thyme (*Clinopodium acinos*), which is more common in rocky ground but can be used in a similar way.

SALAD BURNET
Sanguisorba minor

Season for picking: spring to autumn
Where to find them: grassy banks
Main identifying features: serrated pinnate leaves
Best use: salads

Salad burnet has grown among the chalk-rich land of southern England for as long as people have settled in the area. Pollen records going back to the British Neolithic period (4500– 2500 BC) show it quickly colonising the chalk downs soon after the mass felling of native yew and lime forests. It is tantalising to think that within the settled communities in these areas the plant must have been part of the daily diet, perhaps eaten with the meat of aurochs, a giant prehistoric cow which used to roam the plains of Britain and Europe.

Salad burnet has compound pinnate leaves (a true leaf made up of small leaves or leaflets growing either side of a main stem), the leaflets of which are sharply toothed and of an even size (about as big as a fingernail). Growing from a central point or in a rosette formation, it can grow as a small plant or form large clumps as broad and as tall as two outstretched hands. The flowers, which come throughout the summer, look like a squat feather duster and are blood red – hence the Latin name of the genus, *Sanguisorba*, from the word *sanguinem*, meaning 'blood'.

Look for the plant on the sides of paths and in unmanaged and lightly grazed grass, especially on alkali-rich soils. It grew so reliably on the sides of hillforts in the south and southeast of England that my partner would ask me to pick some up if she knew I was walking in the area, as if I were going shopping.

PREPARATION AND USE
The leaves of salad burnet can be picked, washed and used as a salad leaf or herb. Its cucumber-like flavour makes it a natural companion for all kinds of drinks. I find it works well with lime and elderflower cordial or infused with drinks containing watermelon, kiwi or avocado. In her book *Herbs For All Seasons*, Rosemary Hemphill gives a recipe for a delicious summer drink, similar to Pimm's (which the herb can also be used with). It involves generous amounts of white wine along with a little soda water, brandy, blackcurrant juice, a dozen strawberries and a handful of salad burnet.

English and Dutch recipes from the seventeenth and eighteenth centuries used the herb in a flavoursome soup with other wild greens, such as sorrel and purslane, and herbs. These were cooked in a bouillon or broth and served up with bread or potato dumplings. Napoleon was said to enjoy the herb as part of a green bean salad.

I like to use salad burnet in a fresh tasting salsa, which you can easily make by shredding a handful of salad burnet with a finely chopped red onion and chopped tomatoes, and dressing the mix with olive oil.

CHICORY
Cichorium intybus

Season for picking: spring to summer (autumn to spring for the roots)
Where to find them: disturbed lime or chalk soils
Main identifying features: dandelion-like leaves and blue flowers
Best use: roots as coffee
Not to be mistaken for: dandelion

While out walking I am often aware of how small changes to my route can make a big difference to the plants I might find. Once, on the fringes of Salisbury Plain, I left a wooded copse to head just a few metres out onto an open chalky hilltop. On this plateau I found chicory thriving in the lime-rich soil under a sunny sky, whereas down below in the wood it was largely absent.

Chicory does best in full sun and although it can grow wild in most places, it does prefer a light soil with a high pH, such as chalk or limestone. You'll find it by paths and roadsides, in meadowland and on ground which has been disturbed.

The leaves look very much like those of a dandelion, with a reddish midrib. The flowers are light indigo blue or (rarely) white, and about the size of a large coin. It is easy to mix up the leaves with those of a dandelion by sight but the flavour is quite different. Both have a bitterness to them but the bitter compounds in chicory give it a drier, cooler flavour.

PREPARATION AND USE

Like broccoli, kiwis and green leafy vegetables, the leaves of chicory are useful as a source of vitamin K, a deficiency of which can lead to osteoporosis. They can be rather bitter but not in an unpleasant way and make for an interesting-tasting salad leaf. Like most greens they are best in the spring before they flower, and later in the season they can be boiled in two changes of water to take away the bitterness. They contrast well with a creamy cheese or a sweet fruit, such as apple, in a salad.

CHICORY COFFEE

In the Soviet Union, coffee made from coffee beans barely existed outside of big cities such as Moscow. Instead, the population drank coffee-like drinks made from barley, acorns and chicory. These coffee drinks are still popular among Eastern Europeans and Russians, and you should find a selection of them in any good Eastern European shop. Chicory root is caffeine free, making it a healthier alternative to coffee. It can also be mixed with coffee to reduce the caffeine content and make your supplies last longer.

To make a chicory coffee, harvest the roots in the autumn or spring when they are thick and fleshy and haven't used all their energy up to flower.

1. Wash the chicory roots – this is best done with a hard scrubbing brush.
2. Dry and cut into pieces around 1 cm (half an inch) thick.
3. Roast at 180°C (350°F) for an hour or so, or until the roots have shrunk and crisped up but not blackened.
4. Grind in a coffee grinder.
5. Brew the ground chicory in a cafetière as you would coffee, either on its own or mixed with up to 40 per cent coffee.

YARROW
Achillea millefolium

Season for picking: spring to autumn
Where to find them: meadows, grassy lawns and banks, especially in lime or chalky soils
Main identifying features: feathery leaves
Best use: as a tea
Not to be mistaken for: hogweed, carrot

Yarrow is a common plant which, although it prefers a slightly alkaline soil, will grow in most grassy places, including meadows and lawns of all soil types. The leaves separate beautifully on a main stalk like a Fibonacci sequence, giving them a feathery or fern-like appearance. As a member of the daisy family, the plant's flowers are composite or daisy-like and grow on equal-sized stems in a cluster, shaped like a flat-topped umbrella (a formation known as an umbel). This distinctive flower formation can superficially give yarrow the appearance of a member of the carrot family, but one look at the leaves should set it apart.

PREPARATION AND USE

Yarrow is best known as a medicinal herb with all kinds of properties, and contains a hemostatic or blood-clotting agent called achilleine. In Greek myth, Achilles used it to treat the wounds of his troops in battle – hence its scientific name 'Achillea'. In pre-colonial America, it was widely used among Native American and First Nation peoples: the Haida would use it as a poultice, the Miwok as a cold remedy, the Cherokee would use it to reduce fever and the Zuni would apply it to burns.

Although known as yarrow root in North America, it is the leaves of the plant which are generally used. These can be picked at any time of the year but are best in the spring. Although they can be used in salads, they have a very bitter and medicinal flavour which dominates any milder flavours. Rather than eat them I prefer them in a herbal tea.

Yarrow can also be useful as a culinary herb when mixed with sweet vinegars, sweet red peppers or soy sauce, which will help combat the bitter flavours.

Up until the seventeenth century, before the use of hops became widespread, yarrow was often used as a bittering agent in beer. Northern European brewers sometimes used yarrow with a combination of local herbs such as mugwort and ground ivy to brew a drink called gruit. Some modern brewers now make a delicious modern version of gruit beer using a very scaled down mix of herbs.

WILD CARROT, QUEEN ANNE'S LACE
Daucus carota

Season for picking: spring to autumn
Where to find them: chalk and lime meadows
Main identifying features: feathery leaves
Best use: seeds as a spice
Not to be mistaken for: hemlock

Warning: wild carrot is not a plant for the novice forager because it closely resembles the deadly hemlock plant, which has a hollow and hairless stem with purple blotches, and a 'mouse-like' smell. Be extremely careful when dealing with any plants that resemble hemlock and if in any doubt, do not pick.

Wild carrots have feathery, carrot-like leaves and a slightly furry stalk. The reddish-purple spot in the middle of the flower is said to resemble a spot of blood produced when Queen Anne pricked her finger making lace, thus the plant's nickname. The flower heads hold on to the seeds like a hand closing its fingers, before opening out into a white umbel towards the middle and end of summer. The leaves have a carrot-like scent when crushed.

The roots of the wild carrot are generally white and slightly more spindly than those of a domestic carrot. The latter may have first been bred from the purple-rooted wild carrots of Afghanistan before a Dutch botanist developed the orange strains we know today. Occasionally you will find a root of a wild carrot with a purple hue, which may be a result of interbreeding between wild and domestic flowers.

Wild carrot has beautiful feathery leaves.

PREPARATION AND USE

The leaves of both domestic and wild carrot have a superb flavour and can be picked throughout the year. Use them as you would parsley or make them into a tangy salsa by mixing with oil, a light vinegar, cumin, chilli and sugar.

You should harvest the roots of wild carrot in the autumn or spring of their first year, before they go to flower. Look for the flowering plant first and you should spot the feathery leaves of the smaller, first-year plants alongside. It is an offence to dig up roots without the landowner's permission but if you do find a suitable legal patch, they come up very easily with a small trowel and on thin soils a stick can be all you need to uproot them. If you are expecting a juicy carrot you will be disappointed; the spindly but flavoursome roots are far better put to use to flavour soups and stews. Just like those of the dandelion (see page 126), they roast well to make a very agreeable coffee.

Wild carrot seeds can be used as a spice, much in the same way as caraway seeds. They taste similar to celery seeds, with a resinous note to them. They can be harvested from the late summer onwards.

CHAPTER SEVEN

Acid Soils:
Heaths, Moors, Bogs, Hilltops and Uplands

ACID SOILS, LIKE those found on heaths and moors, support only a small range of specialist plants. You'll find grasses, moss, lichens, cotton grass, bilberries and ferns, along with gorse and heather, and perhaps trees such as rowan, birch and pine. Each summer, as the heather comes into flower, the moors of Britain and Ireland flush a beautiful hue of pinkish purple, as if the landscape has its own natural litmus paper, indicating a strong acid soil. You see changes in the soil as you climb a hill too. Weather can leach away nutrients from the soil, leaving it thin and acidic, and where you once found brambles, raspberries, oak, beech and birch in the lowlands, up on the hilltop only a few mosses, ferns, conifer and rowans survive.

Despite being areas of low diversity, acid habitats are of huge ecological importance worldwide. The plants and animals found there are specialists, honed by millions of years of evolution to thrive in a difficult landscape. You might spot rare species of butterfly, ground-nesting birds, lichens and moss all eking out a living in this harsh environment.

Although soils can acidify as a result of poor farming methods and conifer plantations, in most cases it comes about because of too much or too little water. A free-draining sandy soil, such as the soil that makes up the coastal heaths of northern Europe, can leach nutrients away, turning it acidic. With saturated ground, such as the raised bogs of Großes Torfmoor in Germany or the moors of south-west England, it is the slow decay of organic matter that leads to the acidification of the soil.

We tend to think of moors as extremely wild places, but in fact a good proportion of moorland landscapes are human-made. Around 7000 BC, rather than the open grassland of today, much of the moorland areas of Britain were wooded. Deep in these forests, trees would have given cover for bears, elk and bands of wolves hunting through the prehistoric night. As has been the case throughout history though, humans altered this once pristine landscape. During the Mesolithic (9600–4500 BC) and Neolithic ages (4500–2500 BC) hunters felled the trees in their thousands, first with fire and then with a new technology: stone axes.

Our ancestors cleared vast swathes of forest and scrub to open up hunting grounds, so that their arrows and spears would be better able to target grazing aurochs, elk and European bison. Towards the end of the Neolithic, into the Bronze Age (2500–800 BC) and beyond, humans continued to keep the trees at bay for farming settlements. The climate slowly changed, becoming cooler and wetter. The once-fertile uplands became saturated and the inhabitants, no longer able to farm the newly acidic soil, were forced to move to lower ground. Blanket bog began to take hold and layers of peat were laid down, forming what we now know as moors. The peat soil could not sustain the tree life it once did and this naturally forced back the wildwood, so that areas of natural moorland grew larger and larger. Remnants of this wooded past are often dug up as bog trees, especially bog oaks, in places like Ireland.

On the thin, sandy soil of lowland heaths, such as those found both inland and along the coasts of Europe, something slightly different occurred. The fertile layer of soil drained away, while grazing kept higher plants, such as trees and large shrubs, at bay. Little except grasses, gorse and heather can now grow here. You'll see this on the coastal lowland heaths in parts of the Netherlands, France, Denmark, Northern Ireland and Britain. In upland areas the soil can become acidic if the top layer of alkaline soil is leached away with continuous heavy rainfall, or a wet climate can mean that acid leaches from acidic granite rocks into the soil.

So, what does all this mean for the forager? Regardless of the cause of acidification, the results are much the same: fewer species. First there are the born survivors, tough plants found in most environments; stray hawthorns seeding themselves in cracks in the rock, the odd patch of bramble, scrubby sloes in the hedgerow and hogweed eking out a living wherever it finds a deep-enough patch of ground.

Then there are the specialists, the plants found only in acidic soils. On the moors, the uplands, in bogs and in conifer woodlands, you'll find berries such as bilberry, cranberry and lingonberry, which historically kept scurvy at bay for the indigenous populations of the far north. Rowan trees, with their clusters of bright-orange fruit, seem to defy the thin soils in upland areas and on mountainsides. On these acidic uplands and lowlands, keep your eyes peeled and try to learn the few species that grow there – they are worth the trouble.

GORSE, FURZE, WHIN
Ulex spp.

Season for picking: all year
Where to find them: heaths and moors
Main identifying features: yellow flowers on a prickly bush
Best use: gorse syrup
Not to be mistaken for: broom

An old saying goes, 'Gorse goes out of bloom when kissing goes out of fashion.' In other words, no matter what time of year it is, you can normally find at least one species of gorse in flower. If you head up the east coast of Scotland during the month of May you'll see whole hillsides are coloured a bright, vibrant yellow as gorse bursts into full bloom.

Various species of gorse grow on moors and heaths throughout Europe; the dwarf gorse (*Ulex minor*) favours the east of Britain, while western gorse (*U. gallii*) predictably favours the west. And common gorse, living up to its name, can be found all over.

Alongside its flowers, gorse has spiny, prickly branches, which can give you a nasty scratch, occasionally bad enough to pierce the skin. Outside of its native Europe, it has been planted as a living fence to control livestock. Much of this fence planting has taken hold or escaped and gorse has become an invasive plant in North America, Australia and New Zealand. In Hawaii it has run wild, with whole hillsides coloured yellow, and farmers are urged to control it wherever possible.

Save for mixing up gorse species (they are all used in the same way), the plant's only real lookalike is broom. It is very easy to tell the difference though, as despite both being green shrubs of up to 2 metres (6.5 feet) with yellow, pea-like flowers, broom lacks the prickles of gorse and its flowers do not have the coconut-like scent.

In some parts of Britain, prickly gorse bushes were used in agriculture (long before the harrow was invented) as a tool to work the soil into a fine tilth. The cut plant was weighed down with a log and dragged behind a beast of burden such as a mule or a donkey. The spiny branch would rake the soil and catch vegetation, clearing the land and readying it for seeding. Farmers still use the plant today but as cattle feed rather than as a tool. In Irish folklore gorse fires were said to drive away witches, and on the Isle of Man ceremonial gorse fires were lit on May Eve or Beltane to mark the end of the winter and the coming of summer.

PREPARATION AND USE
The main problem with foraging for gorse in any quantity is the prickles. A good pair of protective gloves, such as gardening gloves, are essential for picking without losing pints of blood in the process.

The flowers have historically been used to colour butter and cheese and were made into a country wine in highland moor communities across Scotland. They have an undertone of coconut or pineapple, as well as a bitter almond-like quality which works well in moderation in salads. The taste can be highly variable and, as it contains toxic alkaloids, the plant should never be eaten in large quantities; I rarely eat more than a nibble or I'll throw a few flowers into a salad. The buds can also be pickled in a sweet vinegar solution and used like capers – an unusual but delicious addition to salads.

GORSE SYRUP

Gorse cordial or syrup is a rich, vibrant yellow with a subtle coconut flavour. It's very versatile – it can be drizzled over ice cream or diluted and mixed with all kinds of drinks, including prosecco, white wine, apple juice and elderflower cordial.

YOU WILL NEED:

- 300 g (10½ oz) caster sugar
- Juice of 1 lemon
- Zest of 1 orange
- 750 ml (3 cups) water
- A 500 ml (2 cup) jug filled with loosely packed gorse flowers

METHOD:

1. Warm the water and dissolve the sugar on a low heat, then bring to the boil for ten minutes.
2. Take off the heat and allow to cool before adding the orange zest, lemon juice and gorse flowers.
3. Cover the pan and leave the mixture overnight.
4. In the morning, drain the mixture through a sieve or muslin cloth.
5. Bottle the sieved liquid and store in the fridge. Enjoy as a mixer for gin or as a cordial drink for children.

BOG MYRTLE, SWEET GALE
Myrica gale

Season for picking: all year
Where to find them: bogs and moorland
Main identifying features: aromatic leaves
Best use: ale

Warning: bog myrtle can cause miscarriage so do not consume if pregnant.

A bundle of bog myrtle kept my partner and I company on a round tour of Scotland. I'd picked it for my brother, an ardent home brewer, who used it in place of hops for one of his home-brew ales. It has a resinous, pine-like scent which pleasantly permeated through the car, and helpfully masked the smell of bog-soaked boots.

Bog myrtle, as you might expect, grows only in boggy soils, such as those found in the peat-rich moorlands of Scotland. The plant looks like a miniature tree, with upright, narrow, lance- or willow-shaped leaves. The leaves are a matt green and the stem a reddish brown, and the plant has yellow elongated pom-pom flowers and scaly buds like a caterpillar cocoon. You can harvest bog myrtle all year, but it is best from spring to October. Harvest only sparingly when populations are small.

PREPARATION AND USE
Myrtle leaves can be used like bay leaves, one or two at a time to flavour soups. Or you could try my adaptation of an ancient Roman recipe, which was usually made with bay rather than myrtle leaves. Make a light dough using flour, whey (or watered-down milk), baking powder, honey and a pinch of ground cinnamon and cardamom. Work these into balls and place on a bed of greased myrtle leaves in a tagine or a covered baking tray.

Cook for 10–15 minutes in a warm oven until risen. Serve with jam or drizzled in a sugary syrup.

The most traditional use for bog myrtle was in place of hops – but I would use sparingly, just 1–2 g per batch of beer. Alternatively, use it to flavour a strong spirit: place a leaf or two in a bottle and add some sugar and some spices of your choice (cloves, cinnamon, etc.), then top with rum or gin.

BILBERRY, BLAEBERRY, WHORTLEBERRY, WHINBERRY, WINDBERRY, MYRTLE BERRY, TERRY BERRY
Vaccinium myrtillus

Season for picking: summer
Where to find them: acidic ground, moors and woodland, especially conifer and occasionally beech
Main identifying features: tiny blueberry-like berries
Best use: straight from the plant

I still have a brilliant mental picture of my son, aged two, sitting on the banks of a crystal-clear wild swimming pool in South Wales, continuously stuffing himself with bilberries. As he popped a small, succulent, dark-purple berry in his mouth with one hand, the other was already reaching for the next. When his lips, tongue, teeth, face and hands had turned a bright shade of purple I knew it was time to tear him away from the berries.

Bilberries thrive on poor acidic soil, like that of the abandoned slate quarry we'd been swimming in (we had, of course, found a safe, shallow pool). However, as abandoned slate quarries aren't all that common, it's best to look for bilberries on moorlands, heaths, acidic uplands and in woodlands, especially conifer throughout northern Europe. As beech leaves are mildly acidic, you sometimes also find bilberries under these trees. When you do find bilberry plants, it is not unusual to see them in their hundreds; whole hillsides can be thick with the tiny-leaved plant.

In parts of Sweden the summer months are synonymous with the bilberry, or *blåbär*, as it's estimated that at least 17 per cent of the country's landmass is host to the plant. The closely related but taller and larger-fruited wild blueberry, *Vaccinium angustifolium*, grows in similar habitats throughout North America, especially towards the east of the continent. In American household manuals dating from the nineteenth century, blueberries are listed as great whortleberries or bilberries, and all-American blueberry pie is referred to as whortleberry or bilberry pie.

Bilberries are about half the size of blueberries and differ in appearance slightly, with a circular rather than crown-like calyx. They are purple-black, sometimes with a frosty sheen, like a sloe. The plant is generally low lying and woody with 2–4 cm (1–1.5 inch) leaves that are pointed at each end. The flavour is similar to that of a blueberry but deliciously more floral – a fresh bilberry easily outshines a shop-bought blueberry. Sunlight seems to encourage the sweetness and I have found those growing out in the open much sweeter than those growing in woodlands.

Picking bilberries in any great number by hand can be difficult without the use of a berry picker or comb harvester. Berry pickers consist of a box to collect the fruit, with a handle and a comb at the mouth of the box. Those with a plastic do not last long, so look for ones with metal forks. You can make a DIY version by cutting the bottom off a plastic milk bottle (handle on top) with the comb in the underside.

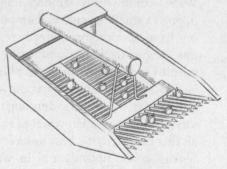

A comb harvester makes picking bilberries much easier.

PREPARATION AND USE

Bilberries can be used in the exact same way as blueberries, raw or cooked. I love them in yoghurt, either fresh or as a big dollop of jam. They are also good in a smoothie, adding vibrant colour, or in place of raisins in flapjacks, muffins and cakes.

SPICY BLÅBÄRSSOPPA

Blåbärssoppa, or bilberry soup, is a traditional Swedish recipe. It is served hot or cold as a drink or dessert, and can even be poured over porridge in the morning. This is my take on it. It will make 4–6 servings.

YOU WILL NEED:

- 500 ml (2 cups) water
- 1 lemon
- 1 tbsp arrowroot powder or potato starch (or use a handful of foraged carrageen)
- 500 g (1 lb 2 oz) bilberries
- 100 g (3½ oz) sugar (or 125 ml (4 fl oz) maple syrup)
- 1 stick of cinnamon
- 1 cm (0.5 inch) piece of ginger, diced into small pieces
- 2 cloves

METHOD:

1. Heat the water in a large pan and stir in the sugar to dissolve.
2. When the liquid is clear, add the berries and bring to the boil.
3. Cook until the berries are soft and mushy.
4. Remove the pan from the heat and blend the mixture with a handheld blender.
5. Add the spices and put back on the heat to simmer.
6. Separately, in a cup, mix the arrowroot or potato starch powder with a little water until it forms a paste. Pour this paste into the pan and heat until thick.
7. Alternatively, if using carrageen, add the carrageen to the pan and heat.
8. Strain the mixture and serve either hot or cold.

CLOUD BERRY
Rubus chamaemorus

Season for picking: summer
Where to find them: arctic tundra
Main identifying features: orange fruit like a blackberry
Best use: jams

Cloud berries are a bright orange blackberry relative which only grow in the acidic, boggy grounds of the far Northern Tundra. You'll find them during the short summers in cold regions of Scotland, Canada, Far Northern USA (including Alaska), Scandinavia and Russia. The berries grow upright on stalks, reaching a height of no more than 30cm or 1ft. The leaves splay outwards; they are lobed, toothed and very much like a blackberry. The fruit will begin red before ripening to a golden orange. Aside from the usual jams, jellies and fruit leather, the juicy, sour-sweet taste of the berry lends itself perfectly to flavour cheesecakes.

CROWBERRY
Empetrum nigrum

Season for picking: late summer/autumn
Where to find them: moors and heaths of the far north
Main identifying features: small heather-like plant
Best use: added to vodka

I first encountered the crowberry on the far northern coast of Scotland. A local gin distiller included it as one of his 'botanicals', a mix of wild and cultivated plants and herbs that he adds to the gin to give it flavour.

The crowberry is a small black berry that grows in little clusters on a heather-like plant. The leaves are tiny, no more than 6 mm long, and they grow alternately along a mainstem, very much like other plants in the heather family.

The crowberry plant can be found on moors, heaths and acid upland throughout the north of the northern hemisphere. They prefer regions north of 60 degrees latitude but you will find them in bogs and uplands at lower latitudes.

For the people of the far north, including the Inuit and Sami, they are an important food. They provide vitamin C and trace minerals, such as copper and vitamin K, within a diet that is otherwise very heavy in fish and sea mammals. In those communities the berries were historically used dried or fresh, mixed with an oil such as seal fat, and whipped into an ice cream-like foam. Known as akutaq in Alaska, it was made with whatever berry was to hand, including cloudberries and low-bush blueberries or bilberries. If this all sounds a little too 'frontier' for your liking, you will be pleased to hear that modern versions of the dish use vegetable shortening (Crisco) and sugar.

PREPARATION AND USE
Crowberries are high in vitamins and antioxidants. They do not have a strong flavour but can be juicy and pleasant to eat. They aren't overly sweet so most recipes call for sugar or other sweeter fruits to be added, or they are mixed with spices such as cinnamon or cloves. They also contain a hard seed which for most recipes will need to be removed. They can be boiled, strained and sweetened to make a juice or cordial, added to vodka to make a schnapps, or simply used in the same way as blueberries.

ROWAN, MOUNTAIN ASH
Sorbus aucuparia

Season for picking: late summer to autumn
Where to find them: acidic uplands, moors and as street trees
Main identifying features: bright-orange umbels of berries
Best use: rowan jelly

Warning: raw rowan berries can cause an upset stomach or worse – they must be cooked before being consumed.

I grew up on a typical late-1930s English housing estate, where the streets were planted with ornamental trees such as cherry, hawthorn and rowan. It took me a while to link these generic street trees with the resplendent wild ones I found on the moors, but once I'd made the connection rowan trees started to appear everywhere, their beautiful red-orange berries marking the end of summer and the start of autumn.

One of the few trees to grow on thin upland soil, the rowan tree can be found in the most unlikely places. I've seen adult trees defying gravity by leaning out from high mountain ridges, growing from tiny cracks or fissures in rocks, or sprouting from dry stone walls. It is perhaps the tree's ability to grow in these inhospitable places, producing bright-red berries from seemingly barren soil, that has led to the belief that it can ward off evil magical beings. In Scotland, people historically planted rowans in their gardens for this very reason. Elsewhere in northern Europe, rowan berries were said to guard against demons and witches.

The trees have ash-like pinnate leaves, which are slightly toothed, and their trunks are a mottled grey-brown. The blossoms are white umbels, like an elder, but the long stamens give a shaggier appearance. The tell-tale identifying characteristic comes when the rowan begins to fruit in the very late summer, producing the fiery red-orange berries that set it apart from any lookalike.

These tart, uniquely flavoured berries have long been used as a food source in human history, most likely in a sauce to accompany meat. It is thought the berries were used as a spice in prehistoric Europe, and in North America the Haida people of the Pacific Northwest would eat the raw berries of the related species *Sorbus sitchensis*, or Sitka mountain ash.

PREPARATION AND USE

As rowan seeds contain cyanide, even small doses of the raw berry can cause stomach upsets and vomiting. In large doses they can be even more dangerous. Needless to say, the berries should never be eaten raw (you'd be unlikely to do this anyway as the berries are so bitter!) As cyanide is destroyed by heat, cooking the berries makes them perfectly safe to eat.

Because of their bitterness, almost any recipe you find for rowan will contain sugar. I've sampled unsweetened rowan berries while preparing them to make a jelly and seldom have I tasted anything quite so unpleasant. Sweetened, however, they are quite different, with a complex flavour like a herb-rich marmalade. Rowan jelly is delicious on toast, or baked into a rowan berry tart. Like a good pickle, the sweet spread improves with age, becoming fuller in flavour.

Some species of *Sorbus* other than rowan have a pleasant flavour when cooked and unsweetened. These variant species lack the pinnate leaves and are often used in ornamental planting, such as on streets. Once correctly identified as a *Sorbus*, you can safely nibble on a single berry and spit it out to test the flavour. Use in the same way as rowan berries.

FORAGER'S TIP

The berries of the rowan tree are greatly improved after a number of frosts, as the cold increases the availability of natural sugars.

With mild winters it is not always possible to eat them after a true frost, but you can simulate this by popping them in the freezer overnight. Repeat this, popping them in and out of the freezer at least twice, if not three or four times, before preparing the fruit.

LIBERTY CAP, MAGIC MUSHROOM
Psilocybe semilanceata

Season for picking: autumn
Where to find them: moors and fields, especially those grazed by sheep
Main identifying features: helmet-like cap
Best use: microdosing in a clinical setting
Not to be mistaken for: conecap

Warning: possession of magic mushrooms can lead to a prison sentence. Moderate to large doses will cause altered perception and hallucinations.

Without fail, on every autumn wild food course, I will be asked about the liberty cap or, as it is more commonly known, the magic mushroom. Even groups of respectable-looking middle-aged people, with their hell-raising years mostly long behind them, are intrigued by these tiny, spindly, grey-brown mushrooms. They grow on open, wet but not sodden grassland, including meadows, heaths and moors – especially land that has been grazed by sheep. For most of the year the body of the fungus is underground seeking out nutrients, so start to look for them after rain in the early autumn. If it's a mild

Liberty caps have a distinctive cap and grow in fields fertilised by sheep.

winter the season can continue, but an early frost will see the mushroom disappear completely.

Liberty cap can be found throughout the UK, northern Europe and parts of the USA and Canada. It is a small unassuming mushroom, with a cap never bigger than 2.5 cm (1 inch), resembling Darth Vader's helmet with a nipple on top. The cap soaks up any moisture around it and can turn a dark yellow-brown or brown olive, becoming more yellowish grey-brown as it dries. Once the mushroom releases its spores, the fringe at the base of the cap can become black. The stalk can grow as long as your finger and sometimes gets twisted as it grows.

The liberty cap has no scent but its poisonous lookalike, the more yellow-brown *Conocybe tenera* or common conecap, with its slimy or sticky cap, will smell mildly mushroomy. If in doubt, take a spore print. Cut the mushroom cap and place it gills-down on a mirror, a sheet of glass or a black piece of paper or card. Leave it overnight and check it in the morning. The conecap will have an orange-brown spore print, the liberty cap's will be dark brown.

Aside from the potentially deadly conecap, in Britain at least, there are countless numbers of small, brown mushrooms, most of which are harmless but some of which can cause an upset stomach if eaten in quantity. Most lack the nipple on top and do not have a helmet-shaped cap. Many do not darken when they are wet and are far less picky than the liberty cap about the time of year they like to rise from the soil, popping up throughout the year. However, always do your research – you should never rely on one single guide to identify any mushroom for the first time.

PREPARATION AND USE

Liberty caps are well known for their LSD-like recreational use, but in recent years studies have been published on the practice of microdosing – taking very small amounts of psychedelics. These studies have found that microdosing can increase creativity and reduce anxiety and depression.[11] There is a possibility that in the future, after further study, use of psychedelics will be explored more thoroughly as a way of alleviating depression and small doses might even be prescribed clinically.

However, possession of magic mushrooms in any form, fresh or dried, has been illegal in the UK since 2005 and could lead to time in prison. If you are outside the UK, check the law in your area and do not rely on second-hand information. The inclusion of the plant in this book does not condone the use of illegal substances.

Reports from those who have eaten magic mushrooms show they are a strong psychedelic and eating them can lead to visual and audible hallucinations, along with an altered perception and mood, both positive and negative. First-time users are said to favour taking the drug in a safe environment with close friends. The biggest danger does not come from the mushroom itself but from misidentification or lack of understanding of its effects. For more information visit www.talktofrank.com and search for 'magic mushrooms'.

SHEEP'S SORREL, SOURWEED
Rumex acetosella

Season for picking: all year, though can be sparse in winter
Where to find them: acidic moors, heaths, close to granite rocks
Main identifying features: little arrow-shaped leaves
Best use: in yoghurt dips
Not to be mistaken for: bindweed, lords and ladies

Sometimes referred to as red sorrel because of its vivid red flowers, sheep's sorrel is a common heath and moorland plant. I once found this tiny plant on a windswept hillside on Dartmoor, and was amazed by its minuscule leaves, which are no more than half an inch long. Up on the moor, it's clear how this plant has evolved to be so small – with the wild weather and lack of nutrients, it struggled to grow to any size and remained a diminutive version of its close cousin common sorrel (see page 234). The two plants are very similar-looking, with leaves often described as arrow-shaped, yet to my mind at least, sheep's sorrel leaves more closely resemble a stubby broadsword. It has a thin leaf blade growing up to 3 cm (1 in) long and two pointed arms at the base. It sends up a flower spike in the same way as common sorrel. In the USA, sheep's sorrel is an invasive weed among blueberry plantations and farmers use a great deal of resources trying to keep it at bay.

It can be confused with bindweed but is easily distinguished as it grows in rosettes rather than a sprawling vine, and it has a distinct lemony flavour (spit it out if it doesn't). Some mistake it for the poisonous lords and ladies plant which is much, much larger, more waxy and has bright-orange berries (see common sorrel, page 234).

PREPARATION AND USE
Sheep's sorrel has a tangy, lemony flavour, packing a much bigger punch than you would expect. Because of its diminutive size, sheep's sorrel is far less useful than common sorrel but it can be used in exactly the same way. I use it as an extra foraged green in sandwiches to eat when I'm out walking. The small leaves are also useful as a garnish to yoghurt-based dips, worked into rice for an extra zing, sprinkled into a frittata or tossed in a salad.

CRANBERRY, LINGONBERRY AND COWBERRY
Vaccinium oxycoccus, V. vitis-idaea

Season for picking: autumn to winter
Where to find them: marshland, bogs, conifer woodland
Main identifying features: little pink flowers and marble-sized red berries
Best use: cranberry sauce

There are a number of plants that produce tart reddish berries and grow on acid soil, marshland and wet bogs. A blanket term for these would be 'cranberry', although botanically that name is

Name(s)	Scientific name
Common cranberry, small cranberry, bog cranberry	*Vaccinium oxycoccus*
American cranberry	*Vaccinium macrocarpon*
Lingonberry, cowberry, partridge berry, mountain cranberry	*Vaccinium vitis-idaea*
Bearberry, smoking berry, hog cranberry, mountain box	*Arctostaphylos uva-ursi*

only used for the small cranberry (*Vaccinium oxycoccus*), which is found in the UK, the American cranberry (*V. macrocarpon*) and one or two other closely related plants. The table above should help clarify the differences between the most commonly found cranberries and cranberry-like plants.

Cranberries are generally the last berries to ripen in the year and you will find them from mid-autumn onwards. As they contain a natural preservative they can sometimes be harvested right up until Christmas. They grow best in wet, boggy soil like upland moors, in areas such as the Scottish Highlands, Scandinavia and the northern parts of the North American continent. As with

Location	Appearance
Boggy, saturated soil and likes to grow on moss. Found in Scandinavia, Russia, Canada, northern USA, Scotland, Wales and the north of England. Occasionally found in south of England	Open pink flowers with petals that bend back in and long stamen. Small (1 cm/½ inch) thread- or thyme-like leaves. Berries flecked red when unripe, turning orange-red when ripe
Mostly north-eastern USA and south-eastern and central Canada, but has escaped into bogland across northern Europe	White to pink flowers. White berries when unripe, turning red when ripe and 9–14 mm across
Throughout northern parts of Europe, Asia and America, where summers are cool. Often as a forest-floor plant on acidic or poor soil	White to pink bell-shaped flowers, similar to bilberry. Fruits are red, 6–10 mm in size. Oval waxy leaves, 0.5–3 cm in size
On poor soil in polar regions or high altitude further south (such as Scotland)	Shiny red berries. Bell-shaped white to pink flowers. Small shrub up to 30 cm (1 foot) high. Waxy, thick evergreen leaves. Less flavoursome than cranberry

the bilberry, it is best to pick them with a berry picker/comb harvester.

PREPARATION AND USE
All kinds of cranberry or berries from the *Vaccinium* genus make a good jam or jelly – you can even find lingonberry jam for sale in Ikea. Traditionally the berries are used to make cranberry sauce as an accompaniment to turkey. However, the sauce is so tangy and delicious it works equally well on toast. To make the sauce, simmer the berries in enough port and/or orange juice to cover. Simmer until the berries have loosely broken up and add a good

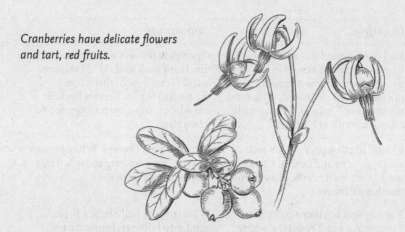

Cranberries have delicate flowers and tart, red fruits.

pinch of cinnamon. Stir in a tablespoon of white or dark-brown sugar – test and add more sugar if needed.

The berries dehydrate very well and add a tangy hit to breakfast cereals. They also pair very well with chocolate in fudge, cakes or chocolate-covered cranberry flapjacks.

HOMEMADE CRANBERRY JUICE

To make a cranberry juice, simply boil 200 g (7 oz) of cranberries in 1 litre (4 cups) of water for 10 to 20 minutes. Add about a teaspoon of lemon juice and 75 g (2½ oz) of sugar, then strain through a sieve and refrigerate.

Serve cool with ice or try it warm with cinnamon and cloves, a little apple juice or cider, or a measure of dark rum.

CHAPTER EIGHT

Meadows and Pastures

D URING THE SUMMER, our family will pack up a
picnic and cycle over to a picturesque local meadow
to meet friends. It's a beautiful, restful place, perched
between a meandering river and a copse of hazel and nationally
rare elms. Swallows swoop overhead and the gentle 'fut-fut-fut'
of grasshoppers emanates from the long summer grass. Dotted
through the grass are the red flower spikes of sorrel, which make
their way into the lunch, mixed in with some pre-cooked pasta or
as an addition to sandwiches. With a strong sense of bravado, the
kids dare each other to eat raw green hogweed, letting the strong,
citrus spiciness build in their mouths before secretly spitting
out the seeds and glugging down water. Scabious, knapweeds,
yarrows and ribwort plantain grow throughout the meadow and
froghoppers, tiny grasshopper-like insects, ping in and out of
lunchboxes.

Over a third of the earth's surface is now made up of grassland,
but less than one-third of this grassland is naturally occurring –
the vast majority has been created by us. We have made pastures
for our animals to graze, meadows to provide a yearly cut of hay
and parks, lawns and fields for nothing more than recreation.

Grasslands are found the world over and they can be highly
varied. There are the great temperate grasslands like the Eura-
sian Steppe, the prairies of the US Midwest, the alpine meadows
of Europe and the Pampas in South America, as well as the tropical savannahs of Australia and Africa. The chalk and acidic

grasslands explored in the earlier chapters of this book can be low-nutrient and species-specific landscapes. But there are also the more human-made or managed areas of grassland which are generally found on fertile soil. These are often there to provide hay or feed grazing animals, such as cows or sheep. Or, increasingly, there are those whose primary aim is to increase biodiversity for wildlife, such as the traditional meadows of Zeeland in the Netherlands,[12] the fertile flower meadows of the Transylvanian countryside (now a popular eco-tourist site) and pocket urban meadows such as Cricklepit Mill in the city of Exeter.

Although there are exceptions, such as flood and water meadows, 'meadowland' usually refers to grasslands that are cut once a year for hay making. This practice allows a wide range of species to thrive between cuts, including a mix of wildflowers, grasses and herbs. The term 'pasture' refers to land that has been set aside for the grazing of animals, usually cows and sheep. The lack of intervention by human hand means these landscapes can also often support a wide range of species (albeit those that can withstand the continuous hungry jaws of livestock).

There's also a type of landscape called 'improved pasture', a term which I always find a contradiction. Improved pasture is easily recognised as it is normally sown with just a few species of grass and a nitrogen-fixing crop, usually clover. It's often present as part of a rotation, left predominantly for the grazing of beef cattle to rest the soil between sowings of arable crops. Improved pastures are disappointing places to forage as even if they have time to establish, they usually only support a handful of weeds (like buttercups and thistles).

Aside from the anomaly of improved pasture, grassland overall can be a fantastic place to look for wild food. Yarrow, musk mallows, chickweed, plantain, sorrel, thistles and dock are almost without fail found nestling within the blades of grass. In my experience, aside from days spent picnicking, grassland is often a corridor between one habitat and another. Yet as most foraging is opportunistic, it would be churlish not to pick a few field mushrooms on the way to a boletus woodland, or to grab some chickweed on my way to my favourite patch of sloes.

Occasionally you will find irresponsible dog owners have left gifts for the would-be forager. That's why I put any greens I find into saltwater to soak before I prepare them, and if in any doubt I'll only pick leaves I can boil, as this kills off any lingering pathogens. But grasslands aren't just good for green leaves – from the spring through to the autumn all kinds of fungi pop up in meadowland and untreated pastures. In a delectable start to the mushroom foraging calendar, the aptly named St George's mushroom comes up around St George's Day on 23 April. In the summer the football-sized giant puffball, along with field and horse mushrooms, makes its way onto kebab sticks for barbecues. Fungi such as the beautiful wide-gilled waxcap, which comes in the colours of the rainbow, are found almost exclusively in untreated grasslands.

Like most habitats, grasslands can have far more to them than first meets the eye – you just have to remember to look down.

CHIVES AND CROW GARLIC
Allium schoenoprasum and *A. vineale*

Season for picking: all year
Where to find them: long grass, grassy banks, lawns, roadside verges
Main identifying features: grass-like blades with an onion scent
Best use: as a herb
Not to be mistaken for: grasses

Chives and crow garlic are different plants, but as there is very little difference in their flavour it is not really necessary to distinguish between the two when picking. Both plants grow on grassy banks and meadows and can hide themselves in the long grass, thanks to their long, hollow stems. One defining feature of both is their garlic-onion scent, a smell which instantly transports me back to my parents' herb garden and my mother's chive-topped mashed potato.

Chives have a tufty pinky-violet flower, whereas the flower of crow garlic is much sparser and slightly darker purple. The seed heads are different too; chives produce many seeds all enclosed within papery husks, whereas crow garlic has hard bulblets at the end of its stem, which sometimes sprout into tiny plants. Crow garlic is a far more common weed than chives – if you have something chive-like in your lawn, nine times out of ten it will be crow garlic.

PREPARATION AND USE
Both chives and crow garlic have that oniony or mild garlic flavour that makes them a welcome addition to many dishes. They will regrow like grass, so there is no need to worry about over-foraging them. I harvest them by hand as they are easy enough to tear from the ground, but scissors can make for a cleaner cut.

A handful can be laid out on a chopping board then rolled over with a knife, cutting them into small shreds to be sprinkled into soups, stews or with wild garlic in garlic bread. Chopped chives go well with dairy products like cheese sauce or fresh goat's cheese, or you could them try with your favourite white fish recipe. My personal favourite, however, is to work them through a pan of cheesy, buttery mashed potatoes.

CHICKWEED
Stellaria media

Season for picking: all year, except height of summer
Where to find them: fertile meadows, farmland, grassy banks
Main identifying features: stems with fur on one side, star-shaped flowers
Best use: salad
Not to be mistaken for: scarlet pimpernel, mouse's ear

Chickweed grows everywhere; I've found it within the Arctic Circle, the mountain principality of Andorra, in Scotland and in my own back garden in Somerset. It has a pleasant flavour – slightly sweet, crisp and grassy – and I can rarely resist having a nibble whenever I see it.

Chickweed can be found all year round (with the exception of a few weeks during the middle of summer) but is at its best when it bursts with fresh green shoots during the spring. It grows in clumps or mats as an arable or garden weed, in open fields, in meadows, and in pastures and disturbed land.

Its scientific name, *Stellaria*, refers to its star-shaped white flowers. At first glance these tiny blooms seem to have ten petals, but on closer inspection you will see they comprise just five, which fork at the base. The leaves are small, paired and grow alternately

Chickweed can be identified by the tiny, furry hairs growing along just one side of the stem.

on the stem. They are no more than 2.5cm (1 inch) in length and ovoid, with a point at the end.

If you hold the stem to the light you should be able to make out tiny white hairs which run down just one side. This is the best way to differentiate the plant from common lookalikes, as most lack a line of fine hairs or, in the case of mouse's ear (also edible), are hairy all over. Other lookalikes, in addition to being smooth, have different coloured flowers – the scarlet pimpernel, for example, has red or yellow flowers.

In British folk tradition chickweed was used to treat all kinds of skin complaints and swelling. Studies have shown that the herb may indeed have mild anti-inflammatory and antioxidant properties when applied to the skin.[13]

PREPARATION AND USE
The flavour of chickweed is mild and somewhat sweet, but with a little hint of the earthy bitterness you sometimes get with wild greens. It can get stringy at the base, so it is best to only use the lush tips of the plant. Use it on its own, mix with wild garlic to make a pesto or chop it finely and add it to a yoghurt dip or raita. Chickweed makes a nutritious addition to soups, but as it cooks down to almost nothing you will need to pick a lot to make this worthwhile.

CHICKWEED SALAD

In our house chickweed is a handy salad ingredient and handfuls of are brought home after a walk and mixed with salad leaves. This is a common recipe I use.

YOU WILL NEED:

- 1 handful chickweed tips, washed and drained)
- 2–3 handfuls mixed leaves, such as lettuce and rocket
- 1 tbsp toasted seeds, such as sunflower
- 1 handful halved grapes
- 5 cm (2 inch) piece of cucumber, finely chopped
- Lemon juice
- Olive oil

METHOD:

Wash and shred the chickweed and salad greens, toss in the grapes, cucumber and toasted seeds, and dress with a splash of olive oil and squeeze of lemon.

RIBWORT PLANTAIN, NARROW-LEAF PLANTAIN
Plantago lanceolata

Season for picking: all year
Where to find them: in grassland
Main identifying features: long lance-shaped leaves
Best use: blanched leaves or to soothe insect bites

My first memories of ribwort plantain are from the school playground. We would wrap the stalks around the seed heads and push, so they would ping off like tiny missiles. Like greater plantain (see page 96) they are effective in soothing nettle stings and insect bites. Just pop a leaf in your mouth and chew a little before applying to the affected area. The flavour is mushroomy and somewhat bitter; you can use them in salads but only sparingly. Blanch or lightly fry the leaves – they go well with strong flavours such as soy, bacon or miso.

ST GEORGE'S MUSHROOM
Calocybe gambosa

Season for picking: spring
Where to find them: fields and grassland
Main identifying features: pale to buff cream
Best use: fried in butter

The St George's mushroom is considered a safe bet for novice foragers as it has a distinctive scent. Predominantly growing in grassland, it appears around St George's Day in April, hence its name.[14] It begins life as a pale-white mushroom, but turns a buff or creamy colour, often with a marbling effect, as it ages. The margins of the cap can be wavy and fold in at the edges. When cut in a cross-section the cap should be predominantly flesh, with very few gills.

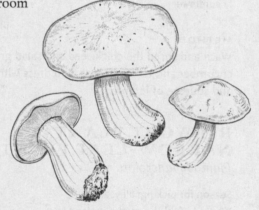

However, the most distinctive thing about this mushroom is its scent. Said to have a 'mealy' aroma, it has been described as everything from sawdust, melon rind and watermelon to bone meal and raw pastry.

FORAGER'S TIP

The mycelium, or the underground part of the organism, grows in a ring and forms a relationship with the roots of grasses, in the same way that woodland species do with the roots of trees (see page 250). Just as with other mycorrhizal species (meaning fungi that form associations with the roots of plants), the host organism is fed with important nutrients in exchange for sugars from the plant, which the fungus cannot create itself. As a result, the ring of grass above the mycelium is greener, heathier, taller and lusher that that of the grass in the field, so ring-forming mushrooms can be spotted from long distances away, especially from a bird's eye view. The St George's mushroom is one of the few species of fungi you might be able to search for using a helicopter or a drone!

PREPARATION AND USE

The St George's mushroom makes an appearance when the wild garlic is at its best, which is serendipitous because the robust flavours of the two mix extremely well. You can't go far wrong with St George's mushroom and wild garlic sautéed in butter and served on a thick slice of toast. Like most mushrooms, it is advisable to cook them first, and they work well in a creamy sauce with pasta or in a risotto with cashews.

CUCKOOFLOWER, MAYFLOWER, LADY'S SMOCK
Cardamine pratensis

Season for picking: spring
Where to find them: meadow banks, grassland
Main identifying features: little pink flower with watercress like leaves
Best use: as a salad

Cuckoo flowers are pretty, little pink flowers which appear around the same time as the first call of the cuckoo in the early spring. The flowers have four petals and the basal, or young leaves, are pinnate, resembling those of watercress or bittercress which it is closely related to. The older leaves remain pinnate but are more lance shaped than oval.

According to popular folklore, the ball of froth on a cuckoo flower comes from a spitting cuckoo. But rather than the product of an anti-social bird, this 'spit' is in fact a protective coating for a froghopper nymph. When they become adults, these tiny grasshopper-like bugs are characterised by pointy head or noise and you will often see jumping around your picnic blanket in the summer.

PREPARATION AND USE
The flavour of the cuckoo flower is spicy, like other cresses, but with an added freshness. The whole of the plant is edible but you may find the stems quite chewy so I stick to the flowers and leaves.

Where the flowers grow abundantly, such as the east of England, they can be gathered in large numbers. However, where I live in the south west, they are sparse at best and I am loath to pick too many. Instead I use them as an occasional nibble or add one to a sandwich along with some more common bittercress. Where they are abundant and you can pick a large number, use as a decorative and spicy addition to salads or make into a pesto with a kick.

DOCK
Rumex spp.

Season for picking: spring (or all year if leached)
Where to find them: everywhere – especially in meadows, grassland, farmland and edgeland
Main identifying features: 20-m-long leaves
Best use: cooked like spinach

Docks are common throughout the world and are found growing on grassland, woodland fringes, wasteland, edgeland – anywhere the seeds take hold. Most of us remember dock leaves from childhood as a remedy for a nettle sting, but this may only be a placebo (the plantain actually works better, page 96). In Europe, especially in the south, docks are commonly eaten as a cooked green similar to spinach. Many of the North American species are bitter to eat and long boiling times may be necessary.

PREPARATION AND USE
Docks have been considered a famine food for centuries as they are readily available and highly nutritious. Due to the presence of oxalates and bitter-tasting compounds in the leaves it is best to only harvest in the spring, when the leaves are light green and very young. The older leaves can be eaten but it is best to leach them first. This is easy to do: simply drop the leaves into boiling water and simmer for around a minute. Discard the water, then repeat the process one more time.

Docks are everywhere so it is easy to forage a lot of them in a very short space of time. They soak up flavours in the same way as spinach and I find them a good side dish with toasted hazelnuts or flaked almonds. Use the leached leaves as you would spinach, pairing with creamy cheeses.

DOCK DOLMADES

Most of us see dolmades as a dish prepared exclusively with vine leaves. But in modern rural Turkey, where the dish is called Sarma, researchers found that at least seventy-one different plants were used to make them – including cabbage, mallow, beetroot and the plantain families, as well as various *Rumex* or dock species.[15] So here is my take on dock dolmades.

YOU WILL NEED:

- 100 g (3½ oz) rice or couscous
- 20–30 dock leaves (either young or leached)
- 180 ml (6 fl oz) vegetable or chicken stock
- Squeeze of lemon juice
- ½ bunch parsley
- Handful pine nuts
- A few sprigs of fresh mint
- 1 tbsp sultanas or currants
- A large pinch of dill
- A slug of olive oil

METHOD:

1. Leach the leaves as per the method above.
2. Cook the rice or couscous in the stock, following the packet instructions.
3. Add the sultanas or currants to the cooked grain.
4. Finely chop the herbs and mix them all together.
5. Add a teaspoon of the rice or couscous mix to the centre of a leaf, sprinkle on the herbs and add a good squeeze of lemon.
6. Roll up the bottom of the leaf into the middle and fold in the sides. Roll the top down, tucking in the sides.
7. Serve with a rich tomato sauce.

THISTLE
Cirsium spp.

Season for picking: spring
Where to find them: meadows, grassland, wasteland, large gardens
Main identifying features: prickly leaves
Best use: stems as a vegetable

It may not be easy to tell the difference between different species of thistle but you usually know when you have sat on one! Thistles are not fussy about where they grow and they inhabit meadows, chalkland, farmland and edgeland. There are various species around the world, ranging from those with heads no bigger than a pea to those that could rival the artichoke. The flowers are normally purple but some have yellow, dandelion-like heads. Beginning in their first year as a prickly rosette of leaves, thistles send up their flower stalks the following spring, which can range from 30 cm (1 foot) to 2 m (6.5 feet) in height.

Thistles have provided food to various populations for centuries. In Portugal, where they are known as *cardos* or *cardinhos* they have endured through recipes such as blanched thistle leaves with beans or chickpeas, and thistle stems in soups. The *Eryngium campestre*, or field eryngo, which grows wild in most of Europe, was a popular food for the Romans, who ate them like carrots. There is evidence too that when much of the Iberian Peninsula was under Arabic rule, from roughly the eighth to the thirteenth century, the thistle was sold as a green vegetable.[16]

Technically all thistles are edible, with one obvious caveat: the prickles. With these as a defence the plant does not need to make bitter compounds to protect itself from predators. Most thistles have a sweet, succulent flavour early in the season, turning bitter as the plant flowers, so are best eaten before they flower which is usually the spring or sometimes early summer. The edible parts are the stem, the leaves and the base of the flower head (think artichoke).

PREPARATION AND USE

To prepare the leaves, remove
a large leaf from the plant
using gloves (or a very
careful hand) and
secateurs. Next cut
around the outside
of the leaf to remove
the prickles (see
illustration). Serve raw
or blanched in salads.

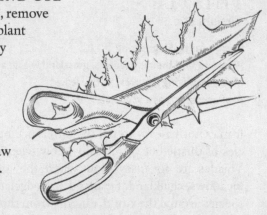

For the stem, cut
at the base of the
plant with a knife or
secateurs. Move your knife downwards to first remove the leaves
then the outside of the stem. Keep working until you are left
with the soft inside. This has a fresh, succulent taste and can be
eaten raw or served slightly blanched with an olive oil and lemon
dressing.

To use the choke, cut the flower head before it comes into
flower. Remove the outer prickles with a knife (gloves are useful
here). Next remove all the fluffy growth on top until you are only
left with the heart. This will be white, like an artichoke heart, and
flattened on one end, varying in size from a flattened pea to the
diameter of a tennis ball. The flavour is usually nutty and pea-
like, much like an artichoke. Eat raw or blanched. From trying
a few types, I've found the woolly thistle, *Cirsium eriophorum*, is
one of the best to eat, because of its nutty flavour and the relative
ease of harvesting it.

FIELD MUSHROOM
Agaricus campestris

Season for picking: spring to autumn
Where to find them: grassland, grazed meadows
Main identifying features: like a shop-bought button mushroom
Best use: stroganoff
Not to be mistaken for: yellow stainer

Field mushrooms are very closely related to the common button or portobello mushroom you normally find in supermarkets. They are abundant in all kinds of grassland, including meadows and pasture. I often find them in sheep or cattle fields when I am out walking and recently came across a prize patch on a grassy bank close to my son's nursery. Field mushrooms can form rings, or fairy rings, so named as they were said to mark the paths of fairies. These rings will be characterised by an outer ring of lush grass and an inner ring of suppressed growth.

Field mushrooms do best on natural grassland that hasn't been sprayed in any way, so unfortunately this once-common mushroom is less abundant than it used to be. They come up in mid to late summer, usually during the school holidays. When you find one, you'll normally find many more, so it is worth hunting around.

As with all mushrooms, you should be very careful to make sure you know for sure what you are looking at. The gills of a field mushroom are pinkish brown when young, turning to a darker brown-black but *never* white. It should have a pleasant mushroom or aniseed smell. Discard anything that has a chemical, acrid or unpleasant scent.

You may mistake the field mushroom for its much bigger relative, the equally edible horse mushroom. Other than size, there is little to distinguish these two – even the taste is near identical. But the field mushroom does have one close lookalike that, although not deadly, is poisonous and has very unpleasant effects.

This is the yellow stainer, *Agaricus xanthodermus*. When bruised or rubbed with a fingernail the cap and the base of the stem of the poisonous yellow stainer will stain a lemon-yellow colour.

COMMON SORREL
Rumex acetosa

Season for picking: spring to autumn
Where to find them: damp or moist grassland, fertile meadows
Main identifying features: arrow-shaped leaves
Best use: salads
Not to be mistaken for: lords and ladies

Sorrel can be hard to spot at first, as its leaves are normally only a touch paler than the surrounding grass, but in the right environment (like a moisture-rich, fertile meadow or pasture) it can be abundant. It does not take to alkaline conditions, such as chalky downs or areas with underlying limestone, so you are unlikely to find it in these environments. It can tolerate a bit of shade, so it sometimes turns up at the base of hedgerows and on the roadside, but it is more common out on the open grass. It is almost completely absent from any improved pasture so give up the search if all you can see is uniform grass and clover. In brief, look for sorrel on slightly damp, iron-rich, often acidic soil. The arrow-shaped leaves grow in rosettes from a central point and are 6 to 20 cm (2½ to 8 inches) or more in length.

The summer can be the easiest time to spot sorrel, when its spike of red flowers announces its presence over the tall grass like a waving arm in a crowded station. However, it is either side of this period when the leaves are at their most sweet and ready to pick. They have a delicious, tangy, lemony flavour, a bit like a grape skin.

For beginners or over-eager foragers, the only potentially dangerous lookalike to sorrel is *Arum maculatum*, better known as lords and ladies (aka waggly willy or the wild arum lily). Both have green, arrow-shaped leaves but lords and ladies tends to grow more in the shade while sorrel prefers a more open environment. Arum lilies have waxy leaves and if you look closely, you will notice a continuous vein running round the inner margin of the leaf, which is absent on the less waxy sorrel leaf. Finally, the flower is completely different: lords and ladies have a modified leaf structure called a spathe, which wraps around a spadix or flowering spike (the 'waggly willy'), giving way to a cluster of red berries. Sorrel, on the other hand, has very red, small, dock-like flowers clustered on a long flowering spike.

PREPARATION AND USE

Sorrel leaves make a good salad ingredient as they provide a hit of sourness without the need for lemon dressing. I like to use them in dairy-based dips as to add a lemony flavour without curdling any milk products. Reduced in butter, perhaps with the addition of some onions and a little garlic, they make a good side to a poached egg on toast. Sorrel soup is delicious – I recommend using an onion and potato base if you want to make your own (page 15). Sorrel sauce is good with fish, especially salmon.

FORAGER'S TIP

Sorrel is high in oxalic acid, a naturally occurring acid present in many foods (like spinach and rhubarb). Although such foods are a regular part of most diets, they can lead to kidney stones when oxalic acid binds with calcium within the body, forming calcium oxalate stones. To reduce the risk of this, keep hydrated when eating sorrel and pair it with calcium-rich foods (like yoghurt), as this enables your body to safely deal with the oxalate. It is always a good idea to vary your diet and not to eat foods high in oxalic acid, such as sorrel, on a daily basis.

GIANT PUFFBALL
Calvatia gigantea

Season for picking: summer
Where to find them: grassy fields, grassy roadside banks
Main identifying features: big ball-shaped white mushroom
Best use: cut into burgers and fried
Not to be mistaken for: egg-stage *Amanita* mushrooms (although unlikely for large ones)

I once had a job as a driver's mate, crossing the country on huge articulated lorries, helping the driver load and unload goods. On my first day, I introduced myself to my driver clutching a football-sized puffball mushroom. I had found it that morning growing on the grass verge outside the depot. The driver kept eyeing it suspiciously in the seat next to him, apparently not reassured by my promises that it was harmless. Thankfully, my friends were rather excited by my find. That weekend we made it into a delicious risotto, cut it into burgers and skewered the final pieces onto kebabs.

It is hard to mistake a giant puffball for anything poisonous, but occasionally optimism might have you crossing a field only to find a plastic bag or lost football. They grow from the size of a grapefruit to the size of a bowling ball or bigger. They are roughly spherical or ovoid and creamy white with a suede-like skin. Although there is little else that looks like them, or grows to such a size, you still need to eliminate any mushrooms which might be poisonous or inedible. Cut the puffball in two; the inside should be uniform white and not black, yellow or brown. It should not look like a cross-section of a mushroom inside, as this can indicate the mushroom is of the poisonous *Amanita* family and in its egg stage. However, as the *Amanita* 'eggs' tend to be golf-ball-sized at best, it is unlikely you will mistake the two.

Puffballs are not rare per se, but the hunt can be challenging as despite their size they are somewhat elusive. In my experience they pop up in different locations every year, so returning to the same area may not yield the same result.

PREPARATION AND USE
Puffballs have an excellent mushroom flavour. They soak up butter and garlic and work in all kinds of mushroom dishes, from pasta and risotto to pies and curries. They can be cut into cubes and barbecued with vegetables on kebab skewers, or cut into burger shapes. You will find recipes for stuffed puffball but this is really only worth doing as a novelty.

PREPARATION AND USE
Follow any recipes for the portobello or button mushroom. I like mine with a creamy sauce served on tagliatelle or as a filling for a jacket potato. Use in curries, soups or simply fried on toast.

PARASOL MUSHROOM
Macrolepiota procera

Season for picking: summer to autumn
Where to find them: grassland
Main identifying features: large mottled cap and long stem
Best use: fried
Not to be mistaken for: shaggy parasol, false or green-spored parasol (North America only)

A mostly grassland species, this very large mushroom appears in late summer. Little else that's edible gets to this size in grassland and its dinner plate-sized caps (30 cm/1 foot) fill a basket very quickly. I've found parasol mushrooms most often on pastureland by the coast, but they are not exclusively maritime. My largest ever haul was inland with easily fifty or more dotted across a hillside.

The parasol is often seen as a good mushroom for the novice forager, but you do have to be very careful not to confuse it with other species which may be poisonous (although not deadly). One of the main signifiers is that it has brown snakeskin marks on the stem caused by the speed at which it grows – a bit like stretch marks. The mushroom doesn't discolour when cut and has a white, not green, spore print. It's particularly important to pay attention to the spore colour in North America, where the poisonous green-spored parasol (*Chlorophyllum molybdites*) also grows.

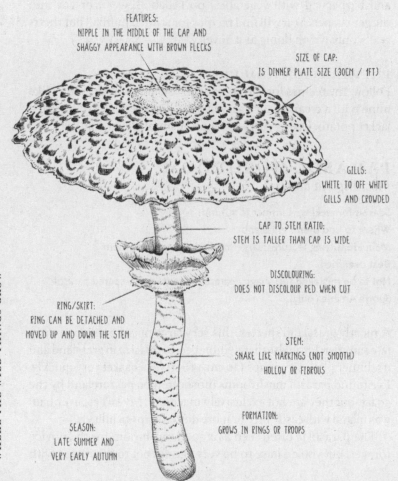

FEATURES:
NIPPLE IN THE MIDDLE OF THE CAP AND
SHAGGY APPEARANCE WITH BROWN FLECKS

SIZE OF CAP:
IS DINNER PLATE SIZE (30CM / 1FT)

GILLS:
WHITE TO OFF WHITE
GILLS AND CROWDED

CAP TO STEM RATIO:
STEM IS TALLER THAN CAP IS WIDE

DISCOLOURING:
DOES NOT DISCOLOUR RED WHEN CUT

RING/SKIRT:
RING CAN BE DETACHED AND
MOVED UP AND DOWN THE STEM

STEM:
SNAKE LIKE MARKINGS (NOT SMOOTH)
HOLLOW OR FIBROUS

FORMATION:
GROWS IN RINGS OR TROOPS

SEASON:
LATE SUMMER AND
VERY EARLY AUTUMN

The shaggy parasol, *Chlorophyllum rhacodes*, has many of the same characteristics but the stem is smooth rather than snake-skinned. It can cause gastric upsets in some, so if you are determined to eat one only consume a little at first and wait a day or two to see if you can tolerate it. Shaggy parasols have been split into three different species and only one of these is thought to cause gastric upset. However, it takes a microscope to tell the difference so for the novice mycologist at least it's best to err on the side of caution.

For ease of identification I've put together this checklist, which will to help you distinguish between a parasol mushroom and a potentially poisonous or stomach-upsetting lookalike.

	Parasol mushroom
Size of cap	Dinner plate size (30 cm/1 foot)
Cap-to-stem ratio	Stem is taller than cap is wide
Discolouring	Does not discolour red when cut
Stem	Snake-like markings (not smooth), hollow or fibrous
Distinctive features	Nipple in the middle of the cap and shaggy appearance with brown flecks
Ring/skirt	The ring can be detached and moved up and down the stem
Gills	White to off-white and crowded
Season	Late summer and very early autumn
Formation	Grows in rings or troops

PREPARATION AND USE

When collecting parasols, because of their large size, it can be easier to break off the fibrous stems and put them to one side of your basket rather than carry the mushroom whole. By boiling with leeks, bay leaves and herbs the stems can be made into a delicious stock, which is suitable as a base for mushroom soup using the heads. The soup is best liquidised, as the mushrooms get a little mushy when boiled.

Parasols are delicious when dipped in a spiced batter and deep-fried. These go well with all kinds of dipping sauces, such as a smooth tomato salsa or a mayonnaise-yoghurt dip with a little mustard. Alternatively, simply fry them whole or sliced in a little olive oil or butter with garlic. Garlicky fried parasols are delicious partnered with a poached egg or bacon on toast.

SILVERWEED
Argentina anserina, syn. *Potentilla anserina*

Season for picking: autumn
Where to find them: compacted land in fields, especially by gates, and in open woodland close to paths
Main identifying features: silver leaves
Best use: roots like potatoes

Silverweed grows in similar habitats to plantain (*Plantago major,* see page 96): on disturbed or compressed soil, the edges of fields, on grassy plains and on open patches of woodland, especially where paths have formed. It is also happy as a coastal plant growing on sandy banks and in shingle.

The plant's sharp-toothed pinnate leaves have a feathery appearance, and are green on top and a matt silver underneath. Occasionally the whole plant will take on a silvery sheen.

Various species of silverweed have been used as a staple food throughout the northern hemisphere. The plant was commonly eaten in the windswept highlands and islands of Scotland, for example, before the introduction of potatoes from the Americas in the late sixteenth century. It went by the Scots Gaelic name of *brisgean* and could be eaten like potatoes or dried to make a bread. Being a wide-spread weed of arable land, it came into its own during the Scottish potato famine in the mid-nineteenth century as it reliably grew in years where other crops failed. Silverweed was also eaten by the Okanagan of Western Canada and the various tribes of Montana. And according to the tradition of the Kwakwaka'wakw, a tribe of the Pacific Northwest of America, the long straight roots were served to the chiefs and high-ranking individuals while low-ranking members of the tribe ate the curly roots (much as misshapen veg is sold cheaply today).

PREPARATION AND USE
Although the leaves are edible, I've never found them to be worthwhile. Instead try the roots in the autumn or spring when they fatten with their winter stores of starch.

It is illegal to dig up roots without the landowner's permission, so half the battle with silverweed is finding a legitimate supply of them. Some roots come up easily but with others you will need to loosen the ground with a fork first.

Blanch the roots prior to frying to remove any bitterness. They make a good replacement for potatoes and I once served 'chips' made of fried swollen silverweed roots (along with chicken of the woods and sorrel omelette) to the TV presenter Ben Fogle.

The roots have a nutty, starchy, potato-like flavour and fried up or lightly boiled they are satisfyingly hearty. If harvested in quantity they can be boiled, then dried and ground to make flour. This can be used to make a flatbread, or mixed with regular flour for added nutrition and a starchy flavour.

MEADOW WAXCAP
Cuphophyllus pratensis, formerly *Hygrocybe coccinea*

Season for picking: late autumn/early winter
Where to find them: untreated grasslands and meadows
Main identifying features: waxy caps and widely spaced gills
Best use: fried
Not to be mistaken for: deadly funnel or fool's funnel

Waxcaps can be very picky about where they grow, preferring meadows and pastures that haven't been treated in any way. As a result, current farming and horticultural practices have led to a decline in some species, including the scarlet waxcap, which has become endangered. However, when they do find the right environment they can grow in abundance. I've found gluts of red, white, yellow and orange-brown-capped waxcaps during blustery walks on rolling coastal downs.

In Britain, at least, there are no deadly poisonous waxcaps, though some are unpleasant to eat. Identification is important as they can look like members of the poisonous *Clitocybe* family. As ever, if in doubt, leave it out.

The meadow waxcap has slightly decurrent gills, meaning the gills run approximately 1 cm (half an inch) down the stem. This is in contrast to a field or button mushroom, where the gills stop at the stem, which can be snapped off without interfering with the gills. Another important signifier of a meadow waxcap is the fact that its gills are widely spaced and fleshy-looking. Poisonous lookalikes like the deadly funnel (*Clitocybe dealbata*) or fool's funnel (*C. rivulosa*) both have tightly packed gills. Finally, it is important to note the time of year – meadow waxcaps pop up in the very late autumn and can last until the early winter.

Meadow waxcaps are also the least endangered variety of waxcap, and thankfully are very good to eat. The cap is a pale brownish-orange, getting lighter as it ages. The gills are also slightly orange and the cap can grow up to 10 cm (4 inches) in diameter. The meadow waxcap grows in rings, so if you see one, step back and you should see the curve of the circle containing more mushrooms.

FORAGER'S TIP

Although many of the waxcaps are endangered and it is advised you should not pick some of the rarer species, they do get knocked over, or picked up and discarded by amateur mycologists. So whereas you can leave those still attached to the ground in place, there is no law against these 'windfalls'.

PREPARATION AND USE

Waxcaps give colour to a dish but the flavour does not rank as highly as other autumnal mushrooms. Use them in risotto with richer-tasting mushrooms, such as wood blewits, or try them in a mixed mushroom curry.

FIELD BLEWIT
Lepista saeva

Season for picking: autumn and winter
Where to find them: fields and hedgerows
Main identifying features: blueish-lilac stem
Best use: risottos
Not to be mistaken for: bruising webcap (*Cortinarius purpurascens*)

The field blewit is a useful mushroom to know in the colder seasons, as it grows in the very late autumn and early winter. It is indistinctive when viewed from above, with a nondescript tan-brown cap. However, the stem sets it apart from most other mushrooms: it is blueish-lilac (the French call the mushroom *pied violet*), as if coloured with a felt-tip pen that is running out of ink. The gills are attached to the stem rather than running down it and it has a pleasant mushroom smell.

To the untrained eye, it can be mistaken for *Cortinarius purpurascens*, the poisonous bruising webcap. Young bruising webcaps will have a web-like structure attaching the cap to the stem – this is absent on young blewits. Another way of determining you have a safe mushroom is to cut it in two: the bruising webcap will stain purple, whereas the flesh of a field blewit remains a creamy white.

If in doubt you can always take a spore print. The way to do this is to remove the stem and place the mushroom gills-down on a mirror, a sheet of glass or a black piece of paper or card. Leave it overnight and check on it in the morning. The field blewit will have left a pale-pink spore print, whereas the webcap will leave a rusty-brown print.

PREPARATION AND USE

Field blewits should not be eaten raw. When fried they can leak a little liquid, which can be drained and used as a mushroom stock. Like most mushrooms, they benefit from a bit of butter and garlic or cream and chives. I've made a good pâté from them, reducing them down with spring onions and garlic in a pan with a knob of butter. Let this cool then blitz it up, adding a bit of cream cheese or olive oil and seasoning with salt, pepper and a little nutmeg if you have it. You can also try field blewits in a pie, or in a risotto with earthy flavours like hazelnuts or beetroot.

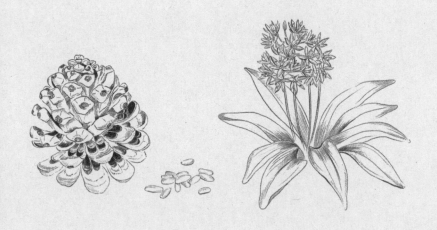

WOODLAND

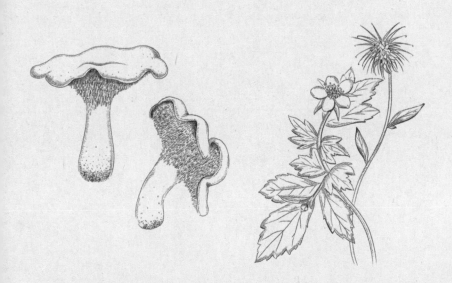

CHAPTER NINE

Mixed Woodland

FORESTS CAN BE dark, cool and mysterious places and to step into the trees is to step into another realm. During the heat of the summer, the light is dappled and soft under the trees, with patches of intense green as the sun pours into grassy clearings. The senses intensify, and every breaking twig, rustling in the undergrowth, is amplified in the deadening silence of the trees. The heat of the sun and warm summer rain stirs up the scents of mosses, lichen and the earthy perfumes of tree resin.

Fiction and folklore often paint the woods as dangerous places; in their adventures both Frodo Baggins in *The Lord of the Rings* and Little Red Riding Hood are told bad things will happen if they stray from the path into the wild wood. When, inevitably, both are tempted into the trees they are faced with life-threating challenges in the form of giant spiders and the big bad wolf. Indeed, in pre-industrial Europe, when the oral tradition of storytelling was at its zenith, the dangers of the woods would have been very real. Wolves, bears and bandits all hid under the leafy canopy and folk stories were cautionary tales to keep children safe as well as entertained.

Outside of fiction and mysteries though, woodlands are essential refuges for our minds. I often counter a stressful day with an evening walking among the trees. The weight of the day lifts, the mind slows and I can breathe more deeply once again. Recent studies show that a walk in the woods can reduce the amount of the stress hormone, cortisol, in the body.[17] In Japan, *shinrin-yoku* or 'forest bathing' has long been popular, and this practice of a woodland walking meditation is gaining popularity in the West as we seek new ways to engage with nature and relieve stress.

There are many different types of woodland, and woodlands do not always fit the neat terminology of 'conifer' or 'deciduous'. 'Mixed woodland' describes an area which has at least 20 per cent cover of either coniferous or deciduous trees. Any less than 20 per cent of the minority tree and it becomes coniferous or deciduous dominated, such as the beech wood and oak wood forests of Sussex. Mixed woodland often occurs naturally, without the intervention of humans, most notably in the Sierra Nevada mountain range of the United States where there is a mixture of pines, firs and oaks. But mixed woodland can also be a man-made phenomenon; the result of regrowth after plantation felling, the planting of a commercial crop alongside a natural woodland, or a mix of trees planted on the whim of a landowner, decades if not centuries ago. Although there can be mature trees present, most of these forests are relatively new habitats. For the majority of us, this mishmash of native stock and imported trees will be the type of woodland we have easiest access to.

Mixed woodlands are ideal places to forage for fungi. Mushrooms tend to pop up where their food source runs out, such as on the boundaries between conifers and deciduous woods, and it's worth following the line between these two kinds of tree during mushroom season. Outside of mushroom season you will find an abundance of shade-tolerant plants, which are not fussy about where they grow. You'll find plants like wood sorrel, with its sharp, sour taste; brambles and raspberries, which tolerate all but the densest shade; and wood avens, a ubiquitous scrap of a plant which seems to actively look for the cover of other plants.

Trees provide an important habitat for animals too, of course. The modern woods may not have the diversity of life of those of old, but you will catch sight of the odd skittish deer, perhaps just glimpsing the white tuft of its tail as it leaps away. Birdsong still fills the branches that stretch up to the sky, while the 'tap-tap-tap' of the woodpecker often echoes around. You'll see tiny treecreepers hopping up the bark of trees and squirrels darting off to bury their winter cache of nuts.

In the spring the woods cycle through the whites and blues of anemones and bluebells, before great pink-purple spikes of fox-gloves and willowherbs rise up. The reds of summer currants and raspberries follow, before the greens of the conifers contrast with the yellows, oranges and browns of the falling broadleaves.

Mushrooms

Although you will find some mushrooms all year round, the first major flush happens towards the end of summer. This is when you'll find highly sought-after boletus mushrooms, and bracket fungi like chicken of the woods which sprout from the trees like bright-orange Cornish pasties. This is quickly followed by a second flush, which can include another round of boletus; the reds, blacks and yellows of the *Russula* species; the tongue-like beefsteak; and delicate amethyst deceivers. Finally come the cold weather mushrooms, such as wood blewits and winter chante-relles. Although there is some crossover between the flushes and mushrooms can have a mind of their own, they do tend to follow these yearly cycles quite closely

I am often asked what the difference is between 'mushroom' and 'fungus'. Mushrooms are a type of fungus, but not all fungi are mushrooms. A fungus refers to a fungal organism; the yeast that helped make your bread is a type of fungus, as is the organism that formed the mould on the old uneaten crust. The mushrooms we see on the surface of the ground, or as a bracket on the side of a tree, are actually just one small part of a much larger fungal organism. Mushrooms, of varying shapes, sizes and colours, are merely the fruiting body, or the sex organs; their purpose is to

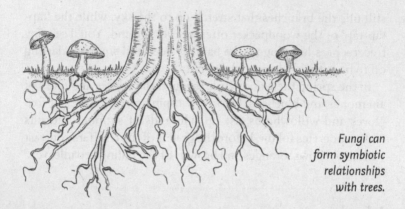

Fungi can form symbiotic relationships with trees.

spread spores and produce the next generation. Under the soil, within a tree or in the leaf litter is where the main organism is found. In some ways this main body is analogous to the roots of a tree. It comprises a mass of tube-like structures called hyphae, which are collectively known as the mycelium. In one teaspoon of forest soil there can be as much as forty miles of this mycelial thread. Occasionally you can spot this part of the organism looking like white hairs threading through compost heaps, or as thick black bootlaces on rotten wood.

The most common edible mushrooms grow in one of three ways: saprophytic, parasitic and symbiotic. Saprophytic means they feed on dead wood or leaf litter. Wood blewits are a good example, and if

Tree	Oak	Beech	Birch
Mushroom	Beefsteak, chicken of the woods, chanterelle, cep (*Boletus edulis*), hen of the woods, wood blewit, wood mushroom	Cep (*Boletus edulis*), hedgehog, chanterelle, oyster mushroom, wood mushroom	Cep (*Boletus edulis*), chanterelle, birch bolete

pulled rather than cut (cutting does the least damage to the organism) a clump of leaf litter will come up with mushroom, threaded together with strands of mycelium. Parasitic fungi live on, and often kill, their host tree – honey fungus is a good example. Symbiotic fungi have a much more benign presence, establishing a more balanced relationship with the tree, where the two organisms can be mutually beneficial to each other.

Some species of fungi can have particularly long-lasting symbiotic relationships with certain trees. Symbiotic mycorrhizal fungi, for example, form a coating around the roots of a tree. This coating helps to 'feed' the tree, accessing nutrients such as phosphorus that are way beyond the normal reach of the tree's roots. In exchange, the tree 'gives' the fungi carbohydrates it cannot make for itself. Most of the year this goes on quite happily under the soil, with little to see above the ground.

Certain mushrooms prefer to grow near, on or under certain trees, such as the morel growing in the leaf litter of elm or the beefsteak growing from a fallen oak. These relationships have built up over hundreds of thousands of years and are as intricate and complex as the relationship between a bee and flower or a lion and a gazelle. The chart below shows a number of common trees and the common, easily identifiable, edible mushrooms you'll find nearby.

The mushroom is the means by which a fungus reproduces. Like most organisms, fungi reproduce either when conditions

Chestnut	Pine	Elm
Beefsteak, chicken of the woods, chestnut bolete (*Gyroporus castaneus*)	Cep (*Boletus edulis*), hedgehog fungus, chanterelle, cauliflower fungus	Morel, velvet shank

are just right, or in times of stress. Running out of territory is one such stress for the fungus and so it will 'fruit' or send up a mushroom as a response. So, rather than going on a wild goose chase expecting to find mushrooms deep in the forest interior, where conditions are uniformly the same, the forager should look in areas where there is some sort of change in territory and the mycelium is likely to run out of food. This can be in clearings within the wood, at the boundary between a forest and a field, or in areas where the species of tree changes, such as where a conifer woodland meets a deciduous one. Quite usefully for us, this boundary can also be the side of a footpath, so mushrooms can be easily stumbled upon when walking.

Timing is also important; most fungi prefer cool, damp conditions, such as those found after the autumn rains, when the heat of the summer subsides. This moisture, combined with a lowering of temperature, also gives the underground mycelium the signal to 'fruit'. The drop in temperature often coincides with an increase in stronger winds, which are just one mechanism that helps to spread the reproductive spores of a fungus far and wide (the other methods are via animals and insects, or thanks to splashing rain).[18]

Autumnal rains can give a sense of anticipation for the mushroom forager, as it is in the days after a heavy downpour, when the sun is out but the damp air still lingers in the trees, that the mushrooms begin to rise up through the leaf litter. During a dry Indian summer, the mycelium will remain deep underground where moisture is at its highest, refusing to expend unnecessary energy producing mushroom spores which will have a hard time germinating in the dry air.

However, even in dry weather there can be pockets of woodland that remain damp. Look for areas of low light, such as north-facing slopes, as these take time to lose their moisture. Areas close to rivers, culverts and drainage ditches may remain damp too. Changes in the leaf litter can also provide clues; small piles of leaves could be hiding emerging mushrooms. Over-management of woodland, such as removal of dead standing trees, can be very detrimental for fungi, as they prefer undisturbed habitat. So, although mushrooms will grow in managed or 'farmed' woods, these would not be my first port of call.

Before you rush out to pick all the mushrooms popping up in your local wood, remember that humans are not the only creatures who enjoy them – something that becomes all too apparent when you find half of your haul infested with maggots. It is good etiquette to take only what you need, especially if you have no means of preserving them, and to leave the largest (so it can spread its many spores) and the smallest (so it can grow for the next forager/ animal/maggot to find). Also, try to ID them on site using a good smartphone app (and further cross-referencing them when you get home), rather than taking home large numbers of poisonous or inedible mushrooms that you will later have to discard.

CEP, PENNY BUN, PORCINI, KING BOLETE
Boletus edulis

Season for picking: summer and autumn, first flush late summer/early September, often a second flush in October
Where to find them: Woodland interior and fringes, and close to trees, especially beech, birch, pine, spruce, occasionally oak
Main identifying features: bread roll-like cap, bulbous stem, white cross-hatch markings
Best use: risottos, soups or on toast
Not to be mistaken for: bitter bolete, devil's bolete

A patch of ceps is always my most thrilling find. They are as beautiful as they are delicious, with a tan-brown cap resembling a freshly cooked bread roll (hence the name penny bun). Rather than gills under the cap (think of the dark folds under a button mushroom), you'll see many white to yellow-olive pores, giving the impression of a sponge. These hundreds of pores release the reproductive spores of the mushroom. The penny bun's stalk is thick, bulbous and club-shaped, and the flesh will remain white when the mushroom is cut in two.

They can be mistaken for the bitter bolete, *Tylopilus felleus*, the scourge of all foraging baskets. To tell the difference, look for the mesh pattern on the stem. A bitter bolete will have a dark mesh pattern, whereas the cep has a white mesh. Once you have gone through all the other identifying characteristics, bite off a tiny piece of the flesh and work it in your mouth (but do not swallow it) – it should taste good, but if it is bitter or bad-tasting spit it out and move on.

Ceps are a gourmet mushroom served in expensive restaurants and sold for high prices on the open market both fresh and dried. They can range in size with the largest growing bigger than your head. They can rise in the same place year after year and most foragers keep their whereabouts a closely guarded secret. Although they are said to favour oak and beech, I have found them in established mixed woodland under both hardwoods and conifers, and in Scotland they are found mostly in conifer woodland.

Unfortunately, the maggots of fungal gnats (*Sciaridae* spp.) love boletus mushrooms almost as much as we do, and all too often you'll find what appears to be a prime specimen is a nursery for maggots. Get out early and often in the season, which can be as early as August, to catch these mushrooms at their best. The gills can become slimy in older specimens. If this is the case, peel off the gills (nine times out of ten the rest of the mushroom will be fine), which contain the reproducing spores, and throw them around the woods as you walk to ensure future crops.

Many other members of the boletus family are edible and excellent to eat, but others are poisonous. Those which can cause you harm tend to have red or pink colours on them somewhere, such as the evocatively named devil's bolete (*Boletus satanas*). An additional sign you should steer clear is that the mushrooms will stain blue or blue-green when cut, like the dotted stem bolete (*B. luridiformis*) and the oldrose bolete (*B. rhodopurpureus*) – both of which also contain some red.

In mainland Europe, most notably France and Italy, there are a number of mushrooms in the boletus family that are every bit as prized as *B. edulis*. Take the summer cep (*B. reticulatus*) for example, which comes up earlier in the season and is also found in the UK. There's also the dark cep (*B aereus*), which is both rarer and smaller than *B. edulis*. And there's the pine tree cep (*B. pinophilus* or *B. pinicola*) which, as the name suggests, grows near pine trees.

After the first summer flush, if conditions are right, ceps may make a second appearance in October and occasionally through to November. Although most boletus mushrooms will grow in the interior of a forest, the best places to look are the fringes; close to paths, clearings or within the first few trees.

FORAGER'S TIP

The cep is believed to grow in close association with the fly agaric (*Amanita mascaria*), the miller (*Clitopilus prunulus*) and the peppery bolete (*Chalciporus piperatus*).[19] The latter two come up around the same time, so if you find these it is likely the *Boletus edulis* is nearby. Fly agaric, the infamous red toadstool with white spots so often depicted in fairy tales, tends to come up after the cep. I mark the location of fly agaric mushrooms using GPS on my smartphone and return to the exact location the following year.

PREPARATION AND USE

No matter how you decide to cook boletus mushrooms you won't be disappointed by their rich, nutty, umami flavour. You can simply fry them in butter and serve them on toast, but to really allow the flavours to build they are best slow cooked in risottos and soups, to which they add a warm autumnal richness.

To dry your harvest, cut into thin slices and place in a dehydrator or on a convection radiator, then store in a sealed container ready to be rehydrated when you need them. When dried, the rich and musky flavour of ceps really comes out beautifully.

I also like to powder a proportion of my boletus mushrooms (of all kinds) to make a delicious umami sprinkle. Once the mushrooms are dehydrated, work them into a powder using a coffee grinder or pestle and mortar. You can use this mushroom powder on its own or add equal amounts of powdered seaweeds, such as gutweed and kelp (see page 384), along with dried wild garlic flakes. You can use this to enhance all kinds of dishes, from soups and stews to ravioli parcels. You can even use it in place of parmesan.

CHANTERELLE, GIROLLE
Cantharellus cibarius

Season for picking: late summer to autumn
Where to find them: mixed, conifer and deciduous woodland
Main identifying features: yellow trumpet shape with ridge-like gills
Best use: cooked in risottos, soups or on toast
Not to be mistaken for: false chanterelle, Jack-o-lantern

Chanterelles are perhaps the most prized symbiotic fungi. They grow in association with hardwood trees, especially oak, poplar, beech and birch, along with conifers such as pine and spruce. A relatively small mushroom (growing up to 8 cm/3 inches), they are mostly yellow in colour and trumpet shaped.

The name 'chanterelle' is given to several edible mushrooms in the same species. The most common and popular is the *Cantharellus cibarius*, an egg-yolk-yellow mushroom with pale-white flesh inside. It can be easily confused with a false chanterelle, *Hygrophoropsis aurantiaca*, which may cause stomach upsets, and it can also be mistaken for the poisonous Jack-o-lantern

(*Omphalotus olearius*), which is rare in Europe but more common in North America. However, there are a few straightforward tell-tale signs to distinguish them all from each other.

Chanterelles do not have the straight gills of most mushrooms but rather primitive or proto-gills, which fork towards the cap. Their gills are more reminiscent of the folds of an air filter. Push hard with your finger and they will rub off, revealing the pale flesh of the cap. The gills of the false chanterelle and the Jack-o-lantern act like true gills, running straight to the cap, and can be hard to break off. The smell is the next giveaway – everything about the scent of a fresh chanterelle says 'eat me'. It has a fruity, almondy, pleasant mushroom scent with hints of apricot. The poisonous Jack-o-lantern grows in clumps, often on stumps or fallen wood, like a honey fungus, rather than the socially distanced chanterelle, which grows in scattered colonies.

There is further confusion between the chanterelle and the winter chanterelle (*Craterellus tubaeformis*). However, this is more of a linguistic problem than one of identification. In France they call the chanterelle (*Cantharellus cibarius)* a *girolle* and the winter chanterelle (*Craterellus tubaeformis*) a *chanterelle*. To add to the confusion, in America the *Craterellus tubaeformis* is known as a yellow leg, on account of its yellow stalk. Whatever you call if, it is a great-tasting mushroom, and has the same proto-gills as *Cantharellus cibarius* – but unlike this mushroom, it can be dried without losing texture or taste.

PREPARATION AND USE

Chanterelles have a beautiful, earthy, mushroomy taste, and partner well with tarragon and parsley. They need to be cooked for a little longer than most mushrooms and make a perfect addition to risottos, soups and pâtés. Or, simply fry them in butter and garlic for around 8 minutes and serve on a slice of toast alongside a poached egg. If you want to preserve chanterelles, pickle them in a lightly spiced vinegar (they become rubbery in texture when dried).

	Chanterelle (*Cantharellus* cibarius)	False chanterelle	Jack-o-Lantern
Smell	Sweet apricot or almond	Mushroomy – slightly unpleasant to some	Unpleasant
Where it grows	Grows singularly (not clump-forming) near trees. More common in broadleaf but also grows in coniferous/pine woods and mixed woodland	Singularly – very common in coniferous/pine woods	On stumps and roots in a clump
Glow in the dark?	No	No	Yes
Gills	Pale folds rather than true gills, like an air filter. Forks towards the cap	Orange, true gills – straight all the way to cap	True gills – clearly defined and straight
Cap	Same colour all over cap. Frays at edge	Dark spot in the centre of cap in young specimens	Sometimes dark spot in centre
Flesh	Pale flesh inside	Pale with streaks of yellow-to-orange flesh inside	Orange flesh inside

COMMON PUFFBALL AND STUMP PUFFBALL
Lycoperdon spp.

Season for picking: late summer/autumn
Where to find them: in woodlands of all kinds
Main identifying features: golf ball size and shape, no gills or pores
Best use: fried in butter or cooked in Asian soups
Not to be mistaken for: egg-stage *Amanita* mushrooms

Puffballs are often among the first mushrooms attempted by novice foragers as they are extremely easy to identify if you follow a few simple guidelines. The most recognisable is the giant puffball, *Calvatia gigantea*, a football-sized mushroom which grows on grassland (see page 219). The much smaller common puffball, *Lycoperdon perlatum*, and stump puffball, *Lycoperdon pyriforme*, are common woodland species, both around the size of a golf ball. Some species, including the common puffball, are attached to a small stalk.

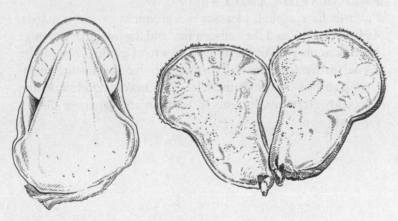

An Amanita *(left) at egg stage alongside
a cross-section of a puffball (right).*

Always pick them young. Older ones may have already started sporing, which will be obvious by the saggy flesh and clouds of dark spores that appear when you poke them. Those about to spore should be rejected too; cut them open, and if the interior has any yellow, brown or even black, the puffball is either reaching maturity or it is an inedible earth ball. Either way you do not want it with your eggs in the morning. Instead, the fleshy inside of the puffball should be a uniform white or cream. If you spot a small or embryonic mushroom inside, or even a small arc, you should discard immediately as this is not a puffball at all but may be the egg stage of the deadly poisonous *Amanita* family masquerading as one.

Lycoperdon, the name of the genus to which the common and stump puffballs belong, translates to 'wolf fart', proving that taxonomists do have a sense of humour. As puffballs lack external gills, their spores are formed inside the body of the mushroom until released as smoke-like puffs (hence the name) when the mushroom is fully mature.

PREPARATION AND USE
Puffballs have a mild, pleasant mushroom taste and a marshmallow texture, and they absorb fats and flavours like a sponge so cook in olive oil or butter with plenty of garlic. They can be served on their own but I like to mix with stronger-tasting mushrooms, such as ceps or chanterelles. They make a good substitute for paddy straw mushrooms in Chinese and Japanese dishes, especially soups.

WOOD BLEWIT
Lepista nuda

Season for picking: autumn and early winter
Where to find them: woodlands, hedges
Main identifying features: streaky lilac stem
Best use: cooked in pies, risottos, soups
Not to be mistaken for: webcap mushroom

Warning: needs to be cooked well before consumption.

Wood blewits are a late-season mushroom, coming up as the nights start to turn chilly. Although most common in woodland, they can also be found in hedges, back gardens and meadows. They are a saprophytic mushroom, feeding from the leaf litter, so should be cut rather than pulled to avoid disturbing the mycelia. The leaves from which they feed can also be an effective camouflage and parting unnatural-looking piles can pay dividends. However, at the right time of year, during the mid to late autumn, the wood blewit can be found in such large numbers it is unlikely you will miss it. You might find more than you can feasibly carry home.

Young specimens have a distinctive blueish-lilac/violet colour to the cap which fades to a pale brown when they age. The gills are closely packed and lilac in colour when young, then fading much paler. The stems have streaks of violet and are a little fibrous. They have a unique, sweet and almost floral scent.

FORAGER'S TIP
It is important to take a spore print (see page 244) when picking this mushroom for the first time as it can resemble the poisonous and unpleasant-smelling bruising webcap (*Cortinarius purpurascens*). The spores of the wood blewit should be

off-white to pale pink, and not a rusty brown like those of the webcap.

PREPARATION AND USE

Wood blewits should never be consumed raw, so be sure to cook them thoroughly before eating them. To be on the safe side, bring them to a rolling boil and discard the water before preparing your preferred way. For an unfortunate few they can also cause an allergic reaction, including profuse sweating and gastric upset. When eating for the first time, cook and consume only a small amount, no more than a quarter to half of a small cap, gradually increasing the quantity on each serving.

Despite all the caveats the wood blewit is an excellent-tasting mushroom, lending itself well to pasta dishes and risottos. It pairs well with tarragon, especially when using a few sprigs of the herb to flavour a mushroom pâté. As it's a substantial mushroom it works well in stroganoffs and pies as the focus of a meal.

HONEY FUNGUS
Armillaria spp.

Season for picking: autumn
Where to find them: dead and dying wood
Main identifying features: bootlace mycelium
Best use: miso soup or risotto, in place of shiitake mushroom
Not to be mistaken for: funeral bell or sulphur tuft

Warning: needs to be cooked well before consumption.

A particularly nasty parasitic fungi, the honey fungus strikes fear into the heart of gardeners and arborists. The mycelia of this mushroom form thick black strands, often nicknamed 'bootlaces', which spread through the living tissue of a tree between the bark and the hardwood interior. These bootlaces starve the tree of essential nutrients, and eventually kill it. Like a hungry predator, the fungus will then actively seek out its next victim by means of an underground mycelial network to find the next weakest tree. Then the whole cycle begins again.

Interestingly, when this mycelium links up with another genetically identical network of honey fungus, the two colonies can fuse together forming an even larger organism. This process has led to some monstrously large specimens, such as the *Armillaria solidipes*, a honey fungus in the Malheur National Forest in Oregon which has grown to 3.4 miles (or 5.5 kilometres) across, covering an area of 2,385 acres. It is estimated that this fungus could be anywhere between 2,400 to 8,650 years old.

It is important to identify the honey fungus correctly as it does have potentially dangerous lookalikes, such as the yellow sulphur tuft (*Hypholoma fasciculare*) and *Galerina marginata*, more commonly known as the funeral bell for obvious reasons. To be certain you have a honey fungus, be sure it is sprouting from dead or dying wood and is growing in dense clusters rather than smaller groups. Look for brown flecks on the yellowish-to-brown cap and a dark spot in the centre, and also look for a ring rather than a membraneous skirt around the stem. It is important to note that it has a white spore print and white gills. Honey fungus is also a tough old mushroom, not at all fragile, unlike other mushroom species which break at the slightest touch.

PREPARATION AND USE
Depending on which mushroom guide you read, the honey fungus is described as edible, inedible, mildly poisonous and 'known to cause gastric upset in some'. The truth is that some happily eat it with no ill effects and others become violently ill. The evidence for why this may be is vague; it may be a case of misidentification or that certain species or even sub-species are more edible than others. So as with all mushrooms it is always

best to cross-reference with as many guides as possible to make sure you have got the right thing.

Having said all that, honey fungus can be worth it: it has an excellent flavour, much like shiitake. I would advise you to begin by consuming a small morsel of the (cooked) mushroom first, and if you have no ill effects after twenty-four hours, try a little more. Never eat them raw – heat destroys otherwise toxic compounds, and even common commercial mushrooms, such as the shitake, can have unpleasant side effects when consumed raw. Honey fungus should really be boiled for at least fifteen minutes, so try it in miso soups, risottos and other dishes that benefit from an extended cooking time.

....

WOOD SORREL
Oxalis acetosella

Season for picking: all year
Where to find them: under trees
Main identifying features: clover-like leaves
Best use: salads, or as an addition to dairy-based dips
Not to be mistaken for: clover

Wood sorrel is a favourite plant among the children who come on my wild food walks. They love its sharp-sour, tangy taste, which is refreshingly lemony or similar to that of grape skins.

It's a low-lying green plant with three small leaflets, which are split in two by a central 'fold'. Superficially, it looks like clover; however, on closer inspection, the two plants are very different. Wood sorrel has heart-shaped leaves and an open, five-petalled white or yellow flower, quite different from the clustered flower of a clover. The habitats of the two plants differ too. Clover will inhabit open fields and grassland, especially improved pasture. Wood sorrel, on the other hand, is found in shade under trees, most often in woodland. Another tell-tale sign is wood sorrel's habit of closing its leaves at night or in harsh weather conditions.

It has been suggested that the original Irish shamrock, which St Patrick used to explain the holy trinity to 'heathen' Celts, may have been wood sorrel rather than clover.[20] Their Irish Gaelic names are very similar – *seamróg* for young clover and *seamsóg* for wood sorrel – so it does seem feasible that the two could have been mixed up.

PREPARATION AND USE
Pluck the leaves by hand and take home in a small plastic bag to keep them fresh. Wood sorrel's lemony flavour adds a sharp top note to any mixed salad. It can be used to flavour yoghurt or cottage cheese. I like to add mint, finely sliced cucumber, a pinch of salt and a twist of black pepper to a yoghurt and sorrel leaf base and use it as a dip for pita or tortilla chips.

WOOD AVENS, HERB BENNET
Geum urbanum

Season for picking: all year but best in autumn or spring
Where to find them: forest floor, hedgerows, under trees and shaded areas in gardens, parks and edgeland
Main identifying features: Spiky seed heads
Best uses: Leaves as greens, root as a clove-like spice

Wood avens or herb bennet grow in snatches of light on the forest floor or under hedgerows. Its leaves have a large three-lobed toothed leaflet at the tip, with smaller leaflets growing either side of the stem down to the base. The plant is most recognisable in the spring and into the summer, when it produces yellow star-shaped flowers with five petals, similar to a buttercup but with prominent green sepals (sepals are petal-like, normally green parts of the flower which protect the flower bud). The flowers give way to small, hooked seeds or burs.

Geum rivale or water avens are a closely related plant growing in wet soils. They can be used in the same way as wood avens but differ in appearance as they have a lovely little bell-shaped flower, the colour of apricot, which pokes out from an enlarged purple sepal.

PREPARATION AND USE

During the winter, wood avens are one of the few plants in leaf, making it a useful wilted green to compliment a poached egg when there is little else around. However, it is the root which has been prized as a spice since

Once familiar with the plant, you will see wood avens everywhere.

medieval times, possibly even earlier. Long before the spice trade brought us exotic flavours from the East, these spindly roots were a source of eugenol, the aromatic compound found in cloves.

Although the scent of wood avens is similar to that of cloves, it has a unique smoky flavour which really shines when it is baked along with fruit. It brings a Christmassy warmth and beautiful smokiness to apple dishes, though it takes around a half a teaspoon of chopped and washed roots to make the equivalent strength of a single clove so use it liberally. Dried roots intensify in flavour.

To combine wood avens with baked apple, start off by carving out the core of an apple. Wash the wood avens roots with a scrubbing brush and try to peel the skin from larger roots by scraping your fingernails or a knife over them, before chopping them roughly. Fill the well of the apples with honey, and around a teaspoon of the chopped roots. You can also coat the apples with honey and more chopped roots for more flavour and sprinkle them with cinnamon. Bake in a moderate-to-hot oven until the apple is soft (30–45 minutes) or, if you're outdoors, wrap it all up in foil and bake on an open fire. The apples are delicious on their own or served up with ice cream.

PIGNUT
Conopodium majus

Season for picking: early spring
Where to find them: edge of woodlands, meadows, pasture
Main identifying features: wispy frond leaves
Best use: as a crunchy snack, in salads, roasted or boiled
Not to be mistaken for: poison hemlock, the (edible) hickory nut and an unrelated plant which is also called pignut

Above the soil, pignuts have wispy fronds for leaves, like a rather sparsely topped young carrot (they are members of the same family). Under the ground, the plant produces a pleasant, nutty-tasting, bulbous tuber at the end of its delicate thin stem. The pignut prefers the margins of a forest to the interior so for the best chance of finding one, follow the edge of the woods. You will also find them in meadows and grazed pasture, most commonly on organic or unsprayed grassland.

Finding a pignut plant is only half the fun. To unearth the tiny tuber, follow its stem all the way into the soil, anything between 3 and 13 cm (1 and 5 inches), being careful not to break it. Then, just before you reach the nut, the plant employs one more form of botanical subterfuge: the stem takes a 90-degree turn, but it is impossible to know in which direction. Rather than guesswork, it can be easier to dig all around and under the plant and then search through the soil for the stem.

Early spring, before the plant flowers, is the best time to find the pignut, when the tuber is swollen with the energy it needs to grow for the following year. As with all wild roots, ensure you have the landowner's permission before digging. Pignuts are also rather uncommon, so should be considered a rare treat rather than a staple carbohydrate. To give them a helping hand, once they go to seed in the late summer, you can scatter the seeds around the local area in places free from competition with other plants. With any luck, what was rare will become more commonplace again.

PREPARATION AND USE

Pignuts have a starchy, nutty flavour, a cross between a hazelnut and a potato. You can normally rub the dirt away from a pignut easily enough and eat it raw, which can be a tasty snack when out in the woods in spring. However, they really come into their own lightly boiled until softened and served with butter.

VIOLET, COMMON VIOLET AND DOG VIOLET
Viola odorata and V. riviniana

Season for picking: spring
Where to find them: woodlands and shaded areas
Main identifying features: heart-shaped leaves
Best use: leaves in salads, flowers in salads, cakes and ice creams

Violets, with their heart-shaped leaves and delicate flowers, are a real treat to find on a bright spring day. They have small, violet-coloured flowers with five overlapping petals, the lowest of which has white centre with thick, darker purple veins. There are two kinds of violet: the common violet, *Viola odorata*, which despite its name is the less common of the two, and the dog violet, *V. riviniana*. They are indistinguishable from each other save for the scent, which is light and fragrant on the violet but completely lacking on the dog violet.

When Napoleon was exiled to the island of Elba, he reportedly said he would return in violet season (they flower from mid-spring to the early summer). For supporters of Napoleon, the flower and the colour violet became a secret symbol for their loyalty to their former emperor.

PREPARATION AND USE

The leaves and flowers of both types of violet can be eaten in salads. They are tasty and sometimes even a little floral (especially *V. odorata*) but they can also be a little tough. It is unlikely you would be able to pick them in any great number and nor should you, as they provide valuable nectar for woodland-dwelling bees. However, a sprinkling of the flowers makes a colourful addition to salads or, once frosted, as decorations for cakes, ice cream or sorbets.

FROSTED VIOLET FLOWERS

Frosted violets give an added touch of class to cakes and desserts. They are simple to make – all you need are the flowers themselves along with a little egg white and caster sugar.

1. Beat an egg white and gently paint the violet flower with the mixture.
2. Carefully dab the whole bloom with fine caster sugar.
3. Leave to dry. At room temperature this will take between 12 and 36 hours, but the process can be sped up by placing in a dehydrator or a very low oven for between 30 minutes and an hour.
4. Check occasionally to see if dried solid.

WILD RASPBERRY
Rubus idaeus

Season for picking: mid-June to late August
Where to find them: woodland, allotments, gardens
Main identifying features: smaller than cultivated raspberry
Best use: sweet snack, desserts

Wild raspberries look very much like their cultivated counterparts only usually a little smaller. The flavour is identical to that of a freshly grown garden raspberry but can feel far sweeter after a day walking in the woods. I've found them as late as mid-September in Scotland, but they are more common from mid-June to late August. They grow in woodlands and as escapees close to allotment sites and gardens. A similar-looking edible berry, the aptly named thimbleberry (*Rubus parviflourus*), grows in the Midwest and western US. Americans may also find a black raspberry, which looks like a blackberry from the outside but has a hollow core.

We humans have a long-standing taste for this sweet wild fruit. Incredibly, raspberry seeds were found at Ohalo II, a 23,000-year-old archaeological site on the south-west shores of the Sea of Galilee. It has been suggested that the settled, hunter-gatherer society who lived there may have loved raspberries so much they dried and stored them for year-round use, making them one of the oldest known preserved fruits, along with figs.[21]

PREPARATION AND USE
I think wild raspberries are best eaten straight from the plant, but if you make it home with some, they are a delicious addition to muffins or yoghurt, and can be made into sorbets and ice cream just as you would with cultivated raspberries. They do make a jam but they tend to have more seeds than a cultivated raspberry, so passing them through a piece of muslin to make a jelly can work better.

CHAPTER TEN

Conifer Woodland

ALTHOUGH I GREW up in a typical English housing estate, as my parents' house backed onto land with a tree preservation order, we ended up with our own tiny pine forest at the end of our garden.

When we were young, my friends and I played hide and seek or built secret dens among the trees. Pine cones became make-believe hand grenades as battles raged on between rival factions of Action Men. Then when we became teenagers, we lit fires and shared sneaky cigarettes, beers and laughter, far from the prying eyes of our disapproving parents. These tall, grey pines are so ingrained in my psyche that if I close my eyes, I can still clearly see the detail of their scaly, knotted trunks and smell their strong resinous scent.

Conifers are ancient trees; they have been around since the time of the dinosaurs. Unlike most broadleaf trees, they do not have a true flower or blossom. Most conifers are evergreen, keeping their needle-like or scale-like leaves all year round. In pagan times clippings of evergreens were brought into the home to celebrate the solstice, a practice that continues with the wreaths and Christmas trees of today. The name comes from the Latin words *conus*, meaning 'cone', and *ferre*, meaning 'to bear' or 'to carry', as all conifers bear some form of cone. These range from the pea-size, scaly cypress cones to the overgrown ones of the stone pine, which can grow to sizes larger than your head. Even the yew has a cone, but it is fleshy and red like a berry.

Some cones are male and some cones are female. The female cones tend to be the dry and woody 'fruit' of the tree – the scales of these open up to reveal the seed, remaining closed before the seed is ripe. As kids we were told the cones of our pines could tell the weather and would only open on a sunny day. The male cones are quite different; on some species of pine they resemble tiny clusters of slightly fluffy corn on the cob. They can be yellow, red or purple and they are generally soft rather than woody, producing clouds of pollen, mostly in the spring.

Conifers include a wide variety of trees, such as the fragrant cedar, upright cypresses, towering redwoods, raggedy junipers, stately yews and the commonly planted spruces, firs and pines that make up much of the planted conifer forests of the world. In the UK there are only three native conifers: yew, juniper and, the only pine tree native to Britain, the Scots pine. Native conifer woodlands are rare in the UK, but there are patches of native pines in Scotland, referred to as the Caledonian Forest and stretching from the Atlantic coast to beyond the Great Glen. These forests support a wide diversity of life: there are spongy mosses underfoot, lichen hangs from branches like tinsel, and at the end of summer there are the vivid white blooms of the rare lady's tresses, peppering the forest floor like confetti. Birds and animals seek a refuge among these trees, which are often considered one of the last remaining true wildernesses of Britain. There are majestic golden eagles, shy red squirrels and pine martens, and the elusive European wildcat.

Down in southern England you can still walk amongst the shade of tangled, centuries-old yews in fragments of ancient woodland. Juniper, a slow growing shrub or small tree, grows both as an understory plant in native pine forests of Scotland and as a scrub on moors and chalk lowlands elsewhere. Aromatic, pine-flavoured juniper berries are mainly used to flavour gin, but can also give jams and pickles an extra layer of flavour.

Elsewhere in the world, native conifer woodlands stretch for hundreds of miles as vast areas of wilderness. In the temperate rainforests of the Pacific Northwest of America, stretching from California, up to Vancouver Island and beyond, mountain lions, wolves, bears and bobcats roam among conifers like the Sitka spruce, western hemlock, Douglas fir and western red cedar. To the far north of the globe, there is a band of boreal woodland, a vast conifer-rich forest which makes up a third of the world's trees and covers the northern parts of Russia, Alaska, Canada, Scandinavia and Scotland. This huge forest, known as taiga in Russia, does have some broadleaf trees, notably birch, but pines dominate. This is untouched wilderness, supporting rare animal and plant life. I've seen first-hand the size the wildlife can get to in these primeval forests after being within metres of elk, or moose as they're known in North America, in the far north of Norway. At ground level, the cranberry-related cowberry follows the line of boreal woodland around the earth. For the Sami people of the far north of Scandinavia and Russia, these berries would have provided valuable vitamins in a meat-rich diet. And berries are not the only edible in the conifer wood: lush springtime spruce and fir tips are deliciously citrusy and pine needles make an aromatic, vitamin C-rich tea.

In the northern reaches of Eurasia, notably in Eastern Europe and into Russia, mushroom picking is deeply embedded in the culture. Historically this was a social affair, a chance to catch up with neighbours; groups of women would thread mushrooms on long strings and hang them up to dry or pickle them in huge jars. In both southern England and the Scottish Highlands, I have found conifer plantations with enough mushrooms to rival those of the Russian wilderness. When the going is good, it is possible to come home with bags full without making a dent in the mushroom population. Sometimes the biggest problem you face is not finding them but what to do with them once you've brought them home.

Like so much of foraging, finding mushrooms in conifer woodland isn't about luck, it's about timing and persistence, which in time will lead to a knowledge of the landscape. Find a seldom-walked wood and visit often. You will learn when to give in and when to keep searching. And once you do find the perfect woodland, keep it to yourself (or just tell me!)

SCOTS PINE
Pinus sylvestris

Season for picking: all year
Where to find them: parks and gardens, also woodland in Britain (especially Scotland), northern Europe and Russia, occasionally in North America
Main identifying features: two-needled leaves; older trees have a peachy-orange colouration on the upper trunk
Best use: needles infused in teas; cold remedies; nuts
Not to be mistaken for: yew, Norfolk Island pine, ponderosa pine, lodgepole pine

---

Warning: do not consume pine needles if pregnant.

I first saw a wild eagle on the edge of a Scots pine woodland in Glen Affric in the Highlands of Scotland. It was perched on a fence post among the grey-brown scaly trunked trees with their blue-green needles. My heart stopped; it was a magnificent bird, nearly a metre in height, eyeing its surroundings for prey. When it heard me coming, the trance was broken and it took off – huge, silent, brown-and-white wings outstretched – and disappeared off into the wilderness.

Scots pine is one of only three native conifers and the only native pine tree found in the UK. The distinctive smell of the Scots pine is thanks to the presence of forty-four different odour compounds – it is a clean, citrusy, resinous scent that I have always found to be both heady and relaxing. A study in Poland found that walking in a pine-rich woodland could reduce negative emotions such as anger and depression, while lowering blood pressure and leading to more positive feelings of well-being.[22]

Scots pine grows as a dominant species in woodlands throughout Scotland or in more mixed woodlands with native hardwood and planted softwood trees. In Europe and Russia other pines join the conifer forests, including Swiss pine, European black pine and Siberian pine. To tell Scots pine apart from other pines, look up. On the older trees, you should see a reddish or peachy-orange colouration on the upper trunk. Scots pine also have two-needled, twisted blue-green 'leaves' and slim 5–8 cm (2–3 inch) cones.

PREPARATION AND USE

Although you can't eat them, the needles of the Scots pine can be infused in hot water for tea, or vinegar, which makes a good salad dressing. The longer you allow the needles to infuse, the deeper the flavour. Just be sure to remove the needles before consuming as they can be nasty things to get stuck in your throat. The tea should be allowed to infuse overnight, the vinegar for around three months.

FORAGER'S TIP

The needles are all too often out of reach and, short of leaning a long ladder against the tree or hiring a cherry picker, there is no way of getting to them. But if you visit the trees after high winds, you'll find more than enough broken branches for tea or vinegar.

The needles are at their best during the spring when the new growth emerges but they can be used at any time of the year. Be very careful not to mix up your pine needles with toxic lookalikes. There is at least one poisonous conifer in the UK, the yew (see page 87). The exotic-looking Norfolk Island pine, with its upturned, fern-like needles, is also highly toxic, and there have been safety concerns regarding the consumption of various other species of pine too (with 111 species of pine worldwide there isn't room to list them all here). The Scots pine is safe to consume infrequently and in moderation, but avoid any pine trees with needles smaller than your finger. Steer clear too of long straight pines such as the ponderosa pine (*Pinus ponderosa*) and the Lodgepole pine (*P. contorta* var. *latifolia*), as these may contain toxic compounds. You should also avoid pine needles if pregnant.

PINE NEEDLE COLD REMEDY

This simple cold remedy is high in vitamin C and with added honey it helps to soothe sore throats.

YOU WILL NEED:

- 50 g (2 oz) pine needles, washed, brown ends removed and cut into 2.5 cm (1 inch) pieces with scissors
- 1 l (4 cups) of apple juice
- 2 tbsp honey
- 2 tbsp lemon juice
- A generous pinch of cinnamon

METHOD:

1. Bring the apple juice to the boil and add all the ingredients except the pine needles.
2. Take off the boil and leave to cool for around five minutes.
3. Add the pine needles.
4. Leave the mixture overnight, with a lid on.
5. Strain and use immediately, or bottle and refrigerate.
6. Serve cold or warm with an optional nip of whisky or dark rum (the latter won't help with the cold but it might cheer you up!)

Pine nuts

All pine trees produce a seed in the form of a pine nut. Although all pine nuts are edible, most including the Scots pine are too tiny to be worth the effort. The rich, creamy, pale-yellow pine nuts which are often served on pasta come from a Mediterranean native called the stone pine, *Pinus pinea*. This distinctive-looking tree has an upper canopy shaped like a flattened broccoli floret and produces broad, flat-based cones. Its nuts, much like a hazel or a walnut, are housed within a hard shell. These beanlike shells sit on cupped grooves, in pairs, tucked into the base of the cone's many scales. They can be accessed only when the nut matures and the pine cone opens to release the seed, when the weather is warm and dry. Outside of southern Europe, the stone pine can be found in parks, gardens and arboretums.

Worldwide, there are twenty species of pine tree with nuts worth eating. In Europe, aside from the stone pine you might also find the Swiss pine, *P. cembra*, and in North America the most highly regarded are the Colorado pinyon (otherwise known as the two-needled pinyon or *P. edulis*), the single-leaf pinyon (*P. monophylla*) and the Mexican pinyon (*P. cembroides*). Although most cones are full of nuts, they can be tough to remove. You can try pulling the nuts out with pliers or you can roast the cone and then bash it with a hammer to release them.

Pine nuts have a nutty taste and a creamy texture, much like a cashew only with a superior, cleaner flavour. They are delicious toasted and sprinkled onto a salad, on top of pizzas or on pasta. They are an important ingredient in pesto and make a sublime ice cream.

All pines produce an edible seed.

SITKA SPRUCE
Picea sitchensis

Season for picking: spring
Where to find them: plantation woodlands worldwide, native to Pacific Northwest of America
Main identifying features: like a Christmas tree with flattened, prickly, blue-green needles
Best use: spruce tip ice cream
Not to be mistaken for: yew

The Sitka spruce's original home is the Pacific shores of North America, where it grows in large forests from Oregon to Alaska. But it is also the most common plantation tree in Europe, representing more than half of Ireland's tree cover and over a quarter of the UK's. These statistics come to life when you visit huge plantations such as the Kielder Forest, close to the Scottish border in Northumberland. Here uniform, straight trunks stand a regimented distance apart and the trees seem to go on for ever. On a misty November morning, these woods have the feel of the Scandinavian forests of dark fairy tales.

In their native Pacific Northwest Sitka spruces have been known to reach over 90 metres (295 feet) tall, but plantation trees are generally cut long before they reach anything like this size. To identify a Sitka tree, look for broad, Christmas tree-like plants with flattened, sharp, blue-green leaves. Sitkas have an uncomfortable prickle when you squeeze on the branches, in contrast to the softer foliage of firs. The leaves have a little woody stub and each group of leaves has a larger woody stalk. They are mostly planted in areas of high rainfall as they do not cope well in dry lowlands.

Historically, the Sitka was a significant tree for many of the First Nation and Native American groups indigenous to the Pacific Northwest. In the Great Bear Rainforest, which covers a stretch of land between Vancouver Island and Alaska and is dominated by Sitka spruce and western red cedar, a rare genetic defect has meant one in ten black bears are born with white fur. These white black bears, called spirit bears, were special creatures to the First Nation Kitasoo and Gitga'at who told stories of a raven who turned the world from snow and ice to green, leaving some bears white to remind the people of the frigid past when the world was covered in snow. They would chew the pitch (the hardened tree sap or resin) of Sitkas like a chewing gum, and used a decoction (concentrated liquid from boiling plant matter) of the branches and tips to treat all kinds of ailments including constipation, rheumatism and even gonorrhoea. The inner bark was sometimes eaten fresh or it could be dried, mixed with berries and made into cakes.

Spruce needles contain large amounts of vitamin C, something local populations relied on for survival. In 1536 French explorer Jacques Cartier and his crew were all suffering badly from scurvy. When the ship's crew found themselves stuck on Canada's frozen Saint Lawrence River, Cartier noticed the local population making a tea from Sitka needles. After copying the locals and drinking this tea, his crew were all cured within four to six days.[23]

PREPARATION AND USE

Although the inner bark of Sitka spruce is technically edible, removal of it can damage the tree so in most situations I would not advise you eat it, especially in a public plantation. However, if you own the tree, or are unlucky enough to find yourself in a survival situation, it can be a valuable source of carbohydrate.

To prepare, dig a knife into the bark until you reach the tough inner core. Then, score a series of lines to make a square or rectangle shape in the bark and peel away the tougher outer bark, leaving the sliver of light, living tissue which sits between the inner core and outer bark. This can be eaten raw, but it is better to boil it, fry it in oil or wrap it around a stick and cook it on a fire.

However, it is the fresh green shoots which grow as little, lighter-green extensions from the tips of the branches in springtime that are the best part of a Sitka spruce to eat. Pick a few shoots from a wide selection of trees, rather than just stripping one. The shoots have a tangy, citrus, resinous flavour and can be eaten raw or infused in liquid (water, milk or even hot chocolate). You can also infuse them in yoghurt, mix them into smoothies, make them into ice cream or pickle them in sweetened and spiced vinegar.

Look for the edible green tips in the spring.

It isn't just the Sitka spruce that has edible tips in the springtime. The Norway spruce (*Picea abies*), white spruce (*P. glauca*) and black spruce (*P. mariana*) have all been used as food by both modern foragers and indigenous groups. The tips of the sweet-smelling Douglas fir (*Pseudotsuga menziesii*) have a mild, tangy flavour which goes really well with yoghurt. Just be sure of a positive ID and do not confuse with the toxic yew, cypress or cedar trees.

SITKA SPRUCE ICE CREAM

Spruce tips have a wonderful resinous, citrusy flavour somewhere between bay and lemon which pairs beautifully with anything sweet and creamy, especially ice cream. I've made this recipe versatile to suit those with a lactose intolerance or those who follow vegan or vegetarian diets. The ice cream is best when eaten fresh but if serving from frozen, leave it to thaw a little before serving.

YOU WILL NEED:

- 15–20 Sitka spruce tips (you can use Norway spruce as an alternative)
- 400 g (14 oz) can of coconut milk or 200 ml (7 fl oz) milk and 200 ml (7 fl oz) double cream
- 2 tsp cornflour
- 50 g (2 oz) Medjool dates, destoned
- 50 ml (2 fl oz) maple or sycamore syrup (see page 293)
- A pinch of salt

METHOD:

1. Set aside roughly 100 ml (3½ fl oz) of the coconut milk (or cow's milk and cream) in a cup.
2. Warm the remaining coconut milk, or cow's milk and cream, in a pan.
3. Add in the spruce tips and simmer for 5 to 10 minutes.
4. Turn off the heat and leave to infuse for at least half an hour.
5. Return to the stove and add the maple or sycamore syrup to the infused milk.
6. Put the cornflour in another cup and mix it into a paste using the coconut milk (or cow's milk and cream) that you set aside at the beginning.
7. Pour this paste into the pan and heat up until the mixture is as thick as custard.
8. Pass through a sieve into a large bowl, then cool in the fridge for 2 hours or more.
9. If you're using an ice cream maker, put all the ingredients into it and churn until thick and creamy (around 30–40 minutes, depending on your device). If you do not have an ice cream maker, place the bowl in the freezer and, at intervals, whisk with a hand or electric whisk until it becomes light and fluffy (normally every 30 minutes over a period of up to three hours).
10. Serve with a fruity strudel or an indulgently rich slice of chocolate brownie.

An alternative method is what I like to call the 'Ice Cream Science Experiment'. To follow this version of the recipe, you'll need to halve the amounts of all ingredients and follow the steps above, but once you have taken the mix from the fridge (step 8), place it instead in a Ziploc bag. Take a larger Ziploc bag and fill it with ice, leaving room for the first bag to fit inside. Liberally sprinkle the ice with salt and place the smaller bag inside the larger one. Wrap the whole thing in a towel and shake for 8–9 minutes. The salt lowers the freezing point and causes the ice to melt faster. As it melts, it 'borrows' heat from the ice cream mix and forms ice crystals, making ice cream. During the spring when the Christmas tree in my garden is sprouting, I can make this more quickly than the walk to my local shop – the perfect recipe for all those times I am in urgent need of ice cream!

BLUSHING WOOD MUSHROOM
Agaricus silvaticus

Season for picking: summer into early autumn
Where to find them: conifer and deciduous woodland, under pine trees.
Main identifying features: flesh bruises ochre red when cut
Best use: as a field or cultivated mushroom
Not to be mistaken for: *Amanita* mushrooms

The blushing wood mushroom is part of the *Agaricus* species and is related to the horse mushroom, field mushroom and cultivated mushroom, which it closely resembles. When exposed to the sun the cap of many mushrooms can turn brown, in much the same we humans develop a tan, and the wood mushroom is no exception. It can be mistaken for the less common (but edible) scaley wood mushroom *Agaricus langei* which has rust brown fibrous scales on the cap rather than the flat scales on the cap of the wood mushroom.

I've found wood mushrooms in all kinds of awkward places, and on more than one occasion I've had to crawl on my hands and knees under the low branches of an ornamental pine to harvest them. Although I have reliably found it under pine and conifer trees they can also be found in mixed and deciduous woodlands. They seem to do well in islands of pine trees, alone within hardwood forests.

The blushing wood mushroom is considered the safest woodland *Agaricus* to eat as it is easy to identify: the flesh bruises ochre red when cut. However, woodland *Agaricus* can resemble deadly poisonous *Amanita* mushrooms. But, as none of the *Amanita* stain this colour when cut, the similarity need only be a superficial one. The gills of the wood mushroom begin a pale pinky colour, turning red before fading to brown with a brown spore print. Another signifier is a pleasant mushroom smell. If it has an unpleasant or chemical scent the mushroom should be discarded. I've found it in the late summer and early autumn but it can come up in the late spring.

PREPARATION AND USE
The blushing wood mushroom tastes very much like a field or cultivated mushroom and can be prepared in the same way. It is good in soups, especially with the addition of other wild mushrooms, or it can be pickled, as it often is in Russia. To pickle mushrooms, you will need to boil them until they are soft before drying on a wire rack. Pack the dried mushrooms in a jar and top with a spiced white vinegar allowing a couple of centimetres headway at the top of the jar. Top with a sliver of olive oil and seal the jars.

CAULIFLOWER FUNGUS
Sparassis crispa

Season for picking: autumn
Where to find them: at the base of conifer trees
Main identifying features: brain-like appearance/coral-like fronds
Best use: cooked in soups, risottos, creamy pasta sauce

You are unlikely to ever mistake the strange, brain-like cauliflower fungus for anything else. It consists of many creamy-white to brownish-white coral-like fronds joined together. It's as close to a Fibonacci sequence as you will ever find in a mushroom.

It can range from 20 cm (8 inches) across to as wide as 60 cm (2 feet), and only ever grows at the base of conifer trees. On one wild food walk it was the very first thing we found, just a few metres into the wood. As it pops up in the same place every year, I now regularly visit the same spot every autumn.

Part of what makes the cauliflower fungus so distinctive is what also makes it hard to prepare, as dirt and insects can get caught in the many folds. Brush these out and cut into smaller pieces to clean it effectively. When harvesting do not remove the whole mushroom – instead, leave a little behind to grow.

PREPARATION AND USE
The cauliflower mushroom has a mild, creamy flavour which despite its name tastes nothing like a cauliflower. It is very useful to carry other flavours, soaking up butter, garlic and cream. It is very versatile, lending itself well to soups, creamy pasta sauces, risottos or pizzas.

CREAMY CAULIFLOWER MUSHROOM PASTA

This is a highly adaptable recipe for a creamy mushroom pasta sauce (dairy or non-dairy). It makes a delicious rich sauce with cauliflower mushrooms but will equally work with whatever you bring back from the woods.

Serves four people.

YOU WILL NEED:

- 200 g (7 oz) cauliflower mushroom
- 2 tbsp butter or margarine
- 2 tbsp plain flour (or gluten-free flour)
- 200 ml (7 fl oz) milk (can use plant-based milk like oat milk)
- A pinch of salt
- Fresh thyme, finely chopped
- 300 g (10½ oz) pasta shells

METHOD:

1. Cook the pasta as per packet instructions.
2. As the pasta cooks, melt half the butter and gently fry the mushrooms in a pan.
3. While the mushrooms are cooking, melt the other half of the butter in a separate pan.
4. Sprinkle the flour into this butter and stir until it forms a lump.
5. Next, add the milk and whisk until the flour and butter has dissolved.
6. Add the salt and thyme.
7. Once the milk has thickened, add the cooked mushrooms to the sauce.
8. Check the seasoning of the sauce and adjust if necessary.
9. Drain the pasta and work into the sauce.

WOOD HEDGEHOG FUNGUS
Hydnum repandum

Season for picking: late summer to late autumn
Where to find them: conifer and deciduous woodland
Main identifying features: yellowish-white caps with spines on their undersides
Best use: cooked in risottos, creamy pasta sauces or on toast
Not to be mistaken for: terracotta hedgehog mushroom

Hedgehog fungi are one of my favourite mushrooms, and I have been known to whoop with delight when stumbling across them. Although they are not particularly rare they are an exciting find as they are utterly delicious. They are also unlikely to be mistaken for anything poisonous.

Rather than gills or pores they have spines underneath their yellowish-white caps. The cap can grow to the size of a stretched hand and is wavy, uneven and asymmetrical, and normally a little darker in the centre.

Rather than gills, hedgehog mushrooms have spines under their caps.

Hedgehog mushrooms start to appear towards the end of summer and although most guides suggest the season ends in October, I have found them as late as December. They grow in both conifer and deciduous woodland but more reliably in the former. The only lookalike is the terracotta hedgehog mushroom, a slightly smaller, orangey mushroom which is equally edible and only slightly less delicious. It can be picked if found in the UK, but in the Netherlands, Belgium or Germany it is on the red data list of endangered species so should be left alone.

PREPARATION AND USE

The hedgehog mushroom is even better tasting than the choicest cep or chanterelle in my view. As I write this, it is autumn outside my window and it is only my impending deadline to deliver this book to my publisher that is keeping me from springing out of my chair to go and look for one. It is great with pasta in a creamy sauce (see cauliflower fungus recipe, page 284), in a risotto or simply cooked in butter and served on toast. It also makes a very good mushroom pâté, fried with onions in butter then blitzed up with a liberal amounts of cream cheese.

SIBERIAN MUSHROOM SHANGI

This recipe is adapted from a Soviet-era cookbook but its roots are far older. The ingredients are simple but filling and hearty and would have been comforting before the onset of a harsh Siberian winter.

Rather than the heavy pie crust more common in the West, this recipe involves a pizza-like dough with a spongy texture, which soaks up gravy or a light sauce. The recipe also calls for smietana (sometimes smetana), a lightly soured cream similar to crème fraîche. This is widely available in Eastern European shops but if you can't find it, use whipped double cream instead as the cooking properties differ from those of crème fraîche. Most wild mushrooms work well in this recipe. It serves three to four people as part of a meal, going particularly well with potatoes, gravy and greens.

For the pie crust:
- 70 ml (2 fl oz) warm (not hot) milk
- 1 tbsp melted butter
- 1 tsp sugar

- 1 egg, beaten
- A pinch of salt
- 200 g (7 oz) white bread flour
- 1 tsp dried yeast or 15 g (0½ oz) fresh yeast

For the filling:
- 250 g (9 oz) hedgehog fungus (or other mixed wild mushrooms)
- Half an onion, finely chopped
- ½ tsp mustard seeds
- 1 tsp fresh thyme

- 1 tsp fresh tarragon
- A twist of black pepper
- A pinch of salt
- 75 ml (2½ fl oz) smietana (or whipped double cream)
- Butter or oil for frying

METHOD:

You can make the pie crust either by hand using the method below (steps 1 to 5) or in a bread machine, by putting the ingredients into the machine in the order listed and running it on a dough setting – this will take approximately one and a half hours, depending on your machine.

1. Sift the flour into a large bowl. Make a large well in the centre of the flour and pour in half the warm milk, then gently dissolve the sugar in the milk.
2. Sprinkle the yeast into the well and gently dissolve it in the liquid, trying not to incorporate any flour.
3. Cover the bowl and leave somewhere warm for 10–15 minutes, giving the yeast a chance to activate.
4. Add in the rest of the ingredients and knead the dough for around 10 minutes until it is no longer sticky.
5. Cover and put somewhere warm (such as an airing cupboard) until it has doubled in size.

6. While the pie dough is rising, melt a generous knob of butter in a pan and sweat the onion.
7. Pre-heat the oven to 200°C (400°F).
8. When the onion is browned, stir in the mustard seeds, cooking for one minute.
9. Add the chopped mushrooms to the pan and cook until they are softened, then add the herbs, seasoning and smietana (or cream). Warm through for a minute or so then take off the heat and set aside.
10. Go back to your dough, now that it has risen, and split it in two. Roll out one half of the dough thinly so it covers a parchment-lined baking tray measuring approximately 30–40 cm (12–16 inches) in length.
11. Spoon the pie filling from the pan onto the dough, leaving a 2 cm (1 inch) lip.
12. Roll out the other half of the pie dough and place on top of the mixture, pinching the sides with the bottom layer of dough until it is sealed.
13. Decorate the top of the pie with any leftover dough pieces.
14. Bake for about 15–20 minutes or until the pie is browned, and then serve hot with potatoes, gravy and vodka.

CHAPTER ELEVEN

Broadleaf Woodland

DECIDUOUS FORESTS UNDERGO a transformation that is one of nature's most breathtaking annual performances. Over the year, they go from a seemingly barren mass of lifeless trunks into a vibrant green landscape bursting with new life, until their leaves transform again into a palette of rich reds, yellows and oranges.

Deciduous trees, or broadleaf trees as they are also known, have adapted to life in areas with cool winters and warm summers, in a band between the polar regions and the warm tropics. Unlike conifer trees, they do not stay green all year but move with the rhythm of the seasons, in an annual dance of death and renewal. In spring, when the days get warmer, new life returns to the woods and the sap in the trees rises, bringing energy in the form of stored sugars from the roots. Buds burst into life with the first leaves of spring. In the 1.75 million-acre Ouachita National Forest on the border of Oklahoma and Arkansas, northern red oaks and winged elms are among the tens of thousands of trees which come into leaf. Here, whole hillsides and deep, plunging valleys are painted a vivid shade of green as far as the eye can see. And in Europe's largest remaining primeval forest, the Białowieska Forest, which straddles Poland and Belarus, many of the trees have gone through this yearly resurrection for at least 350 years.

As spring gives way to summer, forest berries, such as currants, wild strawberries and raspberries, provide food for small mammals and birds. Then, when the days start shortening and autumn arrives, the trees go through a final miraculous display. Across the 105-mile Skyline Drive though the Shenandoah National Park, in the mountains of Virginia, hundreds of thousands of visitors come every year to 'leaf-peep', driving through a breathtaking landscape filled with colour. During these cooler, ever darker days, chlorophyll, the compound responsible for the vivid green of a tree's leaves, starts to go into decline. In the absence of light-absorbing chlorophyll, pigments of flavonoid, carotenoid and anthocyanins are revealed in a kaleidoscope of reds, oranges and yellows. As the chlorophyll declines, the sap goes into reverse, sucking life away from the canopy through a network of vein-like, vascular tissues in the trunk, as the tree reabsorbs sugars into its roots and away from its leaves. As the sugar-rich sap falls, a layer of cells forms at the base of the leaf stalk, preventing any nutrient exchange between the tree and the leaf. And the leaf, effectively no longer part of the larger organism, falls to the ground.

As well as putting on miraculous displays, temperate woodlands are home to complex mysteries which we are only now beginning to unravel. You may have witnessed yourself how, in the late summer, whole forest floors can be thick with a carpet of shiny acorns, rich chestnuts or tiny, triangular beech nuts one year, but be almost completely empty the next. This is because deciduous trees like oak, beech, chestnut and hazel experience abundant years of nuts, known as 'mast' years, only once every few years.

Traditionally, pig farmers would take full advantage of this bounty in mast years, sending their animals into the crisp autumnal woods to gorge on acorns and beech nuts, fattening them up for market. The origin of the word 'mast', or 'mæst' in old English, stems from the West Germanic word *mæsten* meaning to fatten or to feed. This 'all or nothing' strategy gives the tree a chance to put its energy into growth in the intervening down years, but it may serve a further evolutionary purpose. Mammals such as mice, boar and deer love to graze on forest nuts, which provide extra fat stores to help them survive the winter and produce more energy-rich milk for their offspring. However, if the trees provided an abundance of food for these mammals every year, their numbers would soar and the forest floor would be stripped clean. With less frequent mast years, animal numbers are controlled and enough nuts remain uneaten to ensure the next generation of trees germinates.

We don't quite know how this feast-or-famine crop comes about. It may be down to environmental factors, with trees producing more seed in a warm, wet year, or a chemical signal sent through the air with the first blooms of spring. However, recent evidence points to underground fungal networks. Billions of mycelial threads, which form the 'body' of a fungus, extend out from the tree's roots and connect with similar networks from many other trees. This underground network, or 'wood-wide-web', may connect entire forests, aiding nutrient exchange and even facilitating a form of communication between trees. It seems that, through these connections, whole forests – even those that stretch over vast areas – may interactively decide in advance which years to produce seed in and when to concentrate more on growth. In this way, the trees act more like the inhabitants of a beehive or an ant colony than individuals, deciding what is best for the forest as a whole.

One autumn I went out to gather acorns to make coffee but found all the woods bereft. I presumed it was not a mast year and resigned myself to not finding any. Then, in the middle of a field, I found a lone tree that had dropped hundreds of plump, brown acorns. Perhaps, I thought, this isolated tree was dying, throwing down acorns as a last attempt to produce offspring. Or perhaps it had been cut off from the network and had missed the message from the surrounding oaks.

SYCAMORE AND MAPLE
Acer pseudoplatanus and *Acer* spp.

Season for picking: late winter/early spring
Where to find them: woods, edgeland, parks, gardens
Main identifying features: twin key-like seeds
Best use: tapping for sap to make syrup

In Canada and North America, maple syrup is harvested on a grand scale with a network of pipes draining the sap from tens of thousands of *Acer saccharum* or sugar maple trees. In most of Europe, though, the sugar maple struggles to grow. I have seen hopeful gardeners wait years, only to be disappointed both by the size of the tree and the small amount of sap it produces. However, the sap of the sycamore tree, *Acer pseudoplatanus*, is just as rich, sweet and delicious when reduced down, and the tree is common throughout Europe. It can be tapped in the same way as the birch (see page 117) and the sap rises around the same time. To check for the rising sap, look for weeping wounds or snip a branch and see if sap leaks out.

PREPARATION AND USE
The sap of the sycamore can be drunk as it is, and has a refreshing mineral water flavour. It can also be brewed into wine or beer. But it is best reduced into a syrup. The syrup tastes very similar to regular maple syrup, sweet with a honey-like richness, and can be used in place of sugar to sweeten coffee and tea or, of course, can be drizzled over pancakes.

To make the syrup, you can use a slow cooker with the top removed or, for the more experimental forager, get back to nature and camp out in the cold where you can reduce down the sap in a pot on an open fire. Both methods take time and energy so be patient (bring a friend, a deck of cards and some heatproof gloves if you are taking the camping route). You do not need to worry about boiling sycamore sap in the same way as birch, as it doesn't spoil when over-heated (although the syrup will burn if reduced down too far).

Even though the tree is considered a 'weed tree' by some arborists as it can grow quickly and crowd out slower-growing trees, it is best not to damage the sycamore when tapping. Plug up the hole after you have harvested your syrup using wax or a piece of twig the exact size of the hole.

WILD GARLIC, RAMSONS, BEAR GARLIC, RAMPS
Allium ursinum

Season for picking: spring
Where to find them: old woodland floors
Main identifying features: strong garlic smell
Best use: adds a delicious garlic flavour to lots of foods
Not to be mistaken for: lily of the valley

I can still recall the buzz of finding wild garlic for the first time while staying with friends in South Wales. I had read all about it in an old wild food book and rushed out to pick it straight after breakfast the following day. We added it to nettle soup, made garlic bread and threw it in everything from curries to bean stews.

Growing as far west as Ireland and as far east as Russia and Turkey, wild garlic has probably been used by humans for as long as there have been people around to pick it. In Denmark charred wild garlic bulbs were found at a late Mesolithic site in Halsskov, and at a site in Barkær the impression of a leaf dating from the same age was unearthed.

Although a woodland plant, wild garlic can occasionally grow in open pastureland, especially in the north of England. This can be a problem for cattle farmers as the sulphur compounds which cause the garlicky taste can also pass into the cows' milk. Farmers once paid children to 'knock down ramps' (ramps being the old name for wild garlic) or in other words remove the plants from their pastures. Conversely, in parts of Russia, cows were purposely fed the leaves to create butter flavoured with wild garlic.

Like other members of the onion family, wild garlic can help reduce blood pressure and was once prescribed for hypertension. And, if folk tales are to be believed, it's not only humans who recognise the plant's healing properties. The Latin name *ursinum* comes from *ursus*, meaning 'bear', as it was thought that bears would eat wild garlic to regain strength after their long winter hibernation.

Wild garlic thrives in moist but not wet woodland, and is often found in shaded valleys, north-facing hills and areas close to rivers and streams. It likes the same conditions as the bluebell, but it is rare to find the two growing alongside each other. Similarly you are unlikely to find it in woods that are full of bracken, which prefer a dryer soil, or in forests full of bramble, as it struggles to get a foothold among the thorny stems. The plant has long leaves of about 30 cm (1 foot) which taper at one end to a point and at the other to a stalk. Two to three leaves grow from a bulb the size of a single clove of regular garlic. The flowers begin life in a light-green, flame-shaped bud. These buds unfurl into six-petalled, star-shaped white flowers on a single upright stem.

Wild garlic is very safe for a novice forager as its strong garlic scent distinguishes it from any poisonous lookalikes, like lily of the valley. Lords and ladies, *Arum maculatum*, with its strongly irritant, throat-closing leaves, grows alongside wild garlic, so be careful not to pick it by accident – again, it does not have the strong garlic scent. The only garlic-scented lookalike is the close relation *Allium tricoccum*, colloquially known as ramps or wild leek, which grows on the North American continent. This plant is also edible and can be used in exactly the same way as wild garlic.

FORAGER'S TIP
Wild garlic is an indicator of ancient woodland and will thrive in great numbers in older woodlands. If all the trees in a forest are small and young, it is likely this is a newer woodland and the chance of finding wild garlic is greatly reduced.

PREPARATION AND USE
Every part of the wild garlic plant is useful in some way. The leaves are the most commonly used part, but the stems, flowers, buds, bulbs and seeds can all give a beautiful, fiery, garlicky flavour to a host of dishes.

Leaves
Wild garlic leaves are a versatile ingredient. The go-to recipe is pesto, but you can also add the leaves to curries, sauces (it is especially good in cheese sauces), soups, stews or any dish that might be improved with garlic flavour. It is best to chop or shred the leaves and throw them in towards the end of cooking to preserve the flavour. You can make a delicious garlic butter to spread on toast or make garlic bread – just finely chop five or six leaves and massage them into a block of butter. You can mix the finely chopped leaves with oil, mayonnaise or aioli to use as a flavouring or salad dressing. It can also be fun to work them into pasta dough to make beautiful green tagliatelle or spaghetti. In our house we dehydrate the leaves and sprinkle them on dishes throughout the year. You can also mix the dried flakes with dried mushroom powder to enhance the flavour of soups.

Stems

The stems can be used like chives, chopped finely and mixed in with sauces and soups. Unlike the leaves, they need to be added earlier in the cooking process as they are tougher and need longer to break down. In Russia the stems are pickled, with or without the flower buds. Simply blanch and then submerge them in a flavoured vinegar, and use in salads or as a tasty extra in falafel-filled wraps.

Flowers and buds

The flower buds can be pickled by submerging and sealing in a jar of warm, sweet vinegar (see base recipes, page 22). They can then be used like a pungent caper for salads, or as a pizza topping. Alternatively throw them straight into soups for some punchy extra flavour. The raw flowers have an almost overwhelming garlic flavour, but chopped finely and used sparingly they work well in a salad dressing or on pizza, added a couple of minutes towards the end of cooking.

Seed pods

The flowers will eventually give way to tiny, green, ball-like seeds. Although it can be time consuming to remove the thin remnants of the flower (I recommend rubbing them off with your hands in front of the TV or while listening to an audiobook), pickled wild garlic seed pods make an excellent garlic-flavoured substitute for capers.

OKROSHKA

In western Russia, wild garlic leaves are sometimes used as an ingredient in okroshka, a cold vegetable soup like a Russian version of gazpacho. The basis of this refreshing soup is usually radishes, cucumber (fresh or pickled if not in season), boiled potatoes, boiled eggs (you can also use tofu) and of course wild garlic leaves.

A cooked meat such as bologna/baloney or boiled beef is also sometimes added.

The liquid part of the soup is usually made from sour cream and kvass, a drink made from fermented rye bread. Variations of the recipe add yoghurt and mineral water, or the fermented milk drink kefir, instead of the kvass. The dish is flavoured with dill, salt, pepper and mustard to taste. It can be an unusual flavour at first to Western taste buds, and I tend to prefer using yoghurt rather than the sharp taste of kefir. However, on a warm spring day it is refreshingly light and crisp, and the soft potatoes, crisp cucumber, spicy radish and pungent wild garlic leaves all complement each other perfectly.

SCARLET ELF CUP
Sarcoscypha austriaca or *S. coccinea*

Season for picking: winter and early spring
Where to find them: forest floor
Main identifying features: Red cup-shaped fungi
Best use: as a container for other flavours
Not to be mistaken for: orange peel fungus

The scarlet elf cup has a fitting name. It is a scarlet-red, cup-shaped fungus that grows on the forest floor in the depths of winter and into the spring. A pretty-enough mushroom, it is easy to imagine supernatural forest folk using the bowl-shaped fungi for enchanted woodland teas.

PREPARATION AND USE
They can be eaten raw, with a mushroomy flavour but rubbery texture. Their best use is as a container for other things; a natural vol-au-vent case if you will. Try them stuffed with cream cheese, pâtés, pesto or creamy prawn and chicken fillings. They also add texture and colour to soups without altering the flavour.

ASH
Fraxinus excelsior

Season for picking: spring
Where to find them: broadleaf woodlands, roadsides, edgeland woods and thickets, hedgerows
Main identifying features: pinnate leaves, seeds clustered in winged keys
Best use: ash key pickle

Roughly translating as 'ever upward' or 'ever higher', the tree's scientific name describes the incredible speed at which this British native can grow. A fellow gardener once told me that the trouble with English gardens is that they would prefer to be ash forests. Ash self-seeds in the most awkward places and its deep roots are nigh on impossible to weed out. The seeds have spread the tree far and wide, but its preferred habitat is mixed woodland or planted and wild hedgerows.

Ash trees can be identified in the middle of winter by their black, bishop's-hat-shaped buds. They have opposite, pinnate leaves and can reach heights of 12–18 metres (39–59 feet). Close to where I live, there are whole woodlands affected by ash dieback. It is a tragic sight to see – dead branches reach up from green and yellow withering leaves, and the trunks and branches crack open to reveal black scarring as the fungus takes hold. The only hope is that, as a relatively fast-growing tree, the 5 per cent of ashes in Britain that are estimated to be unaffected will bounce back in the decades to come as a more resilient population.

PREPARATION AND USE
My preferred use of the ash is to forage for the immature seeds, or 'ash keys', and eat them pickled.

Ash keys resemble the seeds of a sycamore but grow in clusters rather than pairs. They should be picked in the spring when young – they'll be light green with a translucent casing.

ASH KEY PICKLE

1. Boil the ash keys and discard the water. Do this 3 or 4 times to soften them and remove bitter tannins.
2. Pat dry the keys with a cloth or paper towel and place in a sterilised jar.
3. Sweeten some vinegar with a little brown sugar and add spices such as chilli, cayenne and coriander (a friend of mine likes to use a Jamaican spice mix).
4. Heat but do not boil the vinegar, and then pour it over the ash keys. Seal the jar, screwing the lid tightly.
5. Leave for 3 months or more – the taste improves with age.
6. Use the pickles like capers, as an unusual pizza topping or salad ingredient, or pair with a good strong cheese.

BEECH, EUROPEAN BEECH
Fagus sylvatica

Season for picking: autumn for nuts, early spring for leaves
Where to find them: beech woodland and hedging
Main identifying features: cigar-shaped buds, oval leaves
Best use: toasted nuts
Not to be mistaken for: hornbeam

The European beech is a large, stately tree with a dense, domed canopy of green or copper-brown leaves. During the winter you can spot a beech by its scaly or cigar-like buds, the empty shells of which remain on the tree once the downy, light-green leaves first emerge in the early spring. The leaves are oval in shape with a point at the end and have prominent veins that are evenly spaced like chevrons. They start out as lime green and translucent, and become a darker, glossy green a few weeks after emerging. Like oaks, veteran beeches aged between 125 and 200 years old are full of character with gnarled, knotted trunks reaching a diameter of up to 3 metres (10 feet) and canopies around 40–50 m up from the forest floor. However, few beeches reach this old age and a tree with a 1-metre (3-foot) girth and a height of around 30 metres (100 feet) is more common.

The nuts of a beech tree are small and triangular, with three flat sides and a pointed top. During the first days of autumn, they fall from or with their hard, spiky cases, which open up like flowers to reveal one to three nuts inside each. The nuts contain 40–50 per cent fat and make an oil as rich in flavour as olive or walnut oil. In Albania, the leaves are mixed with nettle and dock and fed to pigs, as it is thought this gives them strength. Remains of the nuts have been found preserved in the sediment under Neolithic dwellings perched on Alpine lakes in both Germany and Switzerland. It is tantalising to gather the nuts knowing our ancestors were doing the same thing 5,000 years ago.

Like many other nut trees, beech trees do not produce an abundance of nuts every year and disease and low fertilisation rates can cause large numbers of hollow or 'dud' nuts. The duds are easily identified, as they have concave sides and are a lighter brown. If you squeeze them between your thumb and forefinger, they will easily crunch flat. If you find that after five to ten minutes of searching you are finding only the odd viable nut then cut your losses and move on.

The American beech, *Fagus grandifolia*, grows throughout eastern North America and occasionally as a park tree in Europe. Its leaves are more pointed than the European beech but the nuts and leaves can be used in exactly the same way.

Beeches are also an important host to a range of mushrooms. Some mushrooms form mycorrhizal fungi associations (see page 250) with the beech while others feed on the leaf litter or the dead or dying wood. You are likely to find woodland puffballs, bay boletes, russula, milk caps, oyster and porcelain mushrooms in the vicinity of the tree. Every autumn a beech wood I know well is flecked with purple as the beautiful amethyst deceiver mushroom pops up in large numbers across the woodland floor.

Gathering the nuts of a beech tree can be time consuming as they are often hidden in the leaf litter or long grass. Look for trees hanging over a quiet stretch of road or tarmacked paths where they will be much easier to spot and gather. On these hard surfaces you can even use a broom to sweep the debris into a large pile and then pick the nuts out.

PREPARATION AND USE

Beech nuts will fall from their cases when they are ripe and ready. It is seldom worth the effort of prizing them from these cases early, especially as they fall in such large numbers and are easily gathered from under the tree. The nuts can be shelled and eaten raw but only in small quantities as they contain toxic glycosides, which in large doses can cause an upset stomach. Roasting the nuts in their shells reduces the levels of glycosides to almost zero, and also makes the nuts a lot easier to crack open. Once roasted and shelled, rub the papery dark coating from the shelled nut and use as you would pine nuts. Alternatively, you can make a delicious beechnut butter by grinding the nuts into a powder, then mixing with a neutral tasting oil (walnut oil is good) a drizzle at a time until it makes a paste, adding a little salt and honey to taste.

The light-green, slightly hairy leaves that emerge from the beech tree in its first flush are also edible, although you should pick them before they start to turn a darker green, at which point they become bitter with tannins. The young leaves have a mild but slightly sharp flavour and can be added to a springtime salad, or can be used to make a beech leaf noyau, a nutty-flavoured liqueur first brewed by Victorian tree workers in the Chilterns. To make the drink, fill two-thirds of a Kilner jar with clean young leaves and then top up with gin. Let this infuse for around 3 weeks in a cool dark cupboard, then drain out the leaves and add a dash of brandy and sugar syrup before sealing into bottles. Leave to rest for a further 6–8 weeks before drinking on its own or with tonic water. You can also try using white rum or vodka in place of the gin, and honey or maple syrup in place of the sugar.

CHESTNUT
Castanea sativa

Season for picking: autumn
Where to find them: woodlands, parks and parkland
Main identifying features: spiky cases, long serrated or toothed leaves
Best use: harvesting the nuts
Not to be mistaken for: horse chestnut

Britain inherited the European sweet chestnut (along with many other edible plants) from the Romans. But the first families to forage for this nut were older still, from the forests surrounding the ancient Persian city of Sardis, in what is now western Turkey. The Greeks called it the Sardinian nut (after the city of Sardis, not the island) and wrote of chubby-cheeked Persian children gorging on the nuts. The Greeks introduced the tree into Europe some time before 400 BC, where it thrived. Chestnuts became popularised in Greek history after the armies of Alexander the Great subsisted on them during their retreat from Anatolia.

The Romans, Greeks and mountain peoples of Western Asia used chestnuts in place of potatoes or ground them down to make flour. The natural sweetness of the chestnuts is amplified when they are ground and in parts of Italy, chestnut flour is used to this day and is known as *farina dolce* ('sweet flour'). It can be added to wheat flour to make pancakes, cakes or castagnole, sweet doughnut-like balls eaten in the north of Italy.

Chestnuts can grow into magnificent trees with stout trunks and rounded canopies, reaching up to 35 metres (115 feet) in height. The leaves are long with a heavily serrated edge. The blossom forms on elongated cream-white or yellow flowering stalks. The nuts come in the autumn, and are dark brown with two to four nuts in a shell. They have a flat back, a rounded front and a point at the bottom. Horse chestnuts, in contrast, are usually completely rounded and lack the point at the bottom. Horse chestnuts are also generally shinier than sweet chestnuts. The cases of a sweet chestnut are covered in hairy, densely packed spikes, rather than the hard spikes (and hard shells) of a horse chestnut.

When a tree produces flat, papery chestnuts rather than full ripe ones, this may be a sign of a chestnut-free year – but it may also indicate that it is too early in the season to expect a crop. The tree drops these reject nuts in much the same way apple trees drop unwanted fruit in June and July, with the main event happening weeks or even months later.

FORAGER'S TIP

When chestnuts fall, some will drop straight from their cases, others will drop with the case half open and some will remain stubbornly closed. After years of practice, I'm now adept at prising half-open nuts from their spiky green cases with my bare hands by pushing the tips of my fingers into the thin opening and pulling; perhaps it is the thought of smelling them roasting (and subsequently eating them) which helps override the discomfort! The stubborn ones can be removed from their case using a pair of gardening gloves or a simple wiggle between the feet.

PREPARATION AND USE

There is a strong characteristic smell to roasted chestnuts, which always reminds me of Christmas markets. Chestnuts, and other foods such as bread, biscuits, marshmallows and even roasted meat, undergo a distinct chemical change when roasted, toasted or baked. This is called the Maillard reaction, named after French chemist Louis Camille Maillard. It occurs when heat breaks down starches and proteins to produce hundreds of different flavour and aroma compounds. It is the Maillard reaction that accounts for why marshmallows are so much better after being cooked in a fire and why roasted chestnuts taste so sweet and creamy.

To prepare the nuts for roasting, score a cross along the flat side of each, leaving one nut unscored. Then place them in the oven at 180–200°C or 350–400°F. My top tip for roasting them is to leave one nut unscored and when you hear the tell-tale 'bang' in the oven you know they are ready.

Aside from roasting, chestnuts can be shelled and boiled, which gives them a creamy, rich texture. The ancient Romans added them to lentil dishes, and they work very well this way, as well as in casseroles or soups in place of meat. I add them whole and peeled to risottos, or chop them alongside homegrown crown prince pumpkin and foraged hazelnuts to make a delicious nut roast.

OYSTER MUSHROOM
Pleurotus spp.

Season for picking: all year – best in early autumn
Where to find them: dead and dying wood
Main identifying features: shelf-like bracket fungus with small stalk
Best use: stroganoff, curries and stir-fries
Not to be mistaken for: angel wings

Oyster mushrooms are both common and prolific. I've spotted them in mid-November by the side of a wet Northumberland road, but they're most common from spring into autumn (slightly favouring the early autumn). Like other bracket fungi they have a habit of growing out of reach on dead standing trees. A long branch or an extendible tree pruner are both methods I've employed to knock them down from great heights. As they are a substantial mushroom they tend not suffer too badly from the fall.

You often see them forced into cellophane-covered packages in supermarkets and it can be worth buying a pack to familiarise yourself with them before you head out to the woods. They are a shelf-like fungus which can form in clusters on dead and dying wood, favouring elms, oaks and beech. The caps vary from 5 to 25 cm (2 to 10 inches), generally coming somewhere in the middle of this. The gills are white or creamy and quite crowded, and they are decurrent, which means they continue from the edge of the cap down the short, stubby stem. Depending on the species the caps of the oyster vary in colour from pale grey to brown or white.

Grey- and brown-topped oyster mushrooms have no poisonous lookalike, but those with pale caps have a potentially deadly one: angel wings (*Pleurocybella porrigens*). These are pure white and do not have the brown or grey suntan tops characteristic of most species of oyster mushroom. The flesh of the angel wings mushroom is also more fragile than that of the oyster. Angel wings are more common in cooler regions, such as the Highlands of Scotland, Scandinavia, Canada and Northern USA. The further south you travel, the less common they become; they are practically non-existent in southern England and lowland southern Europe. Angel wings also grow exclusively from conifer wood stumps, never deciduous stumps like the oyster mushroom. To be 100 per cent sure, take a spore print (see page 244) – oyster mushrooms will have a lilac print while angel wings will have a white one.

PREPARATION AND USE
Oyster mushrooms have a good mushroom flavour and a meaty consistency which remains after cooking. They soak up flavours so are good in curries and stir-fries. Part of their popularity and commercial viability is down to their versatility. You can cook them in pies, stroganoff, pasta, soups, ravioli or any of the many ways mushrooms can be prepared.

Oyster mushrooms can also be dehydrated very easily. Cut off the caps and run a thread through them, then hang them in a cool dry place such as an airing cupboard. Alternatively cut into thin segments and dry in a dehydrator or on the grill of a convection radiator.

CHICKEN OF THE WOODS
Laetiporus sulphureus

Season for picking: May to September
Where to find them: on oak trees or other hardwood trees, stumps or logs
Main identifying features: clustered fan brackets with yellow rims, pores rather than gills
Best use: cooked like chicken pieces

While speeding through a muddy woodland on his mountain bike in mid-September, a friend of mine spotted a large clump of chicken of the woods growing on an old tree stump. He stopped to send me a picture: the mushroom was a vivid yellowy orange, growing close to the ground among a patch of wood sorrel. A couple of days later, I found myself tracking his tyre marks, searching for this distinctive fungus. I finally found it, tucked away on a deciduous stump, surrounded by conifer trees.

Chicken of the woods is a mildly parasitic bracket fungus, which grows on both living and dead wood. I've found it on tree stumps, fallen logs and at the tops of living, healthy trees. It can be sulphur yellow, but is often a shade lighter on the outer rim, with a darker orange inner centre cut into the mushroom. The flesh is ivory white. The brackets form wavy, clustered half-moon or fan shapes, often crammed together as if they are bursting from the log. Chicken of the woods doesn't have gills like a shop-bought mushroom but if you turn it over, you will notice it has tiny, sponge-like, lemon-yellow pores.

I tend to find it between July and September but the season can be longer – some emerge as early as May, and some last until October. The fungus has a particular liking for oak but will grow on most hardwoods, including cherry, willow, sweet chestnut and occasionally beech. It's best to avoid any chicken of the woods you find growing on yew trees, as the wood and leaves of the tree are highly toxic.

PREPARATION AND USE

To say something 'tastes like chicken' is a cliché, but there really is no more accurate way of describing the taste and texture of chicken of the woods. It has a mild and slightly lemony flavour, but it is the meaty texture and sheer abundance of this fungus that make it so sought after. Cooked in much the same way as chicken or Quorn pieces, it will soak up flavours like lemon, butter or soy sauce. It works well in an omelette and really comes into its own in a Thai stir-fry.

SPICY MOROCCAN CHICKEN OF THE WOODS STEW

This is a highly adaptable recipe, making the most of whatever is in season. If you don't have all the ingredients you can easily substitute some for what you do have, for example winter squashes instead of carrot. You can use most kinds of mushroom but the texture of chicken of the woods works best. Serves 2–3 as a main course, or 4–5 as a starter.

YOU WILL NEED:

- 1 medium-sized onion, chopped
- 2 cloves of garlic, crushed (or 2 tsp wild garlic flakes)
- 2 small carrots (or 1 large), diced
- 1 red pepper, sliced
- 1 courgette, sliced
- 380 g (13½ oz) tin chickpeas
- 500 ml (2 cups) stock
- A large handful of dried apricots (roughly halved)
- 5 medium tomatoes, cut into quarters
- 100 g (3½ oz) chicken of the woods, diced
- ½ tsp turmeric
- ½ tsp coriander
- 1 tsp cumin
- ½ tsp ground ginger
- 4 cloves
- A pinch of chilli flakes (optional)
- Oil for frying

METHOD:

1. On a moderate heat, fry the onions in a little oil until they begin to brown.
2. Add the courgette and red pepper to the pan with the crushed garlic (if using wild garlic flakes add these when you add the other spices). Cook on a moderate heat for around two minutes before adding the chicken of the woods.
3. When the vegetables begin to soften, throw in the spices and stir to coat everything in the pan (don't let this burn).
4. Add the carrots and tomatoes, then pour over the stock.
5. Stir the stock, then add the chickpeas and apricots. Cover and simmer until the carrots are softened.
6. Serve on a bed of couscous or in a bowl with warm crusty bread.

BEEFSTEAK FUNGUS, OX TONGUE FUNGUS
Fistulina hepatica

Season for picking: late summer into autumn
Where to find them: hardwood stumps
Main identifying features: 'bleeds' when cut, meat-like appearance
Best use: in place of meat in a range of dishes

The beefsteak fungus is one of the strangest-looking mushrooms you will come across. It is a pinkish, red or reddish-brown bracket fungus and has the appearance of a large tongue or a hunk of meat growing from the base of a tree. In an ironic coincidence, I only ever seem to find it when out with vegan friends.

When they begin life, beefsteak fungi are small, about fist size, and normally pinkish. They darken with age as they grow to 30 cm (1 foot) across and up to 7 cm (3 inches) thick. The fungus is polypore, so the underside is porous or sponge-like rather than gilled and ivory white when young, turning darker as it ages. When cut the mushroom bleeds a red blood-like liquid, and a plastic bag full of them looks disconcertingly like a bag of giblets. The flesh is striated, so it looks like a beef or tuna steak.

With no poisonous lookalikes it is a great mushroom for novices and grows throughout Europe and North America. Look for it on dead and dying oaks and occasionally chestnut trees.

FORAGER'S TIP

It's all too easy to be restricted in the areas in which you look for mushrooms, scouring only the sides of trees facing main pathways. When searching for beefsteak fungi, look for fallen or sickly-looking oaks and search both sides of the tree, front and back. More often than not, this tongue-like fungus likes to poke itself out of the tree away from the path.

PREPARATION AND USE

Beefsteak fungus has a very meaty texture but an acidic, sour, sorrel-like and almost fruity flavour. I personally like it but for some, including very experienced foragers, this sourness is too much. Although the taste is not meaty it is a great substitute for meat, with a superb texture – far less chewy than meat. It's great for soaking up rich, salty flavours like soy sauce or soy sauce substitutes like liquid aminos.

You can soak the fungus overnight in milk or bicarbonate of soda dissolved in water in order to remove the acid flavour before cooking. Salting to remove liquid, peeling and removing the pores also helps to reduce the acidic flavour. But it's definitely worth trying the mushroom on its own first as you might like it as it is. Bizarrely, because of the sourness, some people use it in a fruit salad, but I've found it best to fry up the mushroom with strong flavours like soy sauce, garlic and chilli or to add to a creamy pasta sauce, which counters the acidity. You can also marinate it in strong umami flavours or liquid smoke, as this give it a strong, beefy flavour with only back notes of the acidity.[24]

SMOKY BEEFSTEAK FUNGUS

This way of marinating the mushroom is a great vegan or vegetarian alternative to a Sunday roast if served alongside roast potatoes, Yorkshire pudding and seasonable vegetables. Or try it as beefy fried chunks in a rich tomato sauce on pasta. This recipe serves 4–6 in place of meat, depending on the size of the mushroom.

YOU WILL NEED:

- 1 large beefsteak mushroom
- 2 tsps liquid smoke
- 2 tsps soy sauce or liquid aminos
- 1 tsp yeast extract dissolved in approximately 20 ml (½ fl oz) water
- 1 tsp nutritional yeast flakes

METHOD:

1. Cut your beefsteak mushroom into 2 cm (1 inch) chunks and place in a large bowl.
2. Pour or sprinkle on the marinade ingredients and massage them into the mushroom pieces, then leave in the fridge overnight to soak up the flavours.
3. Fry the mushrooms in oil on a moderate to high heat until the mushroom darkens but does not burn (around 10 minutes) and serve straight away.

HEN OF THE WOODS, MAITAKE MUSHROOM
Grifola frondosa

Season for picking: late summer into autumn
Where to find them: at the base of oak, beech, sweet chestnut and hazel trees
Main identifying features: fan-like brackets
Best use: stews, soups, pasta sauces

Hen of the woods is a parasitic fungus that can be found on the base of oak, beech, sweet chestnut or occasionally hazel trees (in order of preference). As a parasite it feeds off living tissue but every now and then you might find it on what seems to be a dead tree stump. Often on closer examination these stumps are still alive, as neighbouring trees funnel nutrients to them via an interconnected root system, keeping them going for many years after they are cut.

Hen of the woods is on the red list of rare species in Scandinavian countries but is common elsewhere in Europe and the United States. However, it can still be difficult to find as it hides at the base of trees in the scrub and leaf litter. When young and emerg-

You'll find hen of the woods on the bases and stumps of oak, beech and sweet chestnut.

ing, it can look like sea coral until each of the fronds open and fan out like multiple hen's tails sprouting from the tree. In Japan it is called maitake, from the Japanese words *take*, for mushroom (think shiitake), and *mai* meaning 'to dance', as the frilly brackets resemble the sleeves of a woman dancing in a kimono.

Light brown to dusty grey and striated, with white fringes to the brackets, the mushroom has ivory-white flesh and a sponge-like underside made up of hundreds of tiny pores. Although the brackets themselves are small (approximately 10 cm (5 inches)) they can be numerous, easily providing enough for a family meal with leftovers to dehydrate for another day.

In nineteenth-century Rome impoverished tenants sometimes used the mushroom in lieu of late rent to appease angry landlords. During the same era, in the markets of Norwich, traders would sell them at a premium under the spurious name of 'morrel' (see page 187), which is quite a different and highly sought-after mushroom (and would have fetched a much higher price than hen of the woods).

PREPARATION AND USE

Hen of the woods has been called the 'king of mushrooms' for its earthy umami taste. It is particularly highly regarded in Japan. Like chicken of the woods, it has a meaty texture, but its flavour is much more interesting. Go for younger specimens if you can, leaving the older ones to set spores. Like many other mushrooms it needs to be cooked well and can be grilled, fried, seared, or boiled in stews or soups. I love it with a creamy pasta sauce flavoured with thyme or tarragon.

However, you do have to work for your dinner as dirt and insects can get caught between its many frond-like brackets. It's best to cut it up into smaller pieces and run it under the tap to thoroughly clean it. If necessary, give it a further clean with a brush before you eat it. Thankfully the mushroom can be pickled, frozen or dried.

HORN OF PLENTY
Craterellus cornucopioides

Season for picking: autumn
Where to find them: under beech trees
Main identifying features: black or dark grey, trumpet-shaped
Best use: in creamy sauces

Horn of plenty mushrooms are incredibly hard to find. I would recommend foraging for them with children as their young eyes seem better suited to seeking them out (cash bribes can help). Look for a black or dark-grey, trumpet- or funnel-shaped mushroom, which is hollow in the centre with uneven edges. The gills range from black, like the cap, to greyish or brown in colour and run into the stem. I recommend looking under beech trees.

PREPARATION AND USE
They have an excellent, woody, earthy taste but can be overwhelmed by strong spices, garlic or strong-tasting mushrooms. They naturally dry without the need of a dehydrator but need to be cooked in oil to avoid bitterness. Use in stock or soups, or mix with cream.

VELVET SHANK
Flammulina velutipes

Season for picking: winter months, particularly after a frost
Where to find them: dead or dying broadleaf tree stumps
Main identifying features: orange caps, dark at the bottom of the stem
Best use: Asian soups, noodle dishes
Not to be mistaken for: funeral bell

In the depths of winter when little else is around, the orange caps of the velvet shank stand out of the winter gloom. They can be found growing on dead or dying broadleaf tree stumps, particularly elm (if you can find it). Look for them after periods of frost, as they actively need the freezing temperatures.

The scientific name for the velvet shank translates as 'little flame with black foot' which is as close to a perfect description as you can get. It is relatively easily identified; I found it during my earliest days of foraging in my twenties. However, you do have to be careful as there is a potentially deadly lookalike, the aptly named funeral bell mushroom, *Galerina marginata*. Read up on the funeral bell and follow the checklist below to tick off the key characteristics of the velvet shank.

Stems	Older stems turn dark brown to black and feel velvety. No ring or membraneous skirt present
Cap	Orange or yellowy brown, darker in the middle, smooth, slimy in wet weather. 1–10 cm (0.5–4 inches) across
Gills	The gills are white in young mushrooms, turning pale or grey-yellow. Not all the gills reach the stem and, unlike the funeral bell, they are not crowded.
Spore print	Always take a spore print – should be white and not rust- or snuff-coloured

PREPARATION AND USE

Velvet shanks are a delicious mushroom, both fruity and mealy. They taste very much like the related white enokitake mushroom, which is used in a lot of Chinese dishes. Their texture makes them most suited to soups and I like to serve them very simply with noodles, miso, thin matchsticks of root vegetables and some shichimi seasoning.

WATER

CHAPTER TWELVE

Fresh Water and Wetlands

FOR A LITTLE over a year, I rented a quirky old lime-rendered cottage in a small, picturesque Devon hamlet. The cottage had a small brook running around the perimeter of its shared garden, which would wax and wane with the seasons. In the summer it all but dried up, but come winter it ran as fast as a white-water rapid and could be heard all over the house. Thick clumps of tall, shaggy, grass-like sedges had found their way to the water's edge. Sedges are beautiful plants with long, pendulous seed heads. Despite their beauty, I was assigned the task of digging them out as silt would build up around them and the garden was in danger of flooding when the waters returned later in the year.

Sedges thrive in wet woodland. At the cottage, conditions were perfect for them, thanks to the countless, now fully grown Christmas trees our landlady had planted out over the years that kept the garden shaded. I had tried to grow fruit and veg in this garden but the dark and wet proved to be very challenging and the only thing that really succeeded were redcurrants which, like the sedges, are plants naturally adapted to wet wooded areas.

The damp garden brought with it other edibles and brooklime and water mint both grew in abundance along the edges of the stream. But the real bounty came downstream, where this tiny brook met with a larger tributary of the River Dart and a mass of flourishing watercress filled the waters. This abundance was thanks to traditional watercress beds that had been abandoned long ago. No longer tended to, the plants had spilled over the walls of the submerged beds and spread throughout the stream like a weed. Braving the shallow, sometimes icy-cold water, I would wade in as deep as my wellington boots allowed, to pick what I needed for lunch.

As a child of the 1970s and 1980s, I was always told not to pick anything from waterways because they were so polluted. Even today, picking in fresh water after heavy rains can be a problem as raw sewage is sometimes released into the waterways to ease the sewage system.[25] If in doubt, soak any forageables in salt-water and boil them for at least three minutes. In areas close to livestock there is also a risk of the liver fluke parasite (*Fasciola hepatica*), a nasty kind of flatworm which can be fatal. Concerning though this may be, it is easily dealt with, as cooking destroys the parasite – as does soaking in a 6 per cent acidity vinegar (such as a distilled white vinegar) for ten minutes. Thankfully, since the Water Act of 1989, industrial pollutants have declined and as long as you are aware of the risks and take the necessary precautions, rivers, lakes, large ponds and canals can be abundant and beautiful places to forage.

Throughout the wetlands, ponds and drainage ditches of the world, bulrushes (sometimes called cattails), one of the most delicious edible waterside plants, thrive. You'll often spot dense colonies of the plant and its brown, furry, sausage-shaped heads swaying in the breeze. Blanched for just a few minutes, the immature flower heads of bulrushes are as moreish and tender as any corn on the cob. During the spring, I've often risked a soaking by stretching precariously from a bank to reach them.

More safely on dry land, hemp agrimony, valerian, burdock and hogweeds rise above grasses, docks and bistort. On river-banks you'll find the towering Himalayan balsam, with its pink-and-white policeman's helmet-shaped flowers and exploding seed pods, shading out the native marginal plants. Despite their threat to native flora, in remote country streams, I have found signs of native fauna among stands of Himalayan balsam. I've found the scat of otters and the remains of their dinner in the form of empty crayfish claws hiding away among the long, waxy stems of the plant. For the forager, the seeds of the balsam are as tasty as any ripe walnut and just one of the many waterside wild foods you are likely to find in these wildlife havens.

WATERCRESS
Nasturtium officinale

Season for picking: spring to autumn, best avoided when flowering in summer
Where to find them: waterways and rivers in hills, coastal streams
Main identifying features: pinnate leaves, four-petalled white flowers
Best use: soups, salads, pesto or as a herb
Not to be mistaken for: cowbane/water hemlock

Cheap imports have led to the decline of watercress cultivation in Britain but abandoned watercress beds can still be found in and around the country's waterways as reminders of a bygone age. Cultivation of this peppery plant began in Kent, Dorset and Hampshire, where it was cultivated in such numbers the railway through the county was once dubbed 'The Watercress Line'. But I've also stumbled across watercress in Somerset, Devon and all over southern England. It also grows in the mountain streams of North America and throughout the waterways of Europe.

Watercress is also a naturally occurring plant, favouring all kinds of rivers but especially cold, fresh water coming off hills and mountains or in coastal streams heading out to sea. It's sometimes found on its own and at other times with potentially poisonous plants such as cowbane and water hemlock. Correct identification is therefore very important, as the two can tangle together and it's far too easy to pop the wrong one into your basket. Watercress can grow in such abundance that it forms large mats, and from a distance it can give the impression of a lush green meadow rather than a stream of running water.

Wild or abandoned watercress looks just like cultivated watercress, but it can grow in a more chaotic, naturalistic way, with more tangled and less uniform stems. The young leaves are pinnate. They have leaflets on opposite sides with a larger leaflet at the top, and they indent slightly where the veins meet the perimeter of the leaf. Look where the leaves meet the main stem – you should see a tangle of long white roots. The flowers are cross-shaped (four petals), delicate and white and form small clusters. The leaves remain in a pinnate form when they flower but lose some of their ovoid form and become more lance-shaped. It is at this stage where it is easy to confuse the plant with cowbane (see below), so be sure to look for the cross-shaped flowers and the distinctive, peppery, fresh scent.

PREPARATION AND USE
The main caution when it comes to eating watercress is the liver fluke parasite. You should always pick from clear, running water, nowhere near grazing or dead animals, and take only the top part of the watercress, growing above the water line (this will also ensure that the plant replenishes). Even then, you should soak your watercress in vinegar (see introduction) if you wish to eat it raw or blanch for ten minutes before using it cooked. Even supermarket watercress is not without its risks and there have been

mass withdrawals of commercially sold watercress because of outbreaks of E. coli.

One of my favourite soups is made from watercress, and the base recipe at the start of the book works really well with the plant (see page 15). Another really simple and delicious way to eat watercress is blanched and served as a side vegetable with lemon and butter. Watercress both cooked and raw (soaked in vinegar first) is also a great accompaniment to rich cheeses, and you can use a little as a pot-herb to add a peppery kick to otherwise bland soups or stews.

WATERCRESS PESTO

This recipe makes a fresh-tasting but slightly fiery pesto, which is perfect over pasta or in ravioli parcels. Serves 4–5 over pasta.

YOU WILL NEED:

- 80–100 g (3–3½ oz) watercress (around two handfuls)
- 4–5 wild garlic leaves, or 2 tsp wild garlic flakes, or a clove of garlic
- 1 tbsp toasted walnuts
- 60 ml (2 fl oz) olive oil
- 50 g (2 oz) grated parmesan or 25 g (1 oz) nutritional yeast flakes
- Salt and pepper to taste

METHOD:

1. Blanch the watercress and drain (though you can omit this step if you've soaked it in vinegar first).
2. Add all the rest of the ingredients except the oil to the food processer and give it a blitz for one minute.
3. Slowly add the oil, pulsing the mix until it forms a smooth pesto.

Poisonous plants in and by water

Although watercress is distinctive, it is worth remembering there are a few poisonous plants which grow close to or in the water alongside it. They often look and smell fresh and it is all too easy to assume they are edible – a mistake you will only make once.

Cowbane and water hemlock

In parts of the UK, such as Northern Ireland and Cheshire in particular, you may come across the deadly poisonous cowbane, *Cicuta virosa*. In North America, it is more likely you will chance upon its close relative water hemlock, *C. maculata*. Both grow in shallow water, ditches and ponds, and as members of the carrot family both can be easily mistaken for wild celery, parsnips and carrots.

The leaves are quite different from other members of the carrot family and bear more of a resemblance to marijuana leaves. Each leaflet is lance-shaped with a serrated edge and two to three times pinnate, meaning there are two to three leaflets opposite each other on a mainstem, with a long petiole or leaf stem (see illustration). Both plants grow to 1–2 metres (3–6 feet 6 inches) tall and have smooth hollow stems, along with a carrot-like or parsnip-like scent. The flowers are white umbels and each group can be pom-pom like, especially on *C. virosa*. The roots are grouped and swollen, a lot like parsnips.

Hemlock water dropwort

Hemlock water dropwort (*Oenanthe crocata*) is one of the world's most deadly wild plants. What makes it so dangerous is that it looks like a number of edible plants, like alexanders or sweet

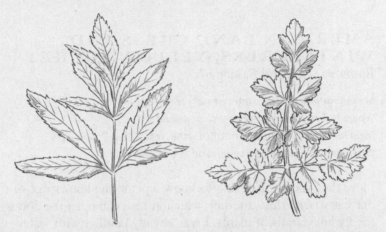

Cowbane (left) and hemlock water dropwort (right) are both deadly, but easily mistaken for other more harmless plants.

cicely, and smells like celery or parsley. As a waterside plant it is most mistaken for water celery and water parsnip, but mix-ups can happen with all members of the carrot family. If aiming to eat any members of this family you should cross-reference with as many sources as possible. Be wary of plant ID apps, as they can dangerously confuse hemlock water dropwort with all kinds of edible plants, which is reason alone not trust them without any cross-reference. I would suggest using a wildflower guide relevant to your country or region, one or two wild food guides and an app, to be on the safe side.

Hemlock water dropwort is a dark-grass to light-green colour. The stems are grooved, hairless and completely hollow and you will hear a satisfying pop when you break them. It can be found as a tufty clump or as towering plants up to 1.5 metres (5 feet) high when it comes into flower. The leaves are lobed and toothed, very similar to flat-leaved parsley, which they are often mistaken for. The flowers are white pom-pom umbels (like a firework or upside-down umbrella).

AMERICAN LAND CRESS AND WINTERCRESS, YELLOW ROCKET
Barbarea verna and *B. vulgaris*

Season for picking: late winter or early spring
Where to find them: grassy banks, wasteland
Main identifying features: similar to watercress with yellow flowers
Best use: as a herb, or as a soup/salad ingredient

I love the process of getting to know a plant; the knowledge of one can cascade into another, which in turn can open the door for a whole family of plants. I was already familiar with watercress when I began to grow American land cress as a substitute. It tastes just like watercress and is remarkably similar-looking, but with yellow rather than white flowers. It soon took up a permanent residency on my allotment, popping up each year alongside my potatoes, squashes and maize.

American land cress self-seeds easily, and so when I began to see a similar plant in hedgerows and around a housing project, I presumed it was the same thing. Yet I was confused to find that at times it tasted mild, like watercress, and bitter at others. I put it down to different soils or lack of rain until I later found out I was actually picking two different but closely related plants: the bitter-tasting wintercress (*Barbarea vulgaris*) and the milder American land cress (*B. verna*).

To cut myself some slack, the leaves of wintercress and American land cress do look remarkably similar. The basal leaves (those at the base of the plant) are pinnate and the leaf shape changes as they flower. American landcress usually has more open, wavy leaflets, like rocket, especially as you move up the stem. Wintercress is normally more ovoid, tightly packed, and has basal leaflets like watercress. The main way to tell the two plants apart is that American land cress has longer seed pods.

PREPARATION AND USE

Both wintercress and land cress have a pungent, wasabi-like kick, though wintercress is decidedly more bitter. If all this sounds confusing, simply try the leaf and if you don't like it, don't pick any more.

The Cherokee would use both plants as a boiled vegetable, a pot-herb or a salad green, but other indigenous peoples of North America, such as the Mohegan and Shinnecock, would use wintercress infused in hot water as a cough medicine.

It's best to pick both kinds in the late winter or early spring, before they have a chance to build up any bitter compounds. Wilt the leaves with onions and butter or cook them in a soup as you would watercress to reduce the bitterness. You could also try them in a tofu salad dressed with a little tabasco, some soy sauce and sesame seeds. Or keep it simple and just pop a few leaves into a sandwich.

MEADOWSWEET
Filipendula ulmaria, formerly *Spiraea ulmaria*

Season for picking: flowers spring into summer, sometimes into early autumn. Leaves best in spring
Where to find them: damp or wet places, water meadows, riversides, drainage ditches
Main identifying features: creamy frothy flowers, honey-sweet scent
Best use: similar to elderflower, for lemonade/cordial
Not to be mistaken for: hemlock (although unlikely)

Warning: not to be consumed by anyone allergic to aspirin, or if pregnant or breastfeeding.

A short walk from where I live, there is a little drainage channel running along a country road. In the summer the white, frothy blooms of meadowsweet unfurl all along this channel and I'll pluck a few of them to prepare a fresh meadowsweet lemonade.

Meadowsweet was commonly used in medieval England as a 'strewing' herb, a sweet-smelling plant that was strewn over floors to cover up the smells of the unwashed householder, at a time when the population were averse to a good wash. Queen Elizabeth I is said to have favoured meadowsweet as her chamber flower.

Meadowsweet flowers burst open during the late spring and early summer, with the odd stray flower still blooming in the autumn. They have a honey-like, slightly antiseptic scent and grow on stems around 1 metre (3 feet) tall. The leaves are dark green with a silvery underside and you are most likely to find the plant in damp or wet places such as water meadows, riversides or drainage ditches.

Surprisingly, meadowsweet gets its name from the word 'mead', rather than 'meadow', as the flowers have a floral flavour and scent much like the honey-brewed wine favoured by the Vikings. In 1830 Swiss pharmacist Johann Pagenstecher discovered that meadowsweet contained significant amounts of salicin, a pain-relieving compound, which is also found in willow bark. This marked the first step towards success for the then-small pharmaceutical company Bayer, who began synthesising a drug called acetylsalicylic acid. The drug became known as aspirin in 1899 and by 1950 had become the bestselling painkilling drug of all time. Meadowsweet is still used by herbalists as an effective painkiller, with a recommended dose of 2.5–3.5 g of the flower or 4–5 g of the leaves. However, just as with over-the-counter drugs, it should be taken with caution and it is not recommended for pregnant or breastfeeding women or anyone allergic to aspirin.

PREPARATION AND USE

The flowers of meadowsweet can be used in any recipe using elderflower, but the flavour is very different. It is more subtle for a start, so the quantities should be at least doubled. But when the flavour does come through it is reminiscent of mead or honey, with a hint of Germolene (in a good way). One of my favourite uses of meadowsweet is to use the flowers as a substitute for elderflower in a lemonade. To give this a bit of colour and extra flavour, I like to drop in my homegrown wineberries (you can also use raspberries) and leave this overnight. The sharp lemon, the fruity berries and the mellow honey flavour of the meadowsweet complement each other beautifully.

You can also submerge a couple of the leaves into apple juice or elderflower cordial, for a little extra flavour. This should be done sparingly, as there is more salicin in the leaves than in other parts of the plant.

LARGE BITTERCRESS AND WAVY BITTERCRESS
Cardamine amara and *C. flexuosa*

Season for picking: spring to autumn
Where to find them: damp woodlands, streams, marshland, moist and shady habitats
Main identifying features: pinnate leaves
Best use: salads

Both large leaf and wavy bittercress are found in damp woodlands, by streams, marsh areas or in moist and shady habitats. As you might expect, large bittercress looks like a much larger form of hairy bittercress (see page 64). Wavy bittercress is also larger than the diminutive hairy bittercress and a little more common than the large-leaf variety. Both have a watercress-like flavour and are good as a tasty salad green. You'll find them at most times of the year, except for the depths of winter.

WATER MINT
Mentha aquatica

Season for picking: spring to autumn
Where to find them: riverbanks, ponds, marshland
Main identifying features: square stem, mint scent
Best use: infusions, flavour for desserts and fruit

Water mint has lilac pom-pom flowers and grows around knee height in shallow water. You might find it by the sides of rivers and ponds or on marshland. Like all mints it has a square stem, opposite leaves and an instantly recognisable scent when crushed. It has a cooling flavour far milder than peppermint or spearmint.

PREPARATION AND USE
Although the flavour is milder than peppermint, it can be used in the same way. Infuse in boiling water for a refreshing tea or try as one of the fresh herbs in a Vietnamese pho (a meat or vegetable broth with rice noodles). Mint also goes well with fruits, such as kiwi and watermelon, in smoothies and fruit salads. Or throw a few leaves into a hot chocolate or chocolate mousse.

BULRUSH, CATTAILS
Typha spp.

Season for picking: shoots in spring, pollen and flower spikes early summer
Where to find them: anywhere near water
Main identifying features: long thin leaves like overgrown grass, sausage-shaped flower
Best use: shoots in salads, tips in desserts and flower heads eaten like corn on the cob

One hot spring day my family and I found a lovely swimming pond, on the edge of a meadow, flanked with bulrushes. We swam to escape the heat then sat on the shore pulling up the shoots of the plant, eating the soft white inner core. They were starchy and a little gooey, yet almost cucumber-like in their freshness – the perfect snack for a hot day.

Finding a bulrush, or cattail, is a sure sign the ground is no longer firm beneath your feet. They grow anywhere that is water-logged: riversides, ponds, lakes, lochs and marshy, swampy areas. They are easy to spot, as the male flowers are shaped like a hot dog sausage with a spike on top and the leaves are thin and long, like overgrown blades of grass.

PREPARATION AND USE
The edible part of a bulrush shoot is the white part at the base, which looks a lot like the white of a leek. Above this the green leaves get tough and inedible. Look for the shoots in the spring when they taste their most fresh and tender. They have a crisp flavour with a little starchiness, and are best eaten raw as part of a salad or with a dip as you would celery or carrot sticks. The base of the leaves are white and crunchy, much the same as the shoots, and can be cut and eaten as a salad leaf or passing snack.

The shoots work well fermented like a Chinese cabbage in a sort of kimchi. I recommend you complement their freshness by fermenting them with stronger flavours like chilli or ginger. Simply weigh the chopped shoots down in a jar in a 3–5 per cent brine solution along with spices of your choice (a Korean red pepper spice mix works well). The process can take up to two weeks, but you often can get good results after two to three days, especially in a hot summer. You can tell if the kimchi is ripe once the shoots take on the colour and flavour of the spices, and are soft but with a little crispness remaining. If it's too sour, it's gone over and you should start again. As soon as it is ripe, put it in the fridge to stop the fermentation.

The green female flower heads of the bulrush can be eaten a little like corn on the cob and are creamy, starchy, mealy and quite delicious. Don't harvest any which have started to go brown – they should be lime green and a little spongy. Blanch these sausage-shaped flowers in hot water until soft and dress with lemon and olive oil. Much like a corn on the cob, you should eat the outer, fleshy part, leaving the tough inner core. Alternatively, once you have blanched them, peel away the outer part and mix with fresh chopped tomatoes and olive oil. The bulrush will work like a creamy feta cheese, mellowing the acidic tomato.

I have an irrepressible sweet tooth, and I love the green flowers with cocoa powder, bananas and honey for a dessert. Don't discard the water you cooked them in, as this makes an excellent, creamy stock which can be drunk like a tea or used to make gravy.

WATER PEPPER, MARSH PEPPER KNOTWEED, TADE
Persicaria hydropiper syn. *Polygonum hydropiper*

Season for picking: summer
Where to find them: damp or marshy places; by streams, ponds, lakes and lochs; heath and moorland
Main identifying features: long thin leaves, drooping white or pink flowers
Best use: spice to add hot flavour to a range of dishes
Not to be mistaken for: redshank

Water pepper has long, thin, lance-shaped leaves, like the leaves of a weeping willow, with drooping greenish-white or pinkish flowers. It can look a lot like another related plant, *Persicaria maculosa*, or redshank, which has similar-shaped leaves and a characteristic dark dot on the centre of the leaf. Although not poisonous, redshank is not great to eat.

Water pepper can reach up to your waist but generally grows between shin and knee height. Look for it in damp or marshy places and the margins of streams, ponds, lakes and lochs. I have also found it during the summer growing on dry land, on the edges of heath and moorland in areas which may have dried up from the heat or dips, hollows and channels which once contained water. It emerges from the early summer and dies back when things start to get colder in the early autumn.

PREPARATION AND USE
I grow the related plant *Persicaria odorata*, also known as rau ram or Vietnamese coriander, in my polytunnel. It has a far less fiery flavour, which lured me into a false sense of security when trying water pepper for the first time. Instead of the mild coriander flavour of rau ram, water pepper creates a burning sensation in your mouth, akin to eating a chilli pepper or horseradish root. So use it judiciously when cooking, as it is a strong spice.

It is best to consider water pepper like a herbal chilli. I like to finely chop a few leaves and add them to stir-fries, egg-fried rice, noodle soup or filled corn tortillas for an extra kick. A few leaves also work well chopped up with red onion, fresh tomatoes and olive oil as a summer salsa. Alternatively, lay a couple of leaves inside a spring roll, as the hotness of the leaves pairs well with fresh, crisp vegetables.

In Japanese cuisine, tade, a cultivated form of water pepper, is used to make tade-zu, a sauce traditionally served with fresh water fish like salmon, trout and perch. To make a similar sauce with water pepper, finely chop 3 tablespoons of the leaves, then in a bowl add 3 tablespoons of rice vinegar and mix with 3 tablespoons of crushed steamed rice (use a pestle and mortar). Add 3 tablespoons of cold-pressed rapeseed or olive oil and a pinch of salt. In Japan, a squeeze of kabosu (a Japanese citrus fruit) is sometimes added to the sauce. I find a dash of lemon juice works as well and cuts through the flavours. For an alternative to serving the sauce with fish, try it mixed into a sweet tomato salad.

REDCURRANT
Ribes rubrum

Season for picking: mid-summer
Where to find them: wet woodlands, dips and hollows
Main identifying features: serrated leaves, red translucent berries
Best use: jelly, cordial, accompaniment to gamey meat
Not to be mistaken for: woody nightshade

Redcurrants thrive in ancient, wet woodlands and during the warm days of July, the forest can be thick with the juicy, red, translucent berries. A short drive from my home is a small, damp broadleaf forest, with mossy rocks, shaggy clumps of hart's tongue ferns, lichen-covered trees and hundreds of redcurrant plants. A narrow river wends its way through the woods and my boys love to hang precariously over the water's edge to harvest the redcurrants growing out of the riverbanks (rather than do anything sensible like pick those on dry land just a few metres away).

Redcurrants seem to love old woodlands like these, but they aren't fussy and you can find them growing in hedges, on roadsides, on edgeland and on waste ground, both under the shade of trees and in full sun.

The leaves closely resemble those of the maple tree. They're serrated and have five lobes – three larger ones with two smaller ones at the base. When ripe the berries are bright red and translucent. They aren't always as prolific or large as those you may have seen in gardens or allotments. The berries hang in clusters, and one or two will ripen first before the whole patch follows. They have a pleasant, currant smell when crushed, very similar to that of Ribena.

Various species of currant exist throughout the northern hemisphere, including red, white, black and yellow. In North America, people of the Goshute and Okanagan-Colville tribes dried the golden currant, *Ribes aureum*, and would add it to flour to make bread and cakes. It is likely the blackcurrant, *R. nigrum*, evolved in Russia where it was made into a juice or fermented into a wine with honey. Blackcurrants have escaped into the wild and can be found in various parts of Britain. Before I learnt to drive and hitch-hiked everywhere, I spent more time in lay-bys waiting for a lift than is reasonable for any human being. Often hungry and thirsty, I would forage for anything to keep me going and on more than one occasion I found blackcurrants. It wasn't until years later when I saw punnets of fresh blackcurrants being sold from a backwater lay-by that I realised the bushes I found must have been the result of self-seeded rollaway currants from these semi-legal markets.

PREPARATION AND USE
Redcurrants can be eaten straight from the plant but they can be a little sharp for modern taste buds, so are more often sweetened with sugar or maple syrup. Try simmering the berries into a pulp

and dissolving a tablespoon or two of caster sugar in the mix. Strain to remove the seeds and pour over ice cream.

Redcurrants are widely eaten in Europe but are most popular in northern countries. In Sweden they are made into a cordial called vinbärssaft (see base recipes, page 25), which can be put on ice cream, diluted as a drink or used as a salad dressing. In Norway a favourite way to eat redcurrants during the long summer days is to mix them with other seasonal berries in a sweet soup, or søtsuppe as it is known.

Redcurrants have a tart flavour and can be suitable as a substitute for barberries in Persian dishes. A jelly made from the currants is delicious on toast or pancakes, or as an accompaniment to gamey meats. In the far north of Norway, for example, the jelly is served alongside reindeer, where it is mixed with goat's cheese and rendered reindeer fat.

HIMALAYAN BALSAM, INDIAN BALSAM, POLICEMAN'S HELMET
Impatiens grandiflora

Season for picking: summer into autumn
Where to find them: waterways and edgelands
Main identifying features: large pink-and-white flowers, tall stems
Best use: seeds (similar use to sesame seeds)

I love the vividly descriptive scientific name of this plant: *Impatiens grandiflora*. The '*grandiflora*' part refers to the fact that it grows to 2 metres (6 feet 6 inches) or more, with pink or white flowers that are dome shaped, like a helmet. The '*Impatiens*' part relates to the seed pods which, somewhat impatiently, explode at the slightest touch. My children both whooped with delight when I first showed them how these trigger-happy pods pop in your hand as you gently squeeze them. Finding edible seeds inside is an added bonus, as is their creamy walnut flavour.

Balsam is an invasive weed, which spreads along waterways very successfully. The exploding pods catapult hundreds of seeds from each plant into the water, so they wash up onto banks and seed themselves by the side of rivers and streams. The plant also turns up randomly on waste ground and edgeland whenever it can get a hold. Once established, balsam can crowd out native plants, so in the UK it is an offence to spread the plant.[26] Bee-keepers, however, have a different view of balsam as its big flowers have a long season, supplying bees with nectar on warm autumn days when most other supplies have long finished.

The young stems and shoots of balsam are edible, but as they are high in oxalates they should be leached (see page 229) before eating. As a way to idle away an afternoon, the outer layer of the stems can be peeled and plaited to make a rough and ready rope. During the summer both my boys will happily sit on a riverbank peeling and twisting the stringy outer layer of the stems and putting them to good use (they make a good rustic swing for Lego men). Sections of the peeled stems (rather than the peelings) can also be used as straws – or, indeed, peashooters.

FORAGER'S TIP

As it is an offence to spread balsam seeds, they need to be harvested carefully. Cup your hands fully around the fattest pods – after a while you will be able to spot the ones which are about to blow. Gently squeeze the pod until you feel it burst inside your hands, making sure no seeds escape.

Clasp your hands around the seed pods and let them pop to prevent spreading the seed.

PREPARATION AND USE

Both the pale and black seeds of Himalayan balsam can be eaten, either raw or cooked. They taste like a cross between a walnut and a sesame seed and can be used in much the same way as either. I like to toast them and sprinkle them over salads, or just eat them on the spot. I have crushed them up to make burgers, adding grated carrot and a little chickpea flour to help them bind and flavouring with cumin, chilli and coriander powder. Press the mixture by hand into patties no bigger than a falafel and then fry them. The flowers are also edible and will brighten up a salad, or they make a beautiful pink syrup or jelly.

WALDO JEFFERS SALAD

This is my take on the Waldorf salad, using toasted Himalayan balsam seeds instead of walnuts. The name is a homage to the character Waldo Jeffers in the Velvet Underground's song 'The Gift'. The dish is a lot less grizzly than the song – the salad is covered within a casing of fresh green leaves so the red apples and white yoghurt sauce burst out when the salad is eaten. This recipe serves two to three people as a good-size starter, or four as a side salad.

YOU WILL NEED:

- 2 red apples
- Juice of half a lemon
- Half a stick of celery
- 60 g (2 oz) Himalayan balsam seeds
- 50 g (2 oz) raisins
- 250 ml (1 cup) low-fat yoghurt (you can use unsweetened vegan yoghurt)
- A pinch of salt
- Some large lettuce leaves

METHOD:

1. Core and cut the apples into approximately 2.5 cm (1 inch) pieces and place in a bowl.
2. Coat the apple pieces in lemon juice.
3. Cut the celery into slices and add to the bowl of apples.
4. Lightly toast the balsam seeds on a low heat.
5. Mix the seeds, raisins and yoghurt in with the apples and celery. Season to taste.
6. Finally, you'll need to 'wrap' the salad in the leaves. Spoon the mix into the lettuce leaves and cover with more leaves, so the salad is like the pearl in an oyster shell.

JEWEL WEED
Impatiens capensis

Season for picking: summer into autumn
Where to find them: riverbanks
Main identifying features: orange helmet-shaped flowers
Best use: flowers in salads, seeds as above

Closely related to Himalayan balsam, with flowers as orange as a 1970s kitchen, jewel weed grows in the UK, mainland Europe and North America. It does not grow as tall as Himalayan balsam but the flowers and seeds can be used in the same way.

PENDULOUS SEDGE
Carex pendula

Season for picking: late summer/early autumn
Where to find them: damp areas, under the cover of trees,
in gardens and edgelands
Main identifying features: triangular-shaped stem, drooping
head of seeds
Best use: seeds can be ground into flour
Not to be mistaken for: grasses and rushes

If you're finding it tricky to work out the difference between sedges, rushes and grasses, rest assured you're not alone. To help see through the confusion, I was taught this useful rhyme by an ecology tutor: 'Sedges have edges, rushes are round, grasses have knees that bend to the ground.' The 'edge' of a sedge refers to its triangular-shaped stem.

Many sedges have edible seeds but most are too small and fiddly to use. The pendulous sedge, however, with its drooping head of seeds, is easy to gather in quantity and has been used as a food source for millennia. The long blades grow in a shaggy clump, just over waist height, sometimes higher, with the seed heads lolloping out on tough stems above and to the sides. You'll find them in wet or damp areas, especially under the cover of trees, in gardens and on edgeland. The seeds are ready to pick when they have turned from green to light brown, which is usually throughout the late summer and into the autumn.

PREPARATION AND USE
Gathering sedge seeds is a way of channelling your inner Stone-Age hunter gatherer. The seeds can be gathered in quantity and mixed with bread flour for added nutrition and an extra nutty flavour.

Firstly though, to harvest sedge seeds, pinch your thumb and forefinger around the bottom of the lowest seed head and pull up, allowing them to gather in your hand. Drop them into a container poised below the plant and then move on to the next sedge and do the same.

You will then need to separate the seed from the fibrous chaff. Traditionally this was done by transferring the seeds between two bowls in a light breeze and allowing the wind to blow away the chaff. I've never found this method to be that practical, and instead use a normal household sieve. To do this, start by placing your harvest in a bag and agitating the seeds to loosen them from the chaff. Next, pass the contents of the bag through a fine sieve a number of times, discarding any chaff left in the sieve. Grind the seeds into a flour in a food mill or with a pestle and mortar. I find the old technology really works well and use a quern stone.

The flour can be added to wheat flour for biscuits or bread, or used on its own to make a 'survival' bread cooked in the hot coals of a fire. Although the latter is worth playing with as a piece of experiential archaeology, it makes for a crumbly loaf which (in my opinion) needs strong-flavoured jams and butter to make it worth eating.

LESSER BURDOCK AND GREATER BURDOCK
Arctium minus and *A. lappa*

Season for picking: autumn and winter or early spring for roots.
Spring for stems
Where to find them: side of rivers and clearings, woodland edges,
paths, roadsides, edgeland, open fields
Main identifying features: big leaves and burs
Best use: roots cooked
Not to be mistaken for: butterbur

There are two main types of burdock: *Arctium minus* (or lesser burdock) and *A. lappa* (greater burdock). The latter is a bigger plant with more spherical flowers. Both types are edible and are similar-tasting, so for the forager it is more important to be able to tell them apart from the non-edible and downy-leaved butterbur plant, which has more rounded leaves, than it is from each other.

Of the two types you are most likely to find greater burdock by the side of water, especially rivers, canals and drainage ditches. Its large leaves, similar in size to those of rhubarb (approximately 50 cm/20 inches), make the most of any scrap of sunlight that touches them. Lesser burdock can also occasionally be found by the water's edge, but along with greater burdock it can also be found growing in clearings and woodland edges, along with more open places such as the sides of paths and roads and in neglected areas of land.

Burdock is commonly described as a biennial, spending part of its life as a low-lying, rosette-forming plant before going to seed in the second year. However, it often behaves as a perennial, taking anything up to five years to flower and go to seed. It is during this flowering stage that the plant is at its most noticeable; the upper leaves reduce in size and the flowering stalk grows up to 1.8 metres (6 feet) high, producing a purple prickly flower of a similar hue to a thistle. The flower later turns into the sticky, hooked bur that gives the plant its name.

The root, which is harvested in the earlier, rosette form of the plant's life is the most useful edible part of the plant. It is illegal to uproot any plant without the permission of the landowner but even if you can obtain this permission, they can be tricky things to dig up. Early spring and late autumn are the best times to forage for the roots – they are swollen with energy, ready to form the flowers for the following year. Burdock roots range from the size of a finger to the size of a stout carrot. Look for lush green growth and you stand a better chance of finding a decent root.

FORAGER'S TIP

Mischievous children like to fling the sticky burdock burs at unsuspecting parents and siblings. And dog owners can find countless burs attached to the fur of their inquisitive hounds, after the scent of a rabbit or fox has sent them rummaging in the bushes. For these reasons, burdock is often found growing close to car parks where parents and dog owners remove the burs and throw them into the bushes.

PREPARATION AND USE

Young roots can be eaten raw and unpeeled, but older roots need to be peeled first as the outer skin can be bitter. In Japan the root is widely sold as 'gobo' and is used to prepare a dish called kinpira. The root is cut into slices and lightly fried with carrot, then cooked further with sugar and soy sauce before being topped with sesame seeds.

The raw root can be finely chopped and mixed into salads, or grated and added to soups and stews. My favourite way of preparing it is to parboil it, then roast it in a mix of chilli, cumin and coriander powder before dipping into a sweet hawthorn ketchup.

Like several other vegetables (notably chicory, Jerusalem artichokes and asparagus), burdock root contains a type of polysaccharide or starch called inulin (see dahlias, page 59). For some individuals this can have a very audible effect on the bowels, especially when eating the root for the first time. The more often you eat it the less likely you are to suffer from 'burdock bottom'.

In the spring, before the plant comes into flower, both the tall main flowering stem and the smaller side shoots are good to eat. They have a fresh, aromatic, vegetable taste, a lot like the stems of an artichoke but with a little bitterness. Both the main stem and the side shoots will need to be peeled as the outer skin is tough and inedible. The inside will be soft, with the consistency of a carrot that has sat in the fridge too long. You can slice the stem and shoots into discs and boil, fry or bake them. Their fresh vegetable taste soaks up other flavours and I like to eat them as a side snack dressed in soy sauce with a sprinkling of toasted sesame seeds. They also make a good pickle, which can be used in salads throughout the year.

CHAPTER THIRTEEN

The Coast

T HERE IS NOTHING quite like that very first glimpse of
the sea on a hot summer's day. You feel the anticipation
of the warm sand between your feet, hear the cry of the
gulls and smell the salty maritime air.

Down on these wild shores the earth's geological past is clearly mapped out, as the sea slowly reclaims the land, exposing great
rocky cliffs towering above the beaches and crashing waves below.
Over many millions of years, geological forces have contorted
layers of rock into wavy, haphazard shapes, like sugar syrup.
And all along the coast, on top of wind-battered headlands, in
remote coves and nestled among sandy dunes, plants have adapted to the struggles and challenges of this often-inhospitable
environment.

For any plants attempting to take root by the coast, there are
a number of obstacles to overcome. Firstly, there's the soil. Sand
particles form large and free-draining soils which do not hold
onto water, making it difficult for new life to grow. Then there's
the water itself. Much of the water by the coast has such a high
salt content that maritime plants cannot use it effectively. Instead
coastal plants have adapted to make the most of any fresh water they take up – with fleshy succulent leaves that behave a little like those of desert plants. We see this in the tiny cactus-like
marsh samphire (page 394) and seablite (page 397). And if you
look closely at other coastal plants such as sea beet, you will see
that although the leaves are not succulent, they are glossier and

fleshier than those of their inland relatives (like beetroot and sugar beet).

Another issue for coastal plants is the strong winds that whip over headlands or across wide, flat and open expanses of beach. Seaside plants have developed many ingenious adaptions to cope with howling gales. The spear-leaved orache, a close relative to inland goosefoot or fat hen, grows prostrate across the sand, literally ducking down to keep out of the wind. The Monterey pine, a tree native to California which can grow up to 45 metres (150 feet) high, has been planted along coastlines across Europe, especially in Spain and southern England. Its roots can grow up to 12 metres (40 feet) deep, an adaption which helps it grow in the thin maritime soil of California. This adaptation holds onto the sandy European soils, preventing erosion from the strong coastal winds.

Sea beet, sea radish, alexanders and fennel have also evolved to have large, energy-rich roots that allow them to lie in suspended animation over the winter until warmer weather springs them back into action. Although this adaptation is common inland too, there is an abundance of edible biennial plants by the coast, which means they can be reliable places to find food at any time of the year. During a long winter walk, when the sun is doing its best to warm my face and seals on beaches outnumber people, I like to pick a little of these winter leaves from here and there, spreading my picking to allow regrowth in the spring. I'll return to the warmth of my kitchen, wilting the leaves in a splash of water, serving with a dash of Worcester sauce and buttery chickpeas on a crispy jacket potato.

On days when the tide times are working in my favour, another rich foraging seam opens up as the sea retreats and glossy seaweeds lie limp on the rocky shores. Living life half in and half out of the water, they are highly adapted organisms, having honed their survival strategies for longer than we can hope to comprehend. Seaweeds evolved from single-celled cyanobacteria – the slime-like organisms that had dominated the planet for more than a billion years – about 1.6 billion years ago. To put that into perspective, evidence of the first embryophytes, or land plants, dates to only 470 million years ago.

Seaweeds are best gathered in the late winter or early spring, as they grow most quickly in the coolest waters. At this time of year, it is easy to quickly fill a basket with kelps for a rich savoury stock, sea lettuces for tasty winter salads and laver for nutritious laverbread and crisp nori flakes. Once the cool of winter starts to fade, coastal greens like alexanders, wild radish and sea beet are at their best. Come the warm summer, it is time to give the seaweeds a break, as this is their main period of reproduction. Among the dunes and alongside coastal paths, wild radish sends out crisp seed pods and on the rocky cliffs, the succulent rock samphire bursts into flower. As the summer moves into autumn, field and parasol mushrooms (page 237) pepper the grassy head-lands overlooking the coast. Sea buckthorn and coastal roses come into fruit, with oranges and reds joining the blues, greens and yellows of the coastal palette.

As the winter returns, it's time to turn again to coastal greens and seaweeds. And on these clear, crisp days, wrapped up warm and watching the late-afternoon sun set on the rippling waves, the coast can be a place of glorious solitude.

SEA BEET, SEA SPINACH
Beta vulgaris subsp. *maritima*

Season for picking: all year
Where to find them: cliff tops, solid ground near the sea, saline tidal estuaries
Main identifying features: glossy triangular leaves like spinach or chard. Grooved flowering stems
Best use: leaves as you would use spinach

Sea beet is common throughout coastal Europe (with the exception of the cold North Sea coast in north-east Scotland) and can occasionally be found on the coasts of sunny California, where it is thought to have been introduced by early settlers. As the wild ancestor of beetroot, chard, sugar beet and perpetual spinach, the shape and form of the leaves will be familiar to farmers and home-growers. It has glossy leaves, which are slightly thicker than spinach or chard but with a similar triangular shape. The grooved flowering stem supports clustered, green flowers which come up in the late spring and summer. The plant grows in a rosette form, from a single fleshy root, sometimes with many plants clustering together.

You'll find sea beet all over the coast, often just a few metres away from the tide line. As it likes high-nutrient soils, look for it close to coastal paths where dog walkers have been, or on cliff tops enriched by sea birds (remember to wash the leaves when you get home!). Look for it too on grassy headlands, upper reaches of sand and shingle where the land is becoming more solid, and close to sea defences. It also inhabits the shores of saline tidal estuaries and I have found it nearly five miles inland from the mouth of the River Avon, on the outskirts of Bristol.

Although sea beet is around all year, it is best to harvest it either side of its late spring and summer flowering time. As it is slow growing in the winter, avoid picking too much in the depths of winter.

PREPARATION AND USE

Sea beet leaves are as versatile as spinach. They can be cooked in much the same way and have a similar soft texture, which soaks up flavours like butter and olive oil and is enhanced with a pinch of nutmeg.

Like spinach, they go well with a wide variety of ingredients from dairy, chicken and eggs to tofu and beans. Small leaves can be eaten raw but I prefer to cook them as, although not bitter, they have a strong, chlorophyll flavour when raw. However, they can work well in salads, especially with the addition of a dressing sweetened with honey.

One of my favourite recipes is to lightly steam them and use them as a filling for a baked potato with cream cheese or chick-peas. For an East African twist, try them sautéed in butter, with onions, peanuts, tabasco sauce and a little grated coconut.

The roots are edible but, in most cases, it is illegal to uproot the plant and as they taste a bit like a woody beetroot, it is seldom worth the effort.

LEBANESE BAKED EGGS

While living in Bristol, a friend of mine from Florida introduced me to what he called 'Mexican eggs'. He would crack eggs into a spicy tomato sauce and bake them until they turned white, retaining their oozing, yellow yolks. As a lover of Lebanese food, I have adapted the recipe to use sea beet leaves and Lebanese spices. The fresh leaves and protein-rich egg make a perfect Saturday morning breakfast after an indulgent Friday night. The recipe below serves 4.

YOU WILL NEED:

- 650 g (1½ lb) sea beet leaves
- 1 onion
- 1 clove of garlic
- 2 tsp Lebanese spice mix (see below)
- A little water
- Olive oil

For the Lebanese spice mix:
- 1 tsp ground cumin
- 1 tsp paprika
- ½ tsp ground cloves
- A large pinch of ground nutmeg
- A large pinch of ground cinnamon
- A small pinch of ground cardamom

METHOD:

1. Chop and gently fry the onion in the oil until it turns translucent.
2. While the onion is cooking, remove any tough stalks from the sea beet.
3. Crush and finely chop the garlic, then sauté with the onions.
4. Shred the sea beet into strips and add to the pan.
5. Sprinkle on the spices, add a dash of water, stir and cover. Allow to simmer until the sea beet is soft and cooked.
6. Next, spoon the sea beet into a ceramic baking tray large enough to accommodate 4 eggs. Make four deep wells in the sea beet and crack an egg into each hole.
7. Bake in the oven at 180°C (350°F) for 5 minutes until the egg is cooked.
8. Serve with flatbreads or pita and hawthorn ketchup (see page 176).

STAG'S HORN PLANTAIN, BUCK'S HORN PLANTAIN, ERBA STELLA
Plantago coronopus

Season for picking: all year, less prevalent in winter
Where to find them: coastal heaths, headlands and on soil above tide line
Main identifying features: narrow leaves shaped like horns
Best use: extra flavour and decoration for salads or pasta
Not to be mistaken for: groundsel

On the much-trodden headlands of Cornwall, carpets of stag's horn plantain grow as thickly as grass. It is an adorable little plant, with narrow leaves which break into 'horns', giving the appearance of tiny antlers. The leaves are generally matt green, slightly fleshy and up to 20 cm (8 inches) long. It's a perennial, so you'll find it all year round, even in the depths of winter especially in sheltered regions.

It favours poor coastal soils so look for it on sea cliffs, rock crevices and coastal heaths, where it tends to grow only in direct light. It is found throughout Europe and has naturalised in coastal North America. Its only lookalikes are other plantains (which are all edible) or groundsel (*Senecio vulgaris*, not American groundsel), which has deeply lobed leaves and a more branched, herbaceous form rather than growing in a rosette form like plantain. Like its inland relations, stag's horn plantain has a flowering spike. This sets it decisively apart from groundsel, which has a wispy, dandelion clock flower.

It is considered a gourmet micro-green and is sometimes sold in specialist markets as erba stella. One grower in Cornwall sends his stag's horn plantain leaves, along with mixed micro-greens, as far afield as Malaysia.

PREPARATION AND USE

The taste of the leaf is somewhat salty with a mushroom-like bitterness, a crisp freshness and a satisfying, succulent texture.

Cut off the leaves with a pair of scissors, if you have them to hand, or snap near the base. They will last for an afternoon in a pocket if you forget your bag (you just have to remember they are there).

I like to blanch the leaves, coat them with butter and add lemon, and sprinkle on toasted almond flakes to make a little side salad. They have a good enough flavour raw that they can be thrown into a mixed salad, going very well with fresh-tasting ingredients like cucumber, pennywort or sedum. Or you can use them to decorate pasta dishes, or mix in with a lemony couscous chicken salad.

ALEXANDERS
Smyrnium olusatrum

Season for picking: shoots in late winter/early spring, stems in late spring, seeds summer to winter
Where to find them: coastal hedgerows and roadsides
Main identifying features: yellow firework-like flowers, toothed glossy leaves
Best use: as a herb similar to parsley
Not to be mistaken for: hemlock water dropwort or other poisonous members of the carrot family.

Along with chestnuts, walnuts, carrots and smallpox, alexanders were introduced to western and central Europe by the Romans. The scent of the plant was reminiscent of myrrh and the Romans sometimes called it 'myrrh of Achaea', referencing a province of Greece where it grew. Along the Mediterranean coast in medieval times it was called *Petroselinum Alexandrium*, 'the parsley of Alexandria'. The Romans loved the strong flavour and used it in

much the same way as parsley is used today, to flavour sauces, soups and stews.

Alexanders stayed in use in Britain for centuries and were even cultivated outside of their usual coastal habitat. As a result, the plant can sometimes be found in the grounds of ruined medieval abbeys. However, tastes in Britain became ever blander and by the eighteenth century the strong-flavoured alexanders had made way for the sweeter cultivated celery from Italy.

Alexanders are commonly found along coastal hedgerows and roadsides, first sprouting up in the winter and early spring. During the spring and early summer, they can be so abundant that whole hedgerows seem to glow with firework-like umbels of yellow flowers. The leaves grow in groups of three on the ends of stalks; they are a glossy, rich green and toothed, with a celery-like smell. The whole plant can reach 1.5 metres (5 feet) high, and the black seeds that emerge after the plant flowers often remain into the winter. The stem starts off solid, becoming hollow as the plant ages.

Alexanders could be mistaken for the poisonous hemlock water dropwort, which grows in and near fresh water and has more fern-like leaves, so correct identification is crucial. Once the yellow flower forms, or the hard jet-black peppery seeds set, it is much harder to mistake the alexanders for anything poisonous.

PREPARATION AND USE

Alexanders are extremely useful for foragers, with edible leaves, stems, flowers and seeds.

Starting in the late winter/early spring (or in mild areas even the early autumn), the fresh shoots of alexanders make an excellent pot-herb. I use them in salads or, as the Romans did, in place of parsley. Try them with fish or seafood, or use in a rich creamy sauce, but add them at the very end of cooking to preserve the flavour. You could also try the shoots finely chopped, mixed with melted butter and a squeeze of lemon, and added to boiled new potatoes.

The growing stems are next to harvest, later in the spring. They have a wonderfully aromatic carrot-celery flavour, and although the outer skin can be tough, once peeled the inner core is soft and succulent. Eat it raw or, better still, blanched as a uniquely ambrosial side vegetable. Though be warned that the stems, like those of fennel and other fragrant members of the carrot family, can overpower a stir-fry unless you use them alongside strong flavours like chilli and ginger.

The flower heads retain the flavour of the stems but in a subtler fashion. These are best dipped in batter and deep-fried, then served with a yoghurt-based or satay dipping sauce. As well as the flower heads, you can harvest the seeds and use them as a spice, similar to pepper but without the heat. Try them in a pepper grinder mixed with peppercorns, or crush with a pestle and mortar.

TREE MALLOW
Lavatera arborea

Season for picking: all year (can die back in the winter)
Where to find them: rich soils, sheltered coastal gardens, sunlit walls
Main identifying features: soft sycamore-shaped leaves, big lilac flowers
Best use: salads, curries, soups, risottos

With a thick central stalk and soft, sycamore-shaped leaves that can be bigger than your hand, the tree mallow is a common seaside perennial in temperate regions. The flowers are beautiful blooms, much like cultivated mallows and hollyhocks. They have five petals and range from pinkish lilac to purple, with a darker centre and delicate scent to invite passing honey bees.

As they favour rich soil and baulk at hard frosts, they do best in sheltered coastal gardens, along sunlit walls and in soil enriched by seabird droppings. Tree mallow is a Mediterranean plant, and grows in climates similar to its native lands, such as the US states of Oregon and California, coastal southern Europe and most of coastal Britain and Ireland (especially the south). It is rare in Scotland and Scandinavia.

The leaves are exceptionally soft and strong and can make a good substitute for toilet paper in desperate times. This has led to a popular botanical folk tale suggesting the plant's scientific name, *Lavatera arborea*, stems from the word 'lavatory' – and people have speculated that the Romans introduced it to Britain for that very reason. But the plant actually gets its name from Johann Jakob Lavater, an eighteenth-century Swiss naturalist, rather than the Roman version of Andrex.

Lavatera maritima or sea mallow, a very similar plant with smaller grey-green leaves, can also be found in coastal regions throughout Europe, or inland as a garden plant. It is equally edible, though has slightly chewier leaves.

PREPARATION AND USE

Tree mallows have a much more defined flavour than most other mallows. They are refreshing to eat raw, with a bean pod taste and a satisfying mouth feel. They are excellent in salads, especially mixed with other seaside leaves such as sea radish, alexanders and young sea beet. Cooked, they reduce down but still keep much of their flavour and integrity, which makes them work well for dolmades (see page 230). They are also good chopped up and added towards the end of cooking a risotto, curry or soup, to add extra texture.

HIERBAS HERVIDAS DEL MAR

In parts of Spain, wild greens like tree mallow are still prepared as they have been for centuries. Ethnobotanists visiting this region in the 1990s found that locals prepared anything up to fifteen different wild greens gathered from the coast or hedgerows.[27] This recipe, which translates from Spanish as 'boiled sea herbs', is perfect for wild leaves as the hot water reduces the bitterness and softens any tough leaves.

YOU WILL NEED:

- A small handful of sea radish leaves
- A few sea rocket leaves
- A handful of sea mallow leaves
- A handful of sea beet leaves
- 1–2 cloves of garlic (or 4–5 wild garlic leaves)
- A generous pinch of cumin
- A generous pinch of cinnamon
- Salt and pepper to taste

YOU COULD ALSO THROW IN THESE OPTIONAL EXTRAS:

- ½ to 1 can chickpeas
- Boiled potatoes
- Chopped tomatoes
- Cooked onion (or raw red onion)
- Fried bacon pieces
- Fried tofu pieces

METHOD:

1. Clean and remove any tough stems from all the wild leaves, then chop them into 2.5 cm (1 inch) pieces.
2. In a large pan, bring some water to the boil, then add the greens and simmer for 3–4 minutes or until they are tender.
3. Add a generous pinch of salt, the chopped garlic cloves (or leaves) and the spices.
4. Simmer for a further minute or two.
5. Drain and adjust seasoning to taste, adding extra spices if required.
6. Serve as a side vegetable or a pie filling, or add any of the optional extras for a more substantial meal.

SEA RADISH
Raphanus maritimus, R. raphanistrum subsp. *maritimus*

Season for picking: leaves throughout the year, seed pods in early summer
Where to find them: headland and close to the beach where the sand becomes solid ground
Main identifying features: rough, scalloped leaves in rosette form; white, pink and yellow flowers
Best use: leaves to add radish-like flavour to dishes, seed pods as a snack or in salads
Not to be mistaken for: thistles (you'll soon know if you pick the wrong thing!)

Once you get an eye for sea radish you will start to see it everywhere. The leaves grow in a rosette from the central root and are scalloped, hairy, dark green and alternately pinnate with a larger leaflet at the terminal (or tip).

The seed pods of sea radish, which look like small, spiky-topped pea pods, form throughout the summer and have a satisfying crunch and delicious radish flavour. A large stand of them grow between the car park and my favourite beach in Dorset, and

I find it impossible to pass by without removing a pod or five for a spicy, crisp munch while hunting for fossils. Prior to the emergence of these seed pods, the plant sends out white, pink or yellow cross-shaped flowers (characteristic of all members in the brassica family) throughout the spring. These can be plucked off and used in salads or munched as a passing snack.

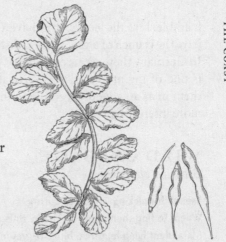

Sea radish leaves are deliciously spicy.

Look for them on headlands and away from the tide line but still close to the beach. They thrive on poor maritime soils throughout Europe, North America and beyond. Away from the coast, on uncultivated areas or fringes of farmland, you might stumble on what looks like a sea radish, but this will be the closely related wild radish, which can be used in exactly the same way.

PREPARATION AND USE

The leaves can be harvested all year round and taste fresh, sharp and peppery – exactly like a crisp red radish or white mooli root. They make an amazing kimchi (see page 24) without the need for much in the way of flavouring. A few leaves mixed into a bigger salad will give it a rounded depth of flavour. Try them too in a stir-fry, to balance rich flavours like beef and pork (or beefsteak mushroom – see page 309). You could also use the leaves to add kick to yoghurt sauces, mixed with mint and cucumber.

The 'rats' tails' or pointed seed pods of sea radish have a short season in the early summer, after which they become tough and inedible. Like the leaves, they have a distinctive radish flavour but have the crunch of a vegetable radish and a mellow, peppery heat. In Germany they are eaten fresh or pickled as a bar snack, which is one of my preferred ways to eat them. Alternatively, throw them in as an added vegetable to make a stir-fry or salad a little more interesting.

WILD CABBAGE
Brassica oleracea

Season for picking: winter to spring
Where to find them: only on chalky cliffs or lime-heavy soil near the sea
Main identifying features: blueish-grey leaves, yellow flowers
Best use: leaves and buds, similar to cultivated cabbage

Warning: do not pick from precarious cliff-tops.

When the Romans invaded England and Wales, they brought with them the contents of their kitchen cupboards. Not content with the British diet, they cultivated plums and damsons to replace the tart sloe. They grew spinach instead of fat hen, and rather than eat the native, bitter wild cabbage, they brought their own sweet cultivated varieties. Most of the foods we now see as purely 'wild' would have been staples of the British pre-Roman diet. I often contemplate this when wincing at the sourness of a raw sloe or munching through some bitter leaves that I've harvested a little too late in the season.

Wild cabbage must have been a challenging crop, not just because of its bitter flavour but also the dangerous places it likes to grow. It is a salt-tolerant, lime-loving plant, so is mostly confined to the chalk cliffs of southern England and northern France. More often than not I spot it just the other side of a 'Danger: Falling Rocks' sign. However, you should look out for the stray plants that crop up by the side of a cliff path or at the bottom, rather than the top, of a sea cliff.

Anyone who has grown any kind of *Brassica*, such as broccoli or Brussel sprouts, should be able to recognise the overall look and form of a wild cabbage. All of these plants are varieties of the same species, *Brassica oleracea*, which can make identifying true wild cabbage rather tricky. Wild kales and mustards will all have the same overall look, especially when young. Wild cabbage differs slightly as the leaves tend to be a greyish or blueish green, sometimes with purple tinges, rather than a lighter green like wild mustard. These leaves are irregular in shape and are stalked, growing to an average of around 30 cm (1 foot) long. When the plant comes into flower the leaves are attached to the stem, rather than on stalks, and much smaller in size. In spring and summer they bloom with a mass of yellow, cross-shaped flowers on a flowering spike up to 2 metres (6 feet 6 inches) tall.

In case you are tempted to nip to the south English coast the day after Christmas, it is considered bad luck to pick cabbage on Boxing Day. The 26 December is also St Stephen's Day, and it is said the saint met his end when he was stoned to death in a cabbage patch.

PREPARATION AND USE

True wild cabbage has a much stronger flavour than its cultivated descendants. It is bitter and overpowering if picked any later than spring, so aim to pick in the late winter or very early spring. One hot summer day, curiosity got the better of me and I decided to sample a leaf when the plant was in full flower. The first bite was fine and I wondered what all the fuss was about, but soon the bitterness started building in my mouth until it was overwhelming. I've not been tempted to try it since.

Cooking helps to reduce the bitterness, as do the old tricks of adding lemon juice, butter, bacon or soy sauce. I shred the leaves into strands and lightly fry them in butter along with sea beet, which often grows right next to wild cabbage. The immature flowering buds are a little less bitter and can be treated like purple sprouting broccoli, which they closely resemble.

Wild cabbage only grows in very particular habitats, and even then only appears in small numbers. Take only one or two leaves from each plant at most, so there is enough of it left to carry on growing.

FENNEL
Foeniculum spp.

Season for picking: spring and summer
Where to find them: poor soils on the edges of dunes and the tops of beaches
Main identifying features: feathery fronds, aniseed scent
Best use: shoots as a vegetable, leaves as a herb, seeds for spice or tea

Growing up to 2 metres (6.5 feet) tall, fennel has yellow umbels of flowers which give way to hard, aromatic seeds. Its feathery fronds are easily distinguished from other plants by their characteristic aniseed scent when crushed. The fennel you find by the coast is a wild variety, lacking the swollen bulb of the common, cultivated vegetable.

In Britain it is a mostly coastal plant but stray plants do find their way inland. In both London and Bristol I've seen them growing through cracks in the pavement close to Indian restaurants and Asian supermarkets, presumably as escapees from spilled spice mixes. By the coast you are most likely to find fennel growing in poor soils on the edges of dunes and at the tops of beaches.

The Romans believed that fennel could bestow great strength on anyone who ate it and gladiators, most of whom were vegetarian or vegan, would mix it in with simple meals of barley and lentils.[28] It wasn't just the gladiators who held it in high esteem in Roman times; Pliny suggested that fennel could restore skin and eyesight back to their youthful vigour.

PREPARATION AND USE

The whole of the fennel plant is edible, and has an aniseed-like flavour from the seeds down to the root. As coastal fennel does not bulb in the same way as the fennel vegetable, it is the fronds, shoots and seeds that are the most useful parts of the plant.

Use the shoots like a vegetable. They go well blanched and mixed with apples and walnuts in a winter salad. Or try them with other members of the carrot family, such as carrots or celery, dressed with mayonnaise.

The leaves are best fresh and used as any other culinary herb, and go very well with fish. Use a few fennel fronds or seeds and a little butter or olive oil to flavour a line-caught sea fish, cooked in tinfoil on a barbecue or hot coals of a fire on a beach. The leaves also work in sparingly in a salad to give it a hint of aniseed.

The flowers and the fruits or unripe seeds make a good passing snack or addition to a salad. The flavour is not subtle and it doesn't work well with everything – something like a creamy mushroom sauce can end up being overpowered. Instead try with flavoursome vegetables in salads and slaws, or in burgers and meatballs.

The seeds are good to freshen the breath and aid digestion after a meal – you might notice that plain or sometimes brightly coloured and sugar-coated fennel seeds are given out in Indian restaurants. A teaspoon of the seeds infused in hot water also makes a very refreshing tea.

SEA ORACHE
Atriplex spp.

Season for picking: spring to autumn
Where to find them: landward tops of beaches
Main identifying features: triangular, goosefoot-shaped leaves, clusters of green to red flowers
Best use: cooked as salty spinach

The name 'sea orache' actually covers various similar species of plant within the *Atriplex* genus. As part of the goosefoot family they are closely related to fat hen, quinoa and amaranth. All these plants share similar-shaped triangular leaves, which are grey-green, with a light dusting or bloom. In the summer, sea orache sends up clusters of tiny green to red flowers.

Some oraches grow prostrate across the ground, others upright. They can grow as single plants in sparsely populated communities or as great dense hedges. It isn't necessary to tell the different species apart as all are equally edible and delicious. However, it is best to harvest oraches from where they are most abundant, leaving solo plants to struggle alone in peace. Like goosefoot, it is great for improvised dishes. I love picking it from the edge of a soft, sandy beach, wilting it in a pan on a portable gas burner, and sautéeing it with summer mushrooms in a little olive oil. I'll serve this with crusty bread and a flask of hot tea – on a warm summer's day, there are few better brunches to be had.

PREPARATION AND USE
The younger leaves can be eaten raw, in the same way as baby spinach. Look for these in the spring when they are at their best. If you intend to cook them, they can be picked at most times of the year, dying back at the first frosts of winter and popping back up in the mid-to-late spring. They have a nutty, salty taste, which works well with creamy flavours. I love to mix them in with a bag

of chips as their fresh flavour cuts through the fat and their salti-ness flavours the chips.

You can also try using orache leaves in Middle Eastern dishes, like a spicy lamb stew served on couscous, mixing with yoghurt and strong spices such as fenugreek. They are also great sautéed with boletus mushrooms or tomatoes, or eaten with pasta or rice.

BURNET ROSE, SCOTCH ROSE
Rosa pimpinellifolia syn. *Rosa spinosissima*

Season for picking: summer and autumn
Where to find them: limestone soils, coastal hedgerows, headlands, sand dunes
Main identifying features: wild rose-like white flowers with a yellow centre
Best use: rose hip vodka

The burnet rose was the symbol for the Jacobite risings of the seventeenth and eighteenth centuries. It was celebrated in poet-ry and song and has remained an important symbol for Scottish independence ever since.

It can be found growing on limestone soils, in coastal thick-ets and hedgerows, on headlands or tucked away in sand dunes. You will also find it on the hedgerows surrounding coastal fields, either as great thickets or scattered individuals. The flowers, which can bloom as early as mid-spring, look very much like wild roses. They are white with five petals and a yellow centre. Like those of many other roses, the leaves are pinnate, but they are smaller and the whole plant has a more diminutive feel to it than the often thuggish *Rosa rugosa* (which can also be found growing by the coast – see page 88).

PREPARATION AND USE
Both the hips and flowers can be used in the same way as those of garden and wild roses. The petals can be added to salads for a

little colour and floral piquancy. Or you could try making a coastal panna cotta. Dissolve a tablespoon of sugar or honey in two glasses of milk, add a handful of fresh carrageen and a few drops of rose essence, and simmer until the mixture starts to turn gelatinous. Fish out the seaweed, fold in a teaspoon of burnet rose petals and pour into ramekins. Allow to cool and set, then sprinkle petals and crushed nuts on top.

The rounded hips are purply black, and make a delicious cordial or syrup. When infused in vodka with sugar they make a beautifully dark liqueur (follow the sloe gin recipe on page 178).

SEA BUCKTHORN
Hippophae rhamnoides

Season for picking: late summer/early autumn
Where to find them: hedgerows and thickets near the sea
Main identifying features: bright-orange berries, silver-green lance-shaped leaves
Best use: juice, sorbet, ice cream
Not to be mistaken for: *Mohave pyracantha*

During a tour of Scotland my partner and I wild-camped on a remote, primeval-looking beach. Scots pines hung to the cliffs above and large stands of silver-green sea buckthorn flanked the upper reach of the shoreline. It was September so the crowds were gone, but a little of the summer heat remained. We awoke to the sound of seabirds and smell of seaweed and, bleary-eyed, dropped squishy, bloated sea buckthorn berries, shaped like Tic Tacs, into our morning porridge to give it a vitamin C kick.

Sea buckthorn is a conspicuous shrub that grows in hedgerows and thickets by the sea, sometimes mixed with other species but more often growing alone. The bush will reach between 2 and 4 metres (7 and 13 feet) and has silver-green, lance- or willow-shaped leaves, a bit like rosemary leaves. The berries are bright orange and cluster onto the mainstem, ripening in the mid-to-late summer or early autumn. Depending on the region, berries sometimes remain on the plant until the winter and if you see them, no matter the time of year, they are always worth a try.

Although sea buckthorn has no poisonous lookalikes, superficially it can look like a *Mohave pyracantha*, which is quite a different garden plant with harder, rounder fruits and greener leaves. Sea buckthorn is considered to be a superfood – the berries owe their bright orange colour to large amounts of beta-carotene (which the body converts into vitamin A). They are also packed with antioxidants and contain much higher amounts of vitamin C than strawberries or oranges.

Sea buckthorn is native to northern Europe but can be found in temperate coastal regions worldwide, including Russia and cooler parts of North and South America. In Mongolia it is grown in environmentally friendly orchards as the strong roots of the plant consolidate the soil and prevent erosion, helping to prevent the spread of the Mongolian desert. The berries are made into a juice and sold throughout Mongolia and Russia, promoted as a healthy, antioxidant-rich drink.

FORAGER'S TIP

Ripe sea buckthorn berries are hard to pick by hand, especially in any quantity, as they can squish into pulp at the slightest squeeze. Some people choose to cut the fruiting branches with a pair of secateurs, freeze them and then remove the hard berries by hand. Cutting a few branches doesn't harm the plant; it will respond to the pruning just like any garden fruit bush. However, if you're planning to turn the berries into a juice anyway, you may prefer to just squeeze them straight into a container. This is best done as a pair, with one of you squeezing the berries and the other holding the bucket or pot.

Sea buckthorn juice is a vivid orange, like fresh carrot juice or one of those horrible, synthetic orange drinks aimed at children. Sometimes called the Siberian pineapple, it is said to have all the flavour of a pineapple without any of the sweetness. I find the berries to have a tangy, slightly sweet, citrusy taste, which reminds me of super-sour gobstoppers or Nerds, deliciously sour American candies I would savour as a boy. The sharpness of the berries can be overpowering but they are easily mellowed with sugar or by pairing with other naturally sweet juices. Sea buckthorn cordial makes a fantastic sorbet, or follow the ice cream recipe on page 281 using sea buckthorn berries rather than conifer tips to make a delicious pinky-orange ice cream.

Seaweeds

There are thousands of types of seaweed. Most are edible but not all are good to eat. Thankfully, those which are good to eat tend to also be the most abundant. The table on page 368 gives an overview of the most commonly found seaweeds, briefly explaining how they look and what their uses are.[29]

I have found the flavour of seaweeds to be more variable than anything on land. They can be rubbery, bland, acrid and fishy, but also delicate, umami, peppery and truffle-like. There are even seaweeds that taste like fried bacon.

Most seaweeds are split into three genetically distinctive groups: browns, reds and greens. Brown seaweed was the first to evolve and is so named because it contains a greenish-brown pigment called fucoxanthin. Rather confusingly, some seaweeds in this group are green (or brownish green). The group contains bladder and serrated wrack, which are flat, green-brown and branching, with tender tips and air-filled bladders. These can dominate a rocky beach in their hundreds and are often the first seaweed most people encounter. The most distinctive of all seaweeds in the brown group is kelp, which evolved relatively recently – around 30 million years ago – in response to a colder climate. More recent on the evolutionary tree are the red seaweeds. These include the dulse, a delicious rockpool regular, which when fried has a delicious savoury bacon like flavour, and carrageen, which has been used in everything from toothpaste to ice cream. As with the brown seaweeds, the name 'red' can be deceptive. Although red pigments often dominate seaweeds in this group are just as likely to be purple, green, yellow or brown.

The most recent seaweeds to evolve were the greens. These include sea lettuce and gutweed, vitamin and mineral rich seaweeds with an intense savoury flavour when dried. This group is by far the least confusing, as they are always bright green thanks to the presence of chlorophyll, the pigment which allows them and land plants to photosynthesize. In fact, green seaweeds are related to land plants, having broken off from a common ancestor way back in their evolutionary history.

Collecting seaweed is not without its concerns.[30] Like any other organic material, seaweed can go bad, so avoid big, rotting piles and instead harvest it straight from the rock. Only harvest what you need. Use scissors to cut just the upper third to two-thirds of the seaweed so the rest can regenerate, and spread your harvesting out as widely as possible. Aim to pick from mid-to-late winter up until late spring, when growth is at its highest and seaweeds are at their most tasty. Try to avoid harvesting much during the summer months when they spawn. If the summer is your only opportunity then by all means taste and sample some – just don't build up your winter's supply.

You must be aware of the tides when foraging by the sea. It's best to forage as the tide is retreating, and this also helps reduce the amount of sand and grit the seaweed can pick up, especially in species such as gutweed. Up past the tide line, you'll find the

	Name	Scientific name	Colour
	Gutweed	*Ulva intestinalis*	Green
	Sea lettuce	*Ulva lactuca* (and other *Ulva*)	Green
	Bladderwrack	*Fucus vesiculosus* or *F. guiryi* (Guiryi's bladderwrack)	Brown
	Serrated wrack	*Fucus serratus*	Brown
	Laver, nori	*Porphyra* spp.	Reddish or greenish purple
	Pepper dulse	*Osmundea pinnatifida*	Variable: reddish brown, purple or dark reddish black

Description	Where found	Uses
Tubular, 10 cm (4 inches) long	Mean high tide	Deep-fried or dried and sprinkled on other foods. Salad ingredient
Thin, papery and light green	Mean high tide	Raw in salads or cooked as crispy seaweed. Can be used to make nori sheets
15–90 cm (6–35 inches) long (often on the smaller side). Branched, brown, with agar-filled, bubble-like bladders. Attached to rocks	High intertidal zone	Tips only, raw or pickled
Branched, greenish brown with large serrated tips. Agar-filled bladders. Attached to rocks	High intertidal zone	Tips only, raw or pickled
Like a melted plastic bag out of the water and like a thin, dark-green-to-purple plastic bag in the water	Mid-to-low intertidal zone	Laver bread and oatcakes, nori crisps, nori sheets
Very small, usually less than 4–8cm. Branched, like a Fibonacci sequence	Mid-to-low intertidal zone	Garlic, truffle or pepper flavouring

	Name	Scientific name	Colour
	Carrageen, Irish moss	*Chondrus crispus*	Variable: reddish brown, dark green
	Dulse	*Palmaria palmata*	Brownish red, slightly purple
	Sea spaghetti	*Himanthalia elongata*	Yellow-green
	Sugar kelp	*Saccharina latissima*	Light to dark brown
	Forest kelp	*Laminaria hyperborea*	Shiny brown

Description	Where found	Uses
Branched, coral-like	Mid-to-low intertidal zone	Less firm vegetarian gelatine, to thicken soups and smoothies.
Ranges from 15–50 cm (6–20 inches) in length. Forked, like a torn piece of paper	Mid-to-low intertidal zone	Fried (it tastes like bacon), or dried and used as a flavouring. Use in soups
Long strands of spaghetti-like seaweed	Low intertidal zone	Mixed with regular spaghetti or noodles
Up to 1.5 metres (5 feet) long, ruffled, feathery fronds	Low tide	As dashi/soup stock, or as a wrap for fish, tofu or tempeh
Large: measures 1.5–3.6 metres (5–12 feet). Like palm trees with long lamina/leaves and a flexible stem/stipe	Mean low tide	As dashi/soup stock, or as a wrap for fish, tofu or tempeh

	Name	Scientific name	Colour
	Oarweed	*Laminaria digitata*	Shiny brown
	Dabberlocks	*Alaria esculenta*	Variable: reddish brown to yellowish brown

usual coastal plants along with rock samphire sprouting from the rock and wild cabbage on the tops of the cliffs.

You should also be aware of the laws in your local area relating to seaweed. In the UK you require a licence to commercially pick seaweed and the landowner's permission for personal seaweed foraging – the National Trust and the Scottish National Trust own many of the beaches and can be contacted prior to a visit. In California it is legal to pick seaweed for personal use but in Washington state you need a licence. If in any doubt, check first.

Description	Where found	Uses
1.5 metres (5 feet) long. Palm-like; usually five leathery segments and a stalk/stipe.	Mean low tide	As dashi/soup stock, or as a wrap for fish, tofu or tempeh
Up to 1.5 metres (5 feet) long. Feathery lamina/leaf with a central stem and smaller sporophylls or leaf-like structures near the base	Lowest spring tide	As dashi/soup stock, or as a wrap for fish, tofu or tempeh

BLADDERWRACK AND SERRATED WRACK
Fucus vesiculosus and *F. serratus*

Season for picking: all year, best in winter
Where to find them: clinging to rocks out of the water
Main identifying features: bladders
Best use: tips, pickled

Bladderwrack and serrated wrack are brown seaweeds and are among the most ancient life forms on the planet. You'll find them clinging to the rocks from the top to the bottom of a rocky shoreline, forming slippery colonies of such large numbers that walking across them is a perilous affair. As they spend much of their life out of the water, they are often easily visible and can cover whole rocky beaches.

Bladderwrack is so named for its characteristic twin bladders running from the tips, right down the stem either side of the midrib. These allow it to float and more effectively photosynthesise, and are as satisfying to pop as a piece of bubble wrap. It has olive-green to brown bladders at the tips of flattened fronds. Serrated wrack is slightly different-looking; it lacks the swim bladders and has branching, rough fronds growing up to 60 cm (2 feet), with a saw-like edge and obvious midrib.

PREPARATION AND USE

The lower part of wracks are tough and unpalatable, so it's best to harvest only their succulent tips. Go for younger plants which haven't yet formed their bladders, or those growing in exposed areas, as these often do not grow any bladders at all. You can nibble on them raw as a passing snack but they really come into their own when pickled in a sweet, spiced pickling vinegar such as rice or white wine vinegar with chilli. To make this, you should first clean and dry your seaweed tips, then pack them in a jar and top with hot, sweet vinegar. The swollen reproductive bladders – the gooey, agar-filled sacks on the tips of the plant – make for an even more interesting pickle, which can be prepared in the same way. When you bite into these pickled bladders, you'll feel the burst of agar soothing the hot spice of the chilli. As the bladders are the seaweed's method of reproduction, it is best to only pick them in moderation – and to try not to think about what you are eating!

Wracks can also be used to make dashi (a seaweed stock) and are often much easier to harvest than kelps.

DULSE
Palmaria palmata

Season for picking: winter and spring
Where to find them: In rockpools, on rocks and growing from larger seaweeds
Main identifying features: purple colour
Best use: fried like bacon

Harvesting seaweed, especially dulse, a gourmet salty seaweed, can be hypnotic. With the gentle rhythm of the sea and the spring sun on your back as you move from rockpool to rockpool in search of its feathery fronds, it is easy to lose all sense of time and place. As dulse grows in the mid-to-low intertidal zone, there is a brief window to find it, so although hunting for it can be all-encompassing you do need to keep an eye on the incoming tide. During one perilous harvesting session in Devon with a good friend, we found ourselves almost cut off by the incoming tide and had to clamber over rocks to get back to dry land.

Dulse is a translucent purple or reddish-brown seaweed belonging to the red seaweed group. It attaches itself to rocks or other seaweeds and branches out from this single point into strips, or fronds, each around 2.5–8 cm (1–3 inches) wide and usually 10–20 cm (4–8 inches) long (but sometimes reaching lengths of 50 cm/20 inches). The name of the genus to which is belongs, *Palmaria*, describes the palm or hand-like formation of the fronds. It grows further out to sea than wracks and green seaweeds but not as deep as kelps.

In the nineteenth century, visitors to the shores of the far north of Scotland would hear the cry of 'dulse and tangle' along the cobblestone coastal streets. These cries would come from 'dulse-wives', lines of women who sat on wooden stools selling dulse and kelp, or 'tangle' as it was often called. Dulse was always the most prized of the two. It would be dried and chewed like tobacco, mixed in to flavour oat or wheat bread or fried.

PREPARATION AND USE

You may need to give dulse a quick wash to remove any sand or sea creatures, but it can be eaten raw. It is tasty but a little chewy. Fried dulse is really moreish; the taste is best described as a savoury vegetable-like bacon. It can be eaten dried or fresh. Fry fresh dulse in a little oil and serve it in a sandwich with a fried egg. Both fried and dried dulse can be cut into pieces and used as a savoury sprinkle for pasta dishes or risottos. It is also good in salads, especially with fresh tomatoes, olives and red onion, drizzled with olive oil.

I like to allow dulse to naturally dehydrate on a washing line before reconstituting it in liquid smoke, a seasoning found in delis and health food shops which gives food the flavour of a smokery without the effort. Fried in a little oil this reconstituted seaweed tastes even more like bacon.

PEPPER DULSE
Osmundea pinnatifida

Season for picking: winter and spring
Where to find them: on rocks
Main identifying features: tiny seaweed with branching fronds
Best use: laverbread, nori sheets or crisps
Not to be mistaken for: other similar-looking but less tasty seaweeds

Pepper dulse is found on the shores of Europe and is most common in Britain and Ireland, the Mediterranean and Portugal. It is a tiny seaweed, ranging between 2–8 cm (1–3 inches) in length. It varies in colour from dark brown to purplish red, and is even sometimes a yellowish green or brown. It has tough, cartilaginous branching and flattened fronds, and covers coastal rocks much in the way that lichen does on land. Look for it on exposed tidal rocks and in rockpools. Like lichen, when it grows in large numbers it can make the rocks look a little furry from a distance. There are some lookalikes but they are bland and tasteless rather than poisonous, and you will quickly know if you have the right seaweed.

Pepper dulse prefers sheltered shores to exposed ones, so look for it in rocky coves and bays in a similar location to dulse, around the low to middle of the intertidal zone. From my experience, it tends to prefer life in waters that are a little deeper than those preferred by dulse, but this is a general observation rather than a hard and fast rule.

PREPARATION AND USE

Pepper dulse is often called the truffle of the sea, as fresh or dried it has a savoury, umami, peppery kick, like a fleshy black pepper with hints of olive. Its flavour intensifies when it is dried but unfortunately it also shrivels away to almost nothing.

Use it as you would black pepper – as a sprinkle for scrambled egg, or with fish or meat. It also works well with tofu. First, marinate the tofu in soy sauce, lime juice and dried coriander. Fry the cubes until crispy and serve on a bed of rice with chopped spring onions and small shreds of fried courgette, along with a sprinkle of finely chopped pepper dulse and toasted sesame seeds. Check for seasoning and dress with soy sauce and sesame oil if need be.

CARRAGEEN, IRISH MOSS
Chondrus crispus

Season for picking: all year, best in spring
Where to find them: on rocks, in rockpools
Main identifying features: branched seaweed, brown to green
Best use: in panna cotta

Carrageen is a highly branched, tree-shaped seaweed. It is in the red seaweed group, but varies in colour from dark or yellowish brown to greenish purple. It grows in rockpools and on rocks, attaching itself on a small stalk or holdfast. It grows throughout Atlantic Europe and Canada and has been found on the shores of Japan and California. It can grow in large numbers and it should not be hard to harvest without disturbing the population as a whole.

If you take a nibble, it doesn't taste of much; it's slightly chewy and a bit fishy, but with no overriding flavour. When boiled, its cell walls break down and it releases a type of polysaccharide or naturally occurring carbohydrate which helps to set liquids. This has led to it being harvested commercially – an extract of the seaweed, called carrageenan, is used as a thickening agent in all kinds of things from toothpaste to plant milk. Carrageenan is a controversial food additive as it has been said to irritate the lining of the gut. But this is true only of the extract, and the seaweed itself is perfectly safe to eat.

PREPARATION AND USE
Carrageen is a magical seaweed. Once boiled in a little water or milk, it will set the liquid much like gelatine. I like to add sugar and cocoa powder to a couple of glasses of milk, then boil this up with 4 or 5 small sprigs of fresh carrageen. Pour this into ramekins and allow to cool in the fridge, where it will set like mousse. Alternatively bring about 1 litre of water to the boil with a large handful of fresh carrageen. Let this cool then put it through a blender until the seaweed is completely macerated. Put this gloop in the fridge and use it to thicken stocks, soups, gravy, sauces and desserts.

LAVER, NORI, SLAKE
Porphyra spp.

Season for picking: winter and spring
Where to find them: on rocks
Main identifying features: look like melted bin bags
Best use: laverbread, nori sheets or crisps

When submerged under the water, laver is a graceful seaweed which delicately swings with the rhythm of the sea. However, when the tide is out, it loses this mystical quality and looks more like a melted bin bag.

Even when prepared traditionally as laverbread, which is not a bread at all but a paste, it doesn't look much better. Laverbread resembles a runny cow pat, something you would wipe from your shoe rather than put in your mouth. Historically, in the UK and Ireland, perhaps partly due to its appearance, laver was rarely considered a regular source of food, but was instead thought of as a last resort when little else was around. During the Irish potato famine, much of the coastal population relied on seaweeds as an important source of protein and minerals, but not with any gusto. A novel dating to the time even called it a 'wretched substitute for food'.[31] Elsewhere in the world, such as East Asia, there is no such negative folk memory attached to eating seaweed and closely related, near identical-tasting species including *Porphyra yezoensis* and *P. tenera* have been used as food for centuries. In Japan it is known as 'nori', in Korea 'gim', and in both countries it is made into sheets and wrapped around rice and other fillings to make sushi nori and gimbap respectively.

Both the names laver and nori refer to a number of species of cold-water red algae in the *Porphyra* and *Pyropia* families. In the UK and Europe there are three main species, the most common of which is *Porphyra umbilicalis* or tough laver, which grows in sheets that look like cut-up plastic bags when submerged under water. The colour varies from a darkish green, through reddish brown to a dark purple. It grows off the shores of the west coast of Britain and east coast of Ireland, where it is called slake. Another species is *P.linearis* which has a more strand-like form, rather than sheets, and *P. leucosticte (syn Porphra leucosticte)* which is common off the coast of Northern Ireland and can also be found off the coasts of south eastern United States from North Carolina to Florida.

PREPARATION AND USE

Laverbread is normally made with *P. umbilicalis* and nori usually refers to either *P. yezoensis* or *P. tenera*, which are found off the coast of Japan. However, all species are somewhat interchangeable and can be prepared as nori or as laverbread.

Laverbread is a puree of cooked laver. It is served up at breakfast, sometimes with the addition of oats. It is rich in protein, vitamins and minerals and has a salty flavour a little like olives, but with distinctive seafood notes. To make laverbread, simmer the seaweed for an extended period of time until it breaks down and forms a mush. I would recommend bringing it to the boil in a pan of water, then transferring this to a slow cooker to cook on a low heat overnight. Drain and fry in butter or bacon fat, then serve on toast with mushrooms or bacon and a generous twist of black pepper. If you do not have a slow cooker, simmer for 3 to 4 hours on the hob, stirring every now and then to prevent burning.

TRADITIONAL LAVER OATCAKES

Laverbread is best mixed in with oats. The two ingredients bind together well and the starchy quality of the oats marries perfectly with the gooey boiled seaweed. You can follow the traditional recipe below or, to add a twist, instead of salt and pepper add a pinch of turmeric, chilli and coriander and a dash of soy sauce. Serves 2–4 as a side:

YOU WILL NEED:
- Approximately 200–250 g (7–9 oz) laverbread (laver simmered overnight in a slow cooker – see above)
- 50–60 g (2 oz) rolled oats
- Salt and pepper
- Butter or olive oil for frying

METHOD:
1. Using a spoon, roughly break apart the cooked laverbread.
2. Drain the laverbread and add the oats a little at a time until the mixture collects as a lump.
3. Add some salt and pepper to taste.
4. Form little patties with your hands – press hard enough to maintain their shape but not too hard as you want the patties to be light and fluffy.
5. Fry the patties in butter until they brown and serve as a snack, or try them as part of a Welsh cooked breakfast with eggs, mushrooms and bacon.

NORI CRISPS

In Japan, preparing nori sheets is an art form more akin to paper-making than cooking. Without the proper equipment it can be difficult to master.

The recipe below will not make perfect nori sheets, but it will make perfectly good nori crisps which, although unsuitable for sushi, work very well in a lunch box.

All you will need to make these crisps is some laver, oil and seasoning, such as soy sauce.

METHOD:
1. Wash the laver in cold water and drain.
2. Blanch for a couple of minutes.
3. Put the blanched laver in a blender, mostly drained with just a splash of the cooking water.

4. Blend on high power for around a minute, then pass through a sieve. Reserve the liquid to make a stock for a soup if you wish.
5. Add seasoning to the pulp – you can use soy sauce, a dash of fish sauce (or vegan fish sauce) or simply salt and pepper.
6. Fold a sheet of kitchen paper in two, open like a book and place the laver pulp on one side. Then close the 'book' and roll it flat with a rolling pin.
7. Take the laver out of the kitchen paper and lay it flat on a baking tray. Sprinkle on oil and soy sauce.
8. Place the laver in an oven on 180°C (350°F) for 20 minutes until crispy, and then cut into seaweed crisps.

SEA LETTUCE
Ulva spp.

Season for picking: all year but best in colder months
Where to find them: from the top of the tide line down to the area of the lowest tide
Main identifying features: bright-green fronds
Best use: raw in salads or fried

Resembling a cross between land lettuce and delicate, transparent green plastic when submerged, sea lettuce grows on rocks and occasionally pebbles, from the top of the tide line right down towards the area of the lowest tide (alongside dulse and pepper dulse). Like all seaweeds it needs something to anchor itself to and although it will occasionally sprout from pebbles, it is more reliably found on rocky shores, especially in rockpools. There are thirteen species of *Ulva* off the coast of the UK, some of which are gutweeds and five of which are the blade-forming, sometimes frilly sea lettuces. Elsewhere there are many more, with at least 100 different species of *Ulva* worldwide.

PREPARATION AND USE

Harvest sea lettuce in the colder winter months when it is at its best. Always cut with a pair of scissors, leaving at least one-third to grow back. Sea lettuce works well eaten fresh and raw in a salad. I advise washing off any bits of sand or grit in the sea rather than under the tap, as washing in fresh water can diminish its flavour. Cutting it from anything other than the most pristine coastline is therefore unwise. More than any other seaweed, the taste of sea lettuce is delicate, distinctly salty and coastal, and works best when not overpowered by other strong flavours. Raw, it pairs well in salads with cucumber, wall pennywort, tomatoes or even fruits like peach or orange.

Dehydrated and powdered, sea lettuce makes an excellent flavouring, still with the briny coastal taste but an overall deeper, richer flavour. I like to use this for a marinade for tofu with soy sauce and a little lime, which I serve on a crisp summer salad.

If you want to cook sea lettuce, shred it and either fry or deep-fry it in oil (it may spit, so dry it off as much as you can before throwing in a pan). Once fried, pat it dry and season to taste. My partner and her mother like to shun convention with this seaweed and wash it in fresh water before use. Once patted dry they crumble ground rock salt over it before adding soy sauce, Worcester sauce or anchovy sauce, and finally lightly frying it until crispy.

SEA LETTUCE SALAD

When I first put this salad together, it was an unseasonably warm spring weekend and as a family we'd spent the day before by the coast, gathering seaweed. My partner and I craved a light, fresh lunch to counter the seaside chip supper followed by ice cream we'd had the night before. I threw this together with what was left in the cupboard and we ate outside in the warm air for the first time that year. This recipe serves 2, as a side.

- 100 g (3½ oz) fresh sea lettuce, washed in seawater
- 60 g (2 oz) cucumber
- 1–2 tsp sesame seeds
- 1 tsp soy sauce
- 2 tsp sesame oil

METHOD:

1. Roughly shred the sea lettuce and pour into a big salad bowl.
2. Cut the cucumber into 1 cm sticks and add to the bowl.
3. Add the soy sauce and sesame oil.
4. In a dry pan, lightly toast the sesame seeds (they can pop so you may need to cover).
5. Sprinkle the toasted seeds over the salad and serve.

KELPS: SUGAR KELP, OARWEED AND FOREST KELP
Saccharina latissima, Laminaria digitata and *L. hyperborea*

Season for picking: all year except summer
Where to find them: lowest tide line
Main identifying features: long, glossy, brown fronds
Best use: Japanese broths, fish dishes

Kelp is one of the most abundant forms of life on earth. Kelp forests cover more than a quarter of the world's coastlines, and off the coast of California, forests of kelp reach more than 60 metres (195 feet) in height. Secured to the seabed by a holdfast, a root-like structure which secures seaweeds to rocks, the fronds wave freely on top of long trunks or 'stipes' and are kept afloat by inflated bladders. Kelp forests can be richer environments than rainforests, providing a home for sea lions, urchins, rays, sea otters and octopuses, all of which directly or indirectly gain sustenance from the giant leaves.

Forest kelp and oarweed are a shiny brown colour, with long linear 'leaves' and a flexible stipe. They spend most of their lives in the water, inhabiting the lowest tide line, with some species, such as the frilly dabberlocks, only emerging during the most extreme lows of the spring tides. This can make harvesting a little tricky and you have to time visits to the lowest tides when piles of kelp can flop on the beach. In Britain you'll find kelp along most shores with the exception of the area from Lincolnshire down to the Thames Estuary, and the coasts to the north and south of Merseyside. Don't be surprised if you don't find 60-metre-high forests of kelp in British waters though – here it tends to be more modest in size, reaching somewhere between 1.5 and 3.6 metres (5 and 12 feet).

In Japan, a species of kelp called kombu, *Saccharina japonica*, has, along with other kelps, been used for centuries to make dashi, a flavoursome seaweed stock for soup. In the early twentieth century, a chemistry professor by the name of Kikunae Ikeda recognised that dashi broth had a unique taste which was neither sweet, sour, bitter nor salty. It had a new type flavour altogether – a satisfying, savoury one – and as such he coined the term 'umami' to describe it.

All kelps are naturally high in sodium and the amino acid glutamate can be seen as white crystals on their surfaces as they dry. This is what gives kelp its unique umami flavour. Ikeda found other foods contained the same substance, and he managed to isolate it from soy beans and wheat, combining it with sodium to create MSG, or monosodium glutamate. MSG is now one of the most widely used flavour enhancers in the world. In the 1960s it was blamed for a condition called 'Chinese restaurant syndrome' where those who consumed it suffered all kinds of symptoms including chest pains, bloating, fatigue and sweating. Studies on the phenomenon found MSG to be safe and free of side effects. It is thought that those who presented these very real symptoms could have been the victims of a reverse placebo effect, known as the nocebo effect.[32] This is where a safe substance is believed to be dangerous and the mind conjures up adverse symptoms as a result. Interestingly the same thing can happen when foragers eat perfectly safe mushrooms believing them to be poisonous.

PREPARATION AND USE

Kelp is best picked young, in the spring when it is at its most tender. Although it can be eaten uncooked, it is rubbery when raw and can feel as if you are chewing on the inner tube of a bicycle tyre. When cooked it will turn a beautiful shade of dark green as the colour pigments respond to the heat. Fry it fresh, or after drying and reconstituting in a soy sauce-rich broth.

As the flavour compounds in kelp are water soluble, the best way to preserve its flavour is to use it in a dashi or stock for soups. I keep dried kelp strips to hand, adding them to soups and ramen so their umami flavour can permeate throughout the dish. Boletus or shiitake mushrooms have another umami flavour compound called guanosine monophosphate (GMP), and cured skipjack tuna has yet another, called inosine monophosphate (IMP) – so including any of these together in a dashi means they work in harmony to enhance the flavour. Knowing this little bit of food chemistry can improve all kinds of dishes. It is worth experimenting using fresh or dried mushrooms, seaweeds and nutritional yeast flakes (which also contain glutamates) in all kinds of cooking from soups to stir-fries.

You can also use long strands of kelp to wrap fish before cooking, to seal in the natural oils while infusing the fish with a subtle umami flavour. This will slightly increase the cooking time but will result in more tender fish. Fresh kelp is ideal but dried kelp can also be used. Its flavour will be further enhanced by drizzling the fish with white wine prior to wrapping. This method works for tempeh too, with dried or fresh kelp, but you will have to leave it wrapped overnight in the kelp prior to cooking.

ROCK SAMPHIRE
Crithmum maritimum

Season for picking: all year, best in spring or early summer
Where to find them: rocks and sea cliffs above the tide line
Main identifying features: fleshy, succulent, grey-green leaves shaped like antlers, white flowers
Best use: noodle soups or stir-fries

Rock samphire grows in perilous places, often just out of reach on dangerous rocks and sea cliffs. Shakespeare himself described picking it as a 'dreadful trade'. Unlike the more familiar and commonly used marsh samphire (related only by name), it doesn't tolerate saltwater and will only grow above the tide line. This knowledge has saved shipwrecked seafarers from death as they have clung to samphire covered rocks overnight, realising that the tides would not take them under.[33]

Despite a tendency for perilous places the fleshy, slightly succulent, grey-green leaves, which are shaped like antlers, can usually be harvested from lower rocks, or those within an easy climb. They can be plucked away, causing little damage unless they are really yanked from their homes and uprooted in the process. It is easy to distinguish them from anything potentially poisonous as there is nothing that looks similar in the same environment. As a member of the carrot family, the plant forms umbels of white-to-green flowers, each with five petals. It has a pungent, oily smell with carrot, fennel and white spirit or creosote overtones. It would have been served up in both ancient Rome and Greece, and in Greek myth Theseus was said to have eaten samphire before battling with the Minotaur. Although rock samphire can be eaten all year round, it is far better in the spring or early summer before it has come into flower.

PREPARATION AND USE

The taste of samphire, especially raw, is not for everyone. To me, its smell and taste is strangely reminiscent of Pepsi. It may be that, like coriander, which can taste unpleasantly soapy to some, a few people are genetically predisposed to disliking the plant. Either way, the flavour is much improved when blanched and/or pickled. Cooked quickly in a little water and dressed with lemon and butter or a strong sauce such as tamari or soy sauce, it makes a pleasant side vegetable. However, I love it as an ingredient in a noodle soup or stir-fry, or mixed with strong salty cheeses like feta in a light cucumber salad.

PICKLED SAMPHIRE

Traditionally samphire was pickled and many still prefer it prepared this way. This method is adapted from an eighteenth-century samphire recipe, but you can also use the pickling guidelines on pages 22 to 23.[34]

1. Put the samphire in a pickle of salt and water (I suggest 8% salt).
2. Change the water every 4 days until the samphire is yellow.
3. Drain, then sandwich the samphire between two cabbage leaves.
4. Place in a pan with enough water to cover and a walnut sized piece of rock sugar (can substitute for brown sugar).
5. Simmer on a moderate heat until the samphire turns green. Then drain and dry, discarding the cabbage leaves.
6. Put the samphire in a jar.
7. Simmer mace, pepper and sliced ginger in vinegar, bring to the boil and pour over the samphire.
8. Seal the jar and store in a cupboard until opened, after which point store in the fridge.

GREEN SAMPHIRE SALAD

Certain foods remind you of certain people. Rock samphire always reminds me of my mother-in-law, who sends me small bundles of it from her seaside home. I first made this recipe during a summer visit to her home in Devon. The mint and cucumber cut through the fats of the feta and avocado, perfectly balancing out this s imple salad.

This recipe serves four as a side or two as an accompaniment to a larger meal.

YOU WILL NEED:

- **A good handful of samphire**
- **Quarter of a cucumber**
- **1 small avocado**
- **4 stalks of mint**
- **Half a block of feta cheese**
- **Juice of 1 lime**
- **Olive oil**

Simply wash and roughly chop the samphire into pieces, and dice the cucumber, feta and avocado, adding them all to a large bowl. Shred the mint and dress the salad with the lime juice, mint and olive oil.

CHAPTER FOURTEEN

Salt Marshes

S ALT MARSHES HOLD a strange beauty, with their wide, flat plains of green broken only by the greys and browns of soft silty mud, which seem to want to suck you down into the earth itself. The added tang of the salt in the air makes any time spent on a salt marsh a full sensory experience. Marshes are neither land nor sea, but somewhere in between; the waves relentlessly, rhythmically, reclaim and release sandbanks, mudflats, gullies and channels shaped by the sea.

Although the plants within the marsh taste different from one another, there are similar flavours that also link them. They are all undoubtedly salty but there is also a complex, iron-incense, floral quality. It is as if they contain the essence of the estuary, taking up the landscape into their cells before releasing it as a burst onto the taste buds.

Salt marshes are created as the flowing waters of estuary rivers deposit beds of silt and mud into sheltered bays. Pioneer species such as marsh samphire and cordon grass, which often form vast colonies, are usually among the first to move in. Unlike most other plants they can withstand being submerged under seawater hundreds of times a year and they thrive in the salt-heavy but nutrient-rich mud. Over time their roots actually help to stabilise the mud flats and prevent estuary deposits washing back out to sea.

On the land that has settled to become the high marsh area, the ground is more solid and easier to navigate, and plant life here has adapted to lower concentrations of salt. It is here you will find the purple blooms of sea aster and the inedible sea lavender alongside edibles such as scurvygrass and sea plantain. Over time, a delta of channels and gullies forms as the estuary and the sea carve up the land, creating a high-nutrient ecosystem brimming with life. Sea creatures like fish, shrimp and crabs navigate these channels and use the area as a nursery for their young, feeding off decaying matter trapped within the marsh. In turn, wading birds can make a good living by feeding off these creatures as they arrive in the winter to breed. As you move away from the sea and the main marsh area, many of the more usual coastal plants start to emerge, such as stag's horn plantain, rock samphire, fiery sea rocket and the soft leaves of tree mallows.Foraging in salt marshes has a long history, especially along the coast of Norfolk. Women would navigate miles of mudflats with exposed bare legs in all weathers to gather Stiffkey blues (or 'Stookey' as the locals pronounce it), a type of cockle or shellfish with a distinctive blue shell. These shellfish get their colour from the anaerobic conditions in the oxygen-starved blue mud around the village of Stiffkey. It was low-paid, difficult and dangerous work, subject to incoming tides. The women would sell cockles along with samphire to supplement their income, even as recently as the 1950s.

I like to time my visits to salt marshes to coincide with the tide retreating. Arriving early is not a problem as it gives time to unwind or play with the children. However, time it too late and at best you will go home empty-handed, or at worst you'll be stuck on a sandbank as the incoming tide cuts you off from land; nature not man dictates when things are done around here.

SCURVYGRASS
Cochlearia spp.

Season for picking: winter to spring, second flush in the summer
Where to find them: coastal areas and roadsides
Main identifying features: fleshy leaves and small clusters of tiny, white, four-petalled flowers
Best use: wasabi-like spice

Scurvygrass will grow around the outer reaches of the high tide mark, often forming patchwork clumps. It doesn't seem to mind rocky ground either and will grow on cliffsides, through cracks between paths and walls and around the bases of concrete sea defences.

Scurvygrass is a catch-all name for around thirty different but closely related species of *Cochlearia*, and occasionally one or two plants of the *Barbarea* genus (although the latter is more commonly referred to as land cress or American land cress).

All *Cochlearia* are relatively small plants, growing in a rosette form with slightly fleshy leaves. Depending on the species, the younger leaves (before flowering) are either strongly heart shaped or heart shaped but loosely lobed, and are 1–5 cm (½–2 inches) long – normally around the size of a large coin. All species have small clusters of tiny, white, four-petalled flowers, rather like those of bittercress. The common name, scurvygrass, comes from the fact that the leaves are extremely high in vitamin C and in the past were used as a remedy for scurvy. Coastal villagers would eat the plant after long winters without any fresh produce. Seafarers, including Captain Cook, would recommend his crew ate the plant when they returned to shore after lengthy voyages.

Long-leaved or English scurvygrass, *Cochlearia anglica*, with its tongue-shaped leaves, is the most commonly found species in tidal marshes. In one spot in the south-west of England, the estuary is peppered white with its tiny flowers in the spring. Danish scurvygrass, *C. danica*, and common scurvygrass, *C. officinalis*, are both found on the coast, often on rocky shores.

Scurvygrass is related to mustard and horseradish, so it's no surprise that the taste can blow your socks off, especially after it has flowered. Once, on a day out by the sea, I had clean forgotten how strong the taste could be and offered some to my ever-game brother-in-law to try. I can still recall his tortured facial expressions and my desperate search through my backpack for some water to wash the taste away. He's been a little more reluctant to try anything I've offered him since then.

Once it flowers, the plant can become decidedly more bitter, so it is best to pick it young. This can be just a few weeks into the new year. As the delicate, cross-shaped flowers come in the middle of spring, scurvygrass can set seed more than once a year and you will sometimes find a second flush of the leaves during the summer.

FORAGER'S TIP

Scurvygrass likes to grow in the same places dogs like to visit, so as with other low-growing leaves, soak in saltwater and rinse well prior to use.

PREPARATION AND USE

Scurvygrass has a fiery flavour, rather like wasabi or horseradish. Chopped up finely and used sparingly, it adds a nice kick (rather than an overwhelming fire) to a salad. It works well in sushi as an alternative to wasabi, mixed with oil and crushed in a pestle and mortar. You can also dehydrate the leaves and powder them for use as a peppery sprinkle in stir-fries, soups or with meat dishes. I love sprinkling the dehydrated leaves into a corn or flour tortilla in place of chilli sauce along with the usual sour cream, guacamole, refried beans and tomato salsa.

MARSH SAMPHIRE, CRAB GRASS, GLASSWORT
Salicornia europaea

Season for picking: spring to late summer
Where to find them: below high tide mark
Main identifying features: thin, cactus-like, bright-green stems
Best use: vegetable side dish, accompaniment to fish dishes
Not to be mistaken for: Virginia glasswort, rock samphire

Perhaps the most well-known inhabitants of a salt marsh and one of the tastiest, these tubular, forked plants can be found growing in the silt and mud looking like tiny Wild West cacti. As a pioneer plant, marsh samphire lives in the lower reaches of the marsh, where the sea covers the land at high tide. The similar-looking species Virginia glasswort, *Salicornia virginica*, is also found in isolated pockets in the UK and is much more widespread across the USA.

There is a lot of confusion between marsh samphire and rock samphire. The samphire you now find in trendy restaurants is marsh samphire, but for centuries it was seen as food for the poor and held in lower esteem than its unrelated namesake, rock samphire. This social stigma ran deep and up until the late twentieth century, no one really ate marsh samphire outside of the rural coastal regions where it grows. In older cookbooks, unless otherwise stated, most recipes for samphire will actually be referring to rock samphire.

In north Norfolk, the plant grows in greater numbers than I have seen anywhere in the world. Locals pronounce it 'sam-fur' and it is sold in neat little bundles by the side of the road.

It starts to poke its head above the ground in the very late spring or early summer, but is at its best during the mid-to-late summer months. Be warned though that much of the land it grows on is protected by law and anyone picking commercially without a licence can be fined.

FORAGER'S TIP

The yellowish base of marsh samphire can get woody, so it is best to harvest just the top two-thirds of the plant. Snip it off with scissors if you have any. This not only allows the plant to regenerate, it also saves you time preparing it when you get home.

PREPARATION AND USE

On camping holidays in Norfolk, I like to pick a good-sized bagful and take it back to the campsite to eat raw as a crisp, salty bar snack with a beer by a camp fire. At home, you can try it as a side dish by lightly boiling or steaming it, then coating it in butter. It also works in stir-fries, particularly with light Japanese flavours such as ume plum sauce, sesame and mirin.

It's a superb accompaniment to fish and seafood; it goes well with everything from scallops, crab and lobster to cod, salmon and bass. The samphire counters the spicy taste and texture of a falafel very well too; I like to pop a handful of them, blanched, into a wrap along with a smear of hummus and some chopped fresh tomatoes. It's also good in a seafood paella.

SEA ASTER

Season for picking: spring to autumn
Where to find them: high tide line
Main identifying features: fleshy, lance-shaped leaves; lilac, daisy-like flowers
Best use: stir-fry, salad, fish dishes
Not to be mistaken for: sea lavender

Growing on the higher tide line, sea aster is a prominent salt marsh plant. It can occasionally be found outside of the salt marsh, on the banks of tidal estuaries and on cliff tops. Sea asters grow to around 50 cm (20 inches) tall and have lance-shaped leaves around 12 cm (5 inches) long. It is easy to confuse the plant with the inedible but non-toxic sea lavender, as they both like to grow in the same regions of the salt marsh. The leaves of sea aster are slightly more fleshy and pleasant to eat, unlike the bitter, fishy-tasting lavender. Once the two plants are in flower there is no mistaking them, as sea aster produces a flower like a Michaelmas daisy, while sea lavender is more heather-like, with long blooms a little like toilet brushes.

Sea aster has only become popular, almost trendy in fact, in the last decade or so. Prior to this it was only really mentioned in ecology books. Over the last few years, a handful of foragers have begun to experiment with the plant and it is now considered something of a gourmet vegetable. Some of this is no doubt due to its novelty, but it is also due to the plant's unique estuary flavour, which goes extremely well with fish.

PREPARATION AND USE

The shoots and leaves of the sea aster are edible and good to eat but benefit from being briefly run under water to wash out some of the salt. The plant has a very distinctive estuary taste: aromatic, edging towards fennel, with floral and pleasantly chemical notes. Lightly blanch the leaves or young shoots and dress them in a little sesame oil and soy sauce to really bring out the flavour. Serve with cucumber and toasted sesame seeds as a side salad.

Sea aster can also be partnered with fish, and goes particularly well with mild-tasting pollock, haddock or whiting. In a stir-fry I pair it with chicken, Quorn pieces or tofu, cashew nuts, chilli and coriander), perhaps finishing off with a sprinkling of soy sauce and some toasted, crushed peanuts.

ANNUAL SEABLITE, SEA SPRAY, HERBACEOUS SEEPWEED
Suaeda maritima

Season for picking: spring through to autumn
Where to find them: just below the high tide mark and above it; in soil with high salt content, rocky shores
Main identifying features: fleshy leaves similar in form to rosemary, vivid green in spring and summer, fading to reddish purple.
Best use: vegetable side dish, salads

Warning: do not pick from polluted areas

Annual seablite sounds like a derogatory name for a plant, but the name actually derives from the Latin *blitum*, which in turn comes from the Greek *bliton*, denoting spinach or spinach-like plants.

Annual seablite can occasionally form dense stands but this is somewhat rare. More often it appears in the lower or middle marsh area, either dotted among the samphire or slightly further up where the sea purslane likes to grow. Like samphire, it is one of the first plants to move into an empty area, and its roots help to stabilise the marsh.

It is a succulent plant, with small, fleshy, pointed green leaves. It looks a lot like rosemary and when I first came across it I flicked through my plant guides looking for 'sea rosemary' rather than seablite. Its flowers are rather like those of the closely related fat hen and made of many clusters rather than individual blooms. It is vivid green for most of the year but towards the end of the autumn it becomes oversaturated with salt and turns a purple-reddish colour. Aside from salt marshes it will turn up on rocky shores and anywhere where the soil has a high salt content, including occasionally by the side of salted roads.

FORAGER'S TIP
Annual seablite can readily take up heavy metals. Although the highest concentrations are in the roots, the leaves should be picked away from polluted areas, including coastlines close to heavy industry.

PREPARATION AND USE
There is an earthy quality to seablite and although salty and estuarine in flavour, it is mild compared to marsh samphire and lacks its succulent bite. You can blanch it for just a minute or so, then use it as a garnish or an accompaniment to fish in both Western or Japanese dishes. Though additional flavours are not necessary thanks to its natural saltiness, it does benefit from a dressing of olive oil, lemon and a good cider or white wine vinegar.

I rarely use seablite on its own, more often adding it to samphire and/or sea purslane. They're great blanched together and added to an avocado salad – the fatty avocado and salty marsh plants make perfect partners.

SEA PURSLANE
Halimione portulacoides

Season for picking: summer
Where to find them: high tide area
Main identifying features: matt-green, fleshy leaves, tiny clusters
of red flowers
Best use: salad ingredient, vegetable side dish, accompaniment to
fish dishes

The matt-green leaves of sea purslane are inviting and can be found growing in the high tide area a little further up from marsh samphire. It can form either a dense carpet or isolated small colonies. It is a perennial, so you will find it throughout the year. However, during the winter months it is slow growing, so keep harvesting to a minimum and spread pickings as widely as possible.

The leaves are fleshy without being succulent and often stand upright, like thousands of hands waving in the air at a concert. The flowers are like those of dock or sorrel – tiny red clusters, rather than anything with a petal.

In the USA, sea purslane is the name given to an unrelated but very similar-tasting and similar-looking plant, *Sesuvium portulacastrum*. This has a glossier green leaf and a small lilac flower. Both plants can be used in the same way.

PREPARATION AND USE
The top few leaves are the best to pick; the lower ones can get woody and can be an effort to harvest. If you can, snip the top leaves with scissors or secateurs, as this does the plant the least amount of harm.

Sea purslane has a naturally salty flavour which it retains even after cooking or washing in fresh water. Using the plant raw in salads gives a salty crunch, which goes particularly well with tomatoes or fiery leaves. Dress with oil, garlic and a dash of low-acid vinegar, such as white wine or rice vinegar.

If cooked, the plant should be quickly blanched rather than boiled, as boiling can destroy the flavour. Lightly frying it is also a good option – just remove any woody stalks and throw into a pan with a little melted butter or margarine for a few minutes. Add generous amounts of fresh lemon juice, stir, and serve. This makes an excellent snack for a barbecue or campfire, washed down with a good beer. Just be sure to make a double helping as it can go quickly.

The salty flavour of sea purslane also blends perfectly with fish – add it to fish cakes or serve alongside grilled Dover sole.

Glossary of Terms

TAXONOMY AND SCIENTIFIC NAMES

In the world of biology, animals and plants are classified using eight taxonomic ranks: domain, kingdom, phylum, class, order, family, genus and species. With each step down in this taxonomy, the group becomes more specific.

In this book, I've referred to three of the taxonomic ranks:

Family: A relatively broad grouping of plants with some similar characteristics – for example, the carrot family encompasses carrots, parsley and celery, which are all aromatic and have feathery leaves. A plant's family is not included in its scientific name.

Genus: The taxonomic rank below family. A plant's genus is the first word in its scientific name. For example, oaks are *Quercus* and pines are *Pinus*.

Species: The next rank down from genus. A plant's species is the second word in its scientific name. For example, the holm oak is *Quercus ilex* – its species name, *ilex*, distinguishes it from other trees in the oak genus (*Quercus*).

Certain abbreviations are also sometimes used with scientific names:

agg.: species complex (a group of closely related but distinct species).
spp.: Several species.
syn.: Synonym, i.e. an alternative scientific name for the same plant.

LEAVES
Bract: Modified leaf which looks much like a flower.
Opposite: Leaf structure with leaflets opposite each other, e.g. nettle.
Ovate: Egg-shaped.
Pinnate: Leaf structure with small leaflets on opposite sides of a stem and a larger leaflet at the top, e.g. ash and watercress.
Serrated: Has a sharply pronounced jagged edge.
Toothed: As 'serrated', but less pronounced.

OTHER PLANT PARTS
Drupe: Fruit containing a seed, e.g. cherry and sumac.
Hip: Fleshy fruit of a rose.
Tuber: Swollen, edible part of a root, e.g. potatoes.

MUSHROOMS AND FUNGI
Bracket: A shelf-like fungal protrusion.
Cap: The top of the mushroom.
Decurrent: Gills which extend down the stipe or stem of the mushroom. Gills can be partially or strongly decurrent, meaning respectively they run down some of the stem or much of the stem.
Fungus: A whole fungal organism. This can be mould, yeast or a woodland mushroom and its underground mycelium.

Gills: Spore-bearing structures on the underside of a mushroom, often resembling folds.

Mushroom: The fruiting body of a fungus.

Mycelium: The vegetative part of a fungus, often underground, consisting of a network of thread-like structures.

Polypore: Has many pores.

Pore (for mushroom): Spore-bearing small holes or tube-like structures on the underside of a mushroom.

Selected Bibliography and Further Reading

Francis Bunker, *Seaweeds of Britain and Ireland*, 2nd edition, Wild Nature Press: 2017

Geoff Dann, *Edible Mushrooms: A Forager's Guide to the Wild Fungi of Britain and Europe*, Green Books: 2016

Alan Davidson, *The Penguin Companion to Food*, Penguin: 2002

Euell Gibbons, *Stalking the Wild Asparagus*, Stackpole Books: 2020 (first published 1962)

Miles Irving, *The Forager Handbook*, Ebury: 2009

Owen Johnson and David More, *Collins Tree Guide*, Collins: 2004

Lisette Kreischer, *Ocean Greens: Explore the World of Edible Seaweed and Sea Vegetables*, The Experiment LLC: 2016

Richard Mabey, *Flora Britannica*, Sinclair Stevenson: 1996

Richard Mabey, *Food for Free*, Collins: 2012 (first published 1972)

Ray Mears and Gordon Hillman, *Wild Food*, Hodder and Stoughton: 2008

Daniel E. Moerman, *Native American Ethnobotany*, Timber Press: 1998

Adele Nozedar, *The Garden Forager*, Square Peg: 2015

Roger Phillips, *Mushrooms*, Macmillan: 2013

Roger Phillips, *Wild Food*, Pan Books: 1983

Jim Pojar and Andy MacKinnon, *Plants of the Pacific Northwest Coast*, Lone Pine Publishing: 2004

Marlow Renton and Eric Biggane, *Foraging Pocket Guide: Food for All Seasons from Britain's Woods, Meadows and Riversides,* Otherwise: 2019.

John Rensten, *The Edible City: A Year of Wild Food,* Boxtree: 2016

Paul Sterry, *British Wild Flowers: A Photographic Guide to Every Common Species,* Collins: 2008

John Wright, *The Forager's Calendar: A Seasonal Guide to Nature's Wild Harvests,* Profile Books: 2020

RECOMMENDED WEBSITES

eattheweeds.com
eatweeds.co.uk
foragerchef.com
gallowaywildfoods.com
handmadeapothecary.co.uk
pfaf.org (Plants for a future)
practicalselfreliance.com
thespruceeats.com
wildfooduk.com

WILD FOOD SUPPLIERS

Totally Wild: Wild mushrooms and wild veg boxes, UK based – https://totallywilduk.co.uk

FORAGING COURSES

I run my own foraging courses and take private bookings in Somerset and the surrounding counties. You'll find me on: davehamilton.co.uk.

For a full list of foraging instructors and suppliers in the UK (and increasingly overseas), go to: Foragers-Association.org.

My recommended courses in the UK are:

Cornwall: Emma Gunn – nevermindtheburdocks.co.uk
Cornwall: Rachel Lambert – wildwalks-southwest.co.uk

Devon: Forage Fine Foods, Liz Knight – foragefinefoods.com

London: Forage London, John Rensten – foragelondon.co.uk

South-east England: Fergus Drennan – fergustheforager.co.uk

Midlands and Home Counties: Wildfood UK – wildfood.co.uk

Northampton and Midlands: Forage Frolics, Richard Mawby – richardmawby.com/foragefrolics

Wales and West England: Adele Nozdar – breconbeaconsforaging.com

North of England: Lisa Cutcliffe – eduliswildfood.co.uk

Leeds: Craig Worrall – edible-leeds.blogspot.com

Northern Ireland: Clare McQuillan – feastingonweeds.wordpress.com

Central Scotland: Monica Wilde –monicawilde.com

South-west Scotland: Mark Williams (also online mentoring worldwide) – gallowaywildfoods.com

My recommended courses outside the UK are:

Germany: Christine Krauss – chirpfood.com

Italy: Eleonora Matarrese – eleonoramatarrese.com

Poland: Lukasz Luczaj – lukaszluczaj.pl

Republic of Ireland: Bill O'Dea – mushroomstuff.com

Lucy O'Hagan – wildawke.ie

Switzerland: François Couplan – couplan.com

USA: Pascal Baudin – urbanoutdoorskills.com/bio.html

Learn your Land, Adam Haritan – learnyourland.com

For a full list of foragers in the USA, visit: eattheweeds.com/foraging/foraging-instructors

For online foraging courses, visit: milesirving.com/courses

Acknowledgements

FIRST AND FOREMOST, I would like to thank my partner Liz for accompanying me on foraging trips, supplying recipe suggestions and bravely sampling my experimental cookery, but most importantly for countless hours of extra childcare during what turned out to be an extremely difficult year. My two boys, Doug and Lenny, also deserve a mention for their willingness to try new foods and explore new places.

I owe a huge debt of thanks to Kirty Topiwala for commissioning and shaping the book, and for her editorial advice and tireless email correspondence. Thank you, Tessa David and Tim Bates at Peters Fraser and Dunlop, for long, friendly phone calls and contract negotiations.

My immense gratitude to all the team at Hodder, including (but not limited to) Amanda, Anna, Caitriona, Vero, Libby and Ian. Not forgetting Sophie Davidson for her author photos and a fun day out in the Cotswolds, May Van Millingen for her excellent illustrations and, of course, Marta Zafra for her amazing book cover.

Thanks to Vivienne Evans for her good-humoured proofreading of early drafts. Perhaps one day we will write the comedy version of this book? Andy and the Karkut-Francis family deserve a mention for days out gathering seaweed and mushrooms, as does Mark Evans for the use of his field as a makeshift campsite when everything was booked up. I'd also like to thank Mark Williams of Galloway Wild Food for his help filling in the blanks in my knowledge, Jo Watson for her help with the base recipe section, Nick Moyle of Two Thirsty Gardeners for homebrew advice and James Wood of Totally Wild UK for his generous gift of mushrooms. Also to Don O'Meara of English Heritage for his archaeobotanical advice, Dr Bethan Stagg for reading through some of the ecology sections, Phil Davidson for the geology bits and Tom Barnsley of Roundfield for his notes on urban planting and landscape architecture.

A big thank-you too to Alys Fowler, for suggesting my name to the *Guardian* for their foraging masterclass, which led to the commissioning of this book. My thanks too to the Mountain Men, to whom this book is dedicated; you are a great bunch of berks and 2020 would not have been nearly as much fun without you. A special thanks to Frag, Dom and John who all clocked up hours of calls between them.

Finally, if you are reading this, thank you for buying this book – an author is nothing without their readers.

Endnotes

1. For a magnolia pickle recipe, see Robin Harford, 'Pickled Magnolia Flowers Recipe', *Eat Weeds*, https://www.eatweeds.co.uk/pickled-magnolia-flowers-recipe, retrieved April 2020. For a magnolia petal honey recipe, see 'Magnolia Petals: Pickles, Honey and More', *Urban Herbology*, https://urban-herbology.org/2012/04/19/magnolia-petals-pickles-honey-cake-and-more, retrieved April 2020.

2. Nicolette Perry and Elaine Perry, *Botanical Brain Balms: Medicinal Plants for Memory, Mood and Mind*, Filbert Press: 2018

3. G. Mazzanti, L. Battinelli, C. Pompeo, A.M. Serrilli, R. Rossi, I. Sauzullo, F. Mengoni and V. Vullo, 'Inhibitory activity of Melissa officinalis L. extract on Herpes simplex virus type 2 replication', *Natural Production Research*, Volume 22, Issue 16, November 2008.

4. Interestingly he also carried with him dried fungi, not to eat as a staple food but to start fires and as medicine to combat internal parasites.

5. Robert Hardwicke, *Hardwicke's Science Gossip*, Volume 9, 1874.

6. J.L. Osborne et al., 'A Landscape-scale Study of Bumble Bee Foraging Range and Constancy, Using Harmonic Radar', *Journal of Applied Ecology*, Volume 36, Issue 4, September 1999.

7. My grandad wasn't quite right – at the height of summer they can grow 10 cm (4 inches) a day but the average is more like 3 cm (1 inch), reaching a height of 3 metres (10 feet) in total.

8. Anastasia Lakhtikova, Angela Brintlinger and Irina Glushchenko (eds), *Seasoned Socialism: Gender and Food in Late Soviet Everyday Life*, Indiana University Press: 2019.

9. D.C. Watts, *Dictionary of Plant Lore*, Academic Press: 2007.

10. French sites such as Chauvet-Pont-d'Arc Cave and Lascaux are famous for their cave painting but in 2007 rock art dating to the Ice Age was also found in Cheddar Gorge. https://www.archaeology.co.uk/articles/features/rare-ice-age-rock-art-found-in-cheddar-gorge.htm

11. T. Anderson, R. Petranker, D. Rosenbaum et al., 'Microdosing psychedelics: personality, mental health, and creativity differences in microdosers', *Psychopharmacology* Volume 236, Issue 2, January 2019, pp.731–740.

12. David Kleijn and Gerard J.C. van Zuiklen, 'The conservation effects of meadow bird agreements on farmland in Zeeland, The Netherlands, in the period 1989–1995,' *Biological Conservation*, Volume 117, Issue 4, 2004, pp. 443–451.

13. Mart Rogowska et al., 'Chemical Composition, Antioxidative and Enzyme Inhibition Activities of Chickweed Herb (*Stelaria media* L., Vill.) Ethanolic and Aqueous Extracts', *Industrial Crops and Products*, Volume 97, March 2017, pp. 448–454.

14. The St George's mushroom usually pops up a week after St George's Day on 30 April, or International Jazz Day. Perhaps a more fitting name would be the jazz mushroom or, as suggested by poet Niall McDevitt, the May Day mushroom.

15. Y. Dogan, A. Nedelcheva and A. Pieroni, 'The diversity of plants used for the traditional dish sarma in Turkey: Nature, garden and traditional cuisine in the modern era', *Emirates Journal of Food and Agriculture*, Volume 29, Issue 6, November 2017, pp. 429–40.

16. Manuel Pardo-de-Santayana, Andrea Pieroni and Rajindra K. Puri (eds.), 'Ethnobotany in the New Europe: People, Health and Wild Plant Resources', *Studies in Environmental Anthropology and Ethnobiology*, Volume 14, Berghahn Books: 2010.

17. M. Antonelli, G. Barbieri and D. Donelli, 'Effects of forest bathing (*shinrin-yoku*) on levels of cortisol as a stress biomarker: a systematic review and meta-analysis', *International Journal of Biometeorology*, Volume 63, Issue 8, August 2019, pp. 1117–1134 (2019).

18. These spores are very small and very numerous. According to the British Mycological Society, a common, shop-bought portobello mushroom, *Agaricus bisporus*, can produce over *one billion* spores which, laid end to end, would stretch for over 5.5 miles!

19. 'Fly agaric (*Amanita mascaria*), the miller (*Clitopilus prunulus*) and peppery boletes (*Chalciporus piperatus*) are often clues to good hunting-grounds, especially under spruce trees. I find the relationship between ceps, spruce trees, the miller and the peppery bolete to be so reliable that I believe (though I've seen no scientific research to prove this) that the relationship is more than just shared habitat, but a complex inter-dependency. It has been known for some years that peppery boletes are parasitic on fly agaric mycelia, but I suspect there is more at play here. Who knows what complex battles, alliances and trades are going

on beneath our feet!?' Mark Williams, 'Cep – Identification, Distribution, Edibility, Ecology, Sustainable Harvesting', *Galloway Wild Foods,* https://gallowaywildfoods.com/cep-identification-distribution-edibility, retrieved December 2020.

20. Miles Irving, *The Forager Handbook: A Guide to the Edible Plants of Britain,* Ebury: 2009.

21. Karen Hardy and Lucy Kubiak-Martens, *Wild Harvest,* Oxbow Books: 2016.

22. Ernest Bielinis et al., 'The Effects of a Short Forest Recreation Program on Physiological and Psychological Relaxation in Young Polish Adults', *Forests,* Volume 10, Issue 1, 2019.

23. J.S. Garrow, W.P.T James and A. Ralph, *Numan Nutrition and Dietetics,* Churchill Livingstone, 10th Edition: 2000.

24. Liquid smoke is a popular flavouring sold in delis, health food stores and bigger supermarkets, which gives foods such as meat, mushrooms and vegetables a smoky flavour without the need for a smoke house.

25. See, for example: Sandra Laville and Niamh McIntyre, 'Exclusive: Water Firms Discharged Raw Sewage into England's Rivers 200,000 Times in 2019', *The Guardian,* https://www.theguardian.com/environment/2020/jul/01/water-firms-raw-sewage-england-rivers, retrieved November 2020.

26. Section 14 of the Wildlife and Countryside Act forbids the release of plants which may 'cause ecological, environmental or socio-economic harm'.

27. Manuel Pardo-de-Santayana, Andrea Pieroni and Rajindra K. Puri (eds.), 'Ethnobotany in the New Europe: People, Health and Wild Plant Resources', *Studies in Environmental Anthropology and Ethnobiology,* Volume 14, Berghahn Books: 2010.

28 Gladiators were mostly vegetarian, BBC Education, retrieved Jan 2021. https://www.bbc.co.uk/news/education-29723384

29. The table was compiled in part from information provided by Mark Williams of Galloway Wild Foods, https://gallowaywildfoods.com/an-introduction-to-seaweed-foraging, retrieved September 2020, and in part from Francis StP. D. Bunker et al, *Seaweeds of Britain and Ireland,* Wild Nature Press: 2017.

30. You shouldn't collect seaweed from anywhere near the shoreline of factories and power plants, where there can be industrial pollutants in the water. Nor should you go out looking for seaweed following heavy rains, when storm drains are sometimes opened, releasing raw sewage into the sea and onto beaches.

31. Mrs Hoare, *Shamrock Leaves: Or, Tales and Sketches of Ireland,* 1851.

32. R.A. Kenney, 'The Chinese Restaurant Syndrome: An Anecdote Revisited', *Food and Chemical Toxicology*, Volume 24, Issue 4, April 1986, pp. 351–354.

33. 'The Rock Samphire', *The Ladies' Garland*, Volumes 1–2, J. Libby: 1838, pp. 159–60. The book tells the story of sailors who were shipwrecked and floating in the sea off Beachy Head only to be saved when they found samphire growing on a rock in the middle of the sea. Armed with the knowledge that samphire never grows in sea water, they clung to the rock until they were rescued. Although the story was repeated many times, *The Ladies' Garland* is amongst the most elaborate and worthy of a read. Available on Google books: https://www.google.co.uk/books/edition/The_Ladies_Garland/DcNBAAAAYAAJ?hl=en&gbpv=1

34. The recipe is taken from Elizabeth Cleland, *A New and Easy Method of Cookery*, 1775. Some of the text is very antiquated but it makes for good reading.

Index

Bold text refers to main entries

413